THE INNOVATIONS OF IDEALISM

This collection of essays, first published in German in 1995, has been written by Rüdiger Bubner, the foremost representative of the hermeneutical approach in German philosophy. It offers an original interpretation of the tradition of German Idealist thinkers – Kant, Fichte, Schelling, Hegel.

Professor Bubner casts fresh light on the genuine philosophical innovations in the complex of issues and aspirations that dominated German intellectual life from 1780 to 1830. His major question is: In what way did the Idealists change philosophy, reformulate traditional issues, and, especially, reinterpret traditional figures? His answer involves focusing on the literary and cultural spirit of the time, thus broadening the question of philosophical innovation and locating it within the wider framework of innovations and continuities of the Western intellectual tradition itself. Professor Bubner thus pays due attention to Plato and Aristotle, Rousseau, Schlegel, Schleiermacher, and Goethe.

In this fine translation by Nicholas Walker, *The Innovations of Idealism* will be of special interest to students of German philosophy, literary theory, and the history of ideas.

Rüdiger Bubner is Professor of Philosophy at the University of Heidelberg.

THE INNOVATIONS
OF IDEALISM

RÜDIGER BUBNER

University of Heidelberg

Translated by Nicholas Walker

CAMBRIDGE
UNIVERSITY PRESS

PUBLISHED BY THE PRESS SYNDICATE OF THE UNIVERSITY OF CAMBRIDGE
The Pitt Building, Trumpington Street, Cambridge, United Kingdom

CAMBRIDGE UNIVERSITY PRESS
The Edinburgh Building, Cambridge CB2 2RU, UK
40 West 20th Street, New York, NY 10011-4211, USA
477 Williamstown Road, Port Melbourne, VIC 3207, Australia
Ruiz de Alarcón 13, 28014 Madrid, Spain
Dock House, The Waterfront, Cape Town 8001, South Africa

http://www.cambridge.org

First published 2003

Printed in the United Kingdom at the University Press, Cambridge

Typeface New Baskerville 10.25/13 pt.   *System* LATEX 2ε [TB]

A catalog record for this book is available from the British Library.

Library of Congress Cataloging in Publication Data
Bubner, Rüdiger, 1941–
[Innovationen des Idealismus. English]
The innovations of idealism/Rüdiger Bubner.
p. cm. – (Modern European philosophy)
Includes bibliographical references and index.
ISBN 0-521-66262-1
1. Idealism, German. I. Title. II. Series.
B2745 .B83   2003
141′.0943–dc21   2002191143

ISBN 0 521 66262 1 hardback

CONTENTS

FOREWORD TO THE ENGLISH EDITION

I am particularly gratified to see the completion of a long and difficult project with the appearance of this collection of essays. Even in our age of instant electronic communication, philosophical texts continue to present persistent problems for the ongoing task of hermeneutic appropriation. Despite all difficulties, Terence Moore at Cambridge University Press has always remained committed to the task of making these essays on the philosophy of German Idealism available in English translation. Robert Pippin, the editor of the Modern European Philosophy series, has also encouraged the project, and I am most grateful for his friendly assistance throughout. I would also like to express my appreciation to Terry Pinkard for his moral and intellectual support.

Above all, I am indebted to the translator, Nicholas Walker, who has undertaken the painstaking and challenging task of appropriate linguistic adaptation and transformation. I feel that the English translation has effectively succeeded in both capturing the thought and reflecting the style of the original essays. To reproduce a specific argument faithfully within the appropriate conceptual framework, and to present it without distortion in another language at once so close to and so remote from German, is no mean achievement.

These considerations are broadly practical in character. But I would also like to make a further point in this connection. The question of the relationship between so-called Continental philosophy and the so-called analytic tradition involves a range of fundamental problems of understanding that, despite the familiar contemporary rhetoric of communicative reason and the universally shared discourse of modern sciences and disciplines, are by no means easy to clarify. My hope was, and remains, carefully and cautiously to suggest something of the deeper potential unity behind the real diversity of approaches that characterise these philosophical traditions. There is no question of assuming some pre-existing unity that could simply be exposed by technical, procedural or purely scholarly means.

During the eighteenth century, philosophy originating from the British Isles exercised a very considerable influence on German thought up to, and of course including, Kant. And German classical philosophy in turn certainly left its mark on many thinkers in Britain and North America in the latter half of the nineteenth century before this tradition was radically challenged in the name of a resurgent and emphatic empiricism by G. E. Moore and Bertrand Russell. The subsequent influence of the emigrant neo-Positivists of the Vienna School also helped to strengthen and intensify this development even further. During the 1960s, I was able to hear Peter Strawson's lectures on Kant, which would result in an important book (*The Bounds of Sense*). It was largely thanks to Strawson that the founder of classical German philosophy became the subject of significantly fresh attention and renewed interest at this time.

The Canadian, Charles Taylor, later helped to initiate a similar breakthrough in relation to Hegel's idealism, which was still widely regarded as little more than an apologetic expression of conservative ideology. Richard Rorty, our highly valued academic guest at the University of Frankfurt in the 1970s, has continued throughout the last two decades to play a key role in building bridges between our different philosophical cultures. And, of course, a number of other thinkers have also lent their voices to the further development of this dialogue.

The once familiar mutual accusations of rationalism and obscurantism have thankfully begun to fade in the light of a genuine exchange of relevant views and perspectives. It is naturally impossible to predict the shape that the emerging philosophy of the new century will take. But one thing at least is clear: without a living re-examination and re-evaluation of the tradition, our philosophical prospects will surely remain unnecessarily limited. As contemporary thinkers, we must be prepared to assume the role of mediators here. And this is a task that is more demanding than it may initially sound.

SYSTEM

SCHELLING'S DISCOVERY AND SCHLEIERMACHER'S APPROPRIATION OF PLATO

Forgive us, sacred Plato! We Have transgressed against thee.

Hölderlin, Preface to *Hyperion*
(penultimate version)

I. The Historical Background

The names of Plato and Aristotle have together accompanied the winding course of European philosophy from the beginning. It is true that Aristotle was regarded during the High Middle Ages simply as 'the philosopher'[1], but the period between Saint Augustine and Nicholas of Cusa also saw the survival of a Platonic tradition that attempted to interpret the relationship between the soul and transcendent reality in a Christian fashion.[2] The Florentine Renaissance celebrated the revival of a theology that, enlivened with the spirit of neo-Platonism, undertook to integrate Plato's treatment of love and beauty into a single doctrine. And a century later, the circle associated with Jacobus Zarabella was striving to renew the Aristotelian interest in the philosophy of nature.[3]

---

[1] Cf. the general discussion by Fr. Cheneval and R. Imbach in the introduction to their edition of Thomas Aquinas, *Prologe zu den Aristoteles-Kommentaren* (Frankfurt am Main 1993).

[2] On this, one should still consult Cl. Baeumker, *Der Platonismus im Mittelalter* (Beiträge zur Geschichte der Philosophie des Mittelalters, 1927); also W. Beierwaltes (ed.), *Platonismus in der Philosophie des Mittelalters* (Darmstadt 1969).

[3] J.H. Randall, *The School of Padua and the Emergence of Modern Science* (Padova 1961). On this, one can also consult the knowledgeable but largely summarising recent study by H. Mikkeli, *An Aristotelian Response to Renaissance Humanism: J. Zabarella on the Nature of the Arts and Sciences* (Helsinki 1992).

Modern scientific thought in general, however, soon began to turn against the verbal subtleties of Scholastic philosophy in favour of an increasingly empirical method of approach. Francis Bacon, the principal protagonist in this, expressly endeavoured in his *Novum Organon* to break with the conceptual hold of Aristotelianism, although he simultaneously appealed to the traditional rhetorical status of *epagōgē* to secure the principle of induction so fundamental to empirical science.[4] To some extent, the Cambridge Platonists grouped around Whichcote and Cudworth subsequently represented a reaction against empiricism, returning to the explicitly theological orientation of the Renaissance and attempting to defend the claims of faith by appealing to Plato.[5] During the intervening period, the Scholastic Aristotelian heritage had passed into Protestant hands, and subsequently exercised a distinct influence on the established eighteenth-century philosophical schools upto the time of Kant.[6] During the same period, the Platonic heritage of the Cambridge School was also kept alive in the Earl of Shaftesbury's aestheticised concept of 'enthusiasm'.[7] The English thinker found a particularly vivid response in German eighteenth-century aesthetics precisely because he seemed to defend a new and versatile freedom in the domain of sensibility over against the still dominant influence of French classicism.[8]

These brief allusions to a number of familiar connections, all of which have been subjected to detailed research, already bring us to the threshold of German Idealist philosophy. It was this tradition of thought that discovered, in an original way of its own, the *authentic Plato* in place of the various mediated substitutes of before, and indeed saw him as a thinker who was to provide continuing inspiration to the needs of post-Kantian philosophy.

Kant's critical revolution had brought the classical metaphysics of the Aristotelian tradition to a decisive end precisely by demanding

[4] Cf. L. Jardine, *Bacon. Discovery and the Art of Discourse* (Cambridge 1974) and my outline of this story, 'Antike und moderne Wissenschaftstheorie', in R. Bubner: *Antike Themen und ihre moderne Verwandlung* (Frankfurt am Main 1992), especially p. 120 ff.

[5] Cf. C. Patrides (ed.), *The Cambridge Platonists* (Cambridge 1969). The anthology also contains a very instructive introduction under the title, 'The High and Aiery Hills of Platonisme'.

[6] Cf. the excellent and still unsurpassed study by P. Peterson, *Geschichte der aristotelischen Philosophie im protestantischen Deutschland* (Leipzig 1921; reprinted Stuttgart 1954).

[7] On this, one should still consult Ernst Cassirer, *Die platonische Renaissance in England und die Schule von Cambridge* (Berlin 1932).

[8] Also cf. M. Wundt, *Die Wiederentdeckung Platons im 18. Jahrhundert*, Blätter für deutsche Philosophie 15, 1941.

self-conscious reflection upon the constitutive limitations of subjectivity in relation to possible experience. At the same time, Kant had discovered the spontaneous character of the synthetic achievements of self-consciousness. For the early idealist thinkers, this situation naturally suggested that the immediate task was that of going beyond Kant by recourse to Kantian means. This meant re-conceiving metaphysics on a quite new basis independent of the traditional approaches, constructing a metaphysics that could effectively present itself as the systematic completion of the philosophy of subjectivity. This itself required a new repertoire of concepts over and above the obsolete ones already discredited by the Critical Philosophy, one that was capable of finally realising the Kantian idea, anticipated but not accomplished by Kant himself, of a new metaphysics that could properly aspire to scientific status.

Such concepts would have to be independent of experience, like Kant's synthetic *a priori*, and yet permit us, through the power of reason alone, to grasp that intrinsic relationship to the world that transcendental philosophy had derived from the *a posteriori* character of contingent experience. For all of his distrust of spurious 'enthusiasm' and irresponsible speculation, Kant himself had emphatically expressed respect, in Plato's name, for the original conception of 'Ideas'[9] in the transcendental dialectic.[10] In this matter, Kant claimed to have 'understood Plato even better than he had understood himself', and thereby provided the classical formulation for all attempts at retrospective reinterpretations of the philosophical past. It was thus quite natural from the post-Kantian perspective on the problem to regard the doctrine of Ideas, and the idea of a dialectic grounded in the latter and capable of producing real knowledge rather than purely apparent sophistical conclusions, as the appropriate point of departure for further intellectual development. And it is this path that the early idealists were in fact to pursue.

II. The Emergence of the History of Philosophy as a Discipline

In this connection, it is important to understand that the early idealist rediscovery of Plato represented far more than a revival of the familiar

---

[9] Cf. Kant's essay of 1796 that was explicitly directed against Schlosser, Goethe's brother-in-law, 'Von einem neuerdings erhobenen vornehmen Ton in der Philosophie'. On this, cf. my study, 'Platon, der Vater aller Schwärmerei', in R. Bubner, *Antike Themen und ihre moderne Verwandlung* (loc. cit.).

[10] *Critique of Pure Reason* B 369 f. Cf. the general discussion in H. Heimsoeth, 'Platon in Kants Werdegang', in: H. Heimsoeth/D. Henrich (eds.), *Studien zu Kants philosophischer Entwicklung* (Hildesheim 1967).

and traditional amalgam of Platonic, neo-Platonic and Christian elements in a new form, since it effectively opened up the Platonic sources themselves for the very first time. The initial stirrings of an authentically philological attitude may have also played a certain role in this respect. But it was, above all, the project of a rationally grounded metaphysics of substance, as mediated through the thought of Spinoza and Leibniz, that helped to realise the possibility of overcoming the traditional philosophy of the Schools.

The contemporary consciousness of the history of philosophy, however, was not alone responsible for these developments. For considerable historical research had already been progressively undertaken by Brucker through to Tiedemann and Tennemann, and the historical scholarship of these writers certainly exceeded the occasional and extremely indeterminate references to the classical thinkers to be found in the works of Kant or Fichte. The revolutionary sense of renewal so characteristic of the early idealist philosophers derived rather from their conviction that they could decisively present the essential questions of philosophy now liberated from the dead weight of tradition, and from the fact that the necessary doxographical support had already been provided by their predecessors.

It is nonetheless the case that the rudiments of something like the history of philosophy in the modern sense had been developed during the eighteenth century.[11] Yet the massive erudition of a Jacob Brucker, so appreciated by his contemporaries, did not prove to be particularly helpful for an actual understanding of Plato.[12] And the *Universal History of Philosophy*, which J.A. Eberhard presented as a 'pragmatic history' in terms of progressive development, dedicated only a few pages to Plato, and treated him in a rather condescending manner.[13] Dietrich

---

[11] Moses Mendelssohn's famous reworking of Plato, his *Phaidon* of 1764, simply presents the school of philosophy of his own time in antique garb. J.J. Engel's *Versuch einer Methode, die Vernunftlehre aus platonischen Dialogen zu entwickeln* (Berlin 1780) is similarly designed as a pedagogical manual for school teachers that is supposed to introduce the contents of Aristotle's *Organon* in an easy and attractive manner: 'more as delightful play than as challenging labour' (p. 5).

[12] J. Brucker, *Historia critica philosophiae* (Leipzig 1742). On this topic, cf. A. Neschke (*Revue de Métaphysique et de Morale*, 1993).

[13] Eberhard's compendium 'for use in the course of academic lectures' seeks rather laboriously to disclose the 'systematic structure' behind the 'dialogical form' and the 'poetic diction' (Halle 1788, p. 139). He thus sets 'dialectics' and 'physics' over against 'theology' and 'ethics'. A. Neschke is not entirely convincing when she attempts to trace Schleiermacher's understanding of Plato's system back to Eberhard. It is true that Eberhard was Schleiermacher's teacher in philosophy, and the synopsis of Platonism as handed down

Tiedemann's history of 1791, which surveys *The Spirit of Speculative Philosophy from Thales to Plato* in the firm conviction of narrating an 'uninterrupted progress of reason', represents a certain advance on Eberhard. Wilhelm Gottlieb Tennemann's *History of Philosophy* of 1798 produced an even more thorough examination of the subject.[14] As his four-volume *System of Platonic Philosophy* of 1792–95 already reveals, he was himself a Kantian, and regarded the history of philosophy very much in the spirit of the final chapter of Kant's *Critique of Pure Reason*, which brings the 'history of pure reason' to an end with its emphatic announcement that 'the critical path alone now lies open before us'.[15]

III. The Earliest System Programme of German Idealism

The early idealist appeal to Plato, however, takes place quite independently of all these still rather modest efforts. We know that Plato was already being read in the original at the Tübingen Theological Seminary, the *Stift*, at the beginning of the last decade of the eighteenth century.[16] The famous and much-debated text generally known as the *Earliest System Programme of German Idealism*, probably composed around 1796–97, is a kind of summary that emerged from an immediate exchange of views between Hegel, Schelling[17] and Hölderlin. It addresses

by Alkinoos may also have exerted a remote early influence upon him, as Neschke surmises ('Platonisme et le tournant herméneutique au début du XIX. Siècle', in: A. Laks/A. Neschke (eds.), *La naissance du paradigme herméneutique*, Lille 1990, 139 ff.). But the few pages that Eberhard dedicates to the subject are so arid and schematic that it is impossible to find any interesting traces of this treatment in Schleiermacher's own interpretation of Plato.

[14] Plato is extensively discussed in the second volume, which appeared in 1799.

[15] Critique of Pure Reason B 884.

[16] As a small example, one might compare the way in which Schelling casually weaves a reference to the *Meno* (70c) into a letter of 1795 to Hegel, who had just moved to Bern. 'You wish to know how things are with us? – by God in Heaven an *auchmos* has come upon us which will only give renewed succour to the ancient weeds. Who will pull them up?' This learned allusion to that 'dearth of wisdom' lamented by Socrates in the opening scene of Plato's dialogue, delivered *en passant* in a personal letter to a friend with shared interests, surely presupposes an extraordinary familiarity with the text in question. Schelling's commentary on the *Timaeus* also refers a number of times, and always affirmatively, to the Latin paraphrase of Plato by D. Tiedemann, *Dialogorum Platonis argumenta* (Zweibrücken 1786), which also discusses the *Timaeus* on p. 302 ff.

[17] Some knowledge of Plato on Schelling's part is documented even for his time in Bebenhausen before he took up his university studies in 1790 (according to the biographical fragment by his son K.F.A. Schelling, as cited by G.L. Plitt, *Aus Schellings Leben in Briefen*, Leipzig 1869, I, p. 25). Schelling also mentions Plato in the dissertation he wrote in Tübingen, *De malorum origine* (AA I, p. 83, p. 128).

all the themes that would be involved in the ensuing rise of systematic
idealist thought, and concludes by placing the Platonic 'Idea' at the
centre of attention.

Beginning with the ego as an 'absolutely free being', there 'simultaneously emerges an entire world out of nothing'. This new philosophy
of nature, which attempts 'once again to give wings to the physics that
slowly and laboriously advances by means of experiment', requires certain 'ideas' that can only be supplied by a philosophy that poses the
fundamental and systematic question, 'How must the world be constituted for a moral being?' After the domain of nature, we confront the
'work of man' – the issues of the state, peace and history. This is followed by the 'moral world' of free spirits in which God and immortality
represent more than the mere postulates permitted at the end of Kant's
Critique of Practical Reason.

'Last of all the Idea that unites all the rest, the Idea of beauty, taking the word in its higher Platonic sense. I am now convinced that
the highest act of Reason [*Vernunft*], through which it encompasses all
Ideas, is an aesthetic act, and that truth and goodness only become
sisters in beauty. The philosopher must possess just as much aesthetic
power as the poet. Men without aesthetic sense is what the philosophers-
of-the-letter of our times are. The philosophy of spirit is an aesthetic
philosophy. [. . . .] Here it ought to become clear what it is that men
who understand no Ideas properly lack. [. . . .] Poetry thereby acquires
a higher dignity, and she becomes at the end once more what she was
in the beginning – the teacher of humanity; for there is no longer any
philosophy or any history here, and the art of poetry alone will survive
all other arts and sciences'. This ardent appeal concludes by turning to
contemplate an 'idea which, so far as I know, has never yet occurred to
anyone else', namely that of a 'new mythology'.[18]

This is not the appropriate place to discuss the numerous questions
provoked by this textual fragment, which, like a prism, casts a refracted
light upon the entire subsequent development of systematic idealist

---

[18] Cited from the text in *Hegel-Studien*, Beiheft 9, 1973. For the recent state of research, cf.
Chr. Jamme/H. Schneider (eds.), *Mythologie der Vernunft. Hegels 'ältestes Systemprogramm
des deutschen Idealismus'* (Frankfurt am Main 1984). The authors follow their teacher
Otto Pöggeler in ascribing the still-contested authorship of the fragment to Hegel. F.P.
Hansen has published an entire book on the 'Systemprogramm' (Berlin 1989), which
thoroughly documents the history of previous interpretations. Cf. also Section IV, and K.
Düsing, 'Ästhetischer Platonismus bei Hölderlin und Hegel', in: Ch. Jame/O. Pöggeler
(eds.), *Homburg vor der Höhe in der deutschen Geistesgeschichte* (Stuttgart 1981).

thought through to its culmination in Hegel, and beyond this into the post-Hegelian debate surrounding the question of 'theory and praxis'. The grounding of the ego in a theory of subjectivity provides the perspective from which both nature and the realm of spirit are to be reconstructed. In this process, it is aesthetics that comes to represent the culminating point of this unifying approach since it is precisely in beauty that the natural and the spiritual merge indistinguishably into one another.

This involves a central claim quite unparalleled in the previous Kantian tradition of aesthetic thought – namely, that the task is to develop, under the aegis of Plato, a form of philosophy so fused with poetry that art and science will no longer have to travel separately upon their divided ways as they have typically done since the beginning of the modern period. From the perspective of the history of philosophy, therefore, the true *telos* of modernity leads us back to the very beginning of the tradition. According to the ancient way of thinking, Homer and Hesiod represented teachers for the Greeks precisely because they had helped to make the world intelligible by creating that collective fabric of explanation mediated by images and imagination that we call a 'mythology'.

The ambitious early idealists wanted to restore this original and transfigured condition of a shared relationship to the world, where people and priests, the many and the wise, were not yet separated one from another. Thus the wounds inflicted by the abstract and alienating reflection of an age now remote from its origins could in future be healed again by recourse to the most advanced means available to thought. The hope was precisely to re-establish through philosophy that connection between life and thought whose loss the Germans felt so keenly in the wake of Rousseau's influential critique of culture. An intellectually independent and publicly effective philosophy would be the specific agent for transforming the shattered reality of the post-revolutionary present into something better. That is precisely what the promised new mythology would help to achieve. But even the more sober conception of a philosophy that seeks to comprehend its time in thought, as Hegel had always demanded from his first publication right through to the mature expression of his thought in the *Philosophy of Right*, also has its origins in this constellation of early idealism.

The central concept that is to unlock the treasures of all these previously sealed chambers of thought is the 'Idea'. The latter names a content that can only be grasped through the dedicated commitment to rational insight beyond the domain of empirical data and sensible experience, that presents the essence of something in its perfect form as determined through the untrammelled exercise of reason in accordance with its own intrinsic character. The *System Programme* itself gives as yet no inkling that the methodical art of dialectic will eventually be required here. The relevant insight in this respect represents Hegel's true breakthrough, which thereby brings him into a proximity with Plato with which none of the aforementioned historical variants of the Platonising tradition can bear comparison.[19] Since the relationship between Plato and Hegel with regard to the 'dialectic' has often been treated before, and I have already contributed to this debate in detail elsewhere[20], this complex of questions will be relegated to the background in the following discussion. This difference of emphasis, determined by the present context, does not of course affect the real importance that must still be ascribed to the question of the dialectic.[21]

IV. A Return to Schelling's Beginnings

The *System Programme* arose from a confluence of ideas shared by the three famous students – Hegel, Hölderlin, Schelling – at the Tübingen *Stift*. We have simply recalled some of the elements involved in this synthesis here, but the task now is to take *a further step back* into the origins of Schelling's thought. Alongside the various early student pieces relating to Plato and Aristotle, all of them corrected by a foreign hand, and some elementary studies of Fichte's thought, Schelling's literary remains

---

[19] We are particularly indebted to the contributions of French scholarship for comprehensive clarification of the role played by classical Greek thought in German idealist philosophy. Cf. J. Taminiaux, *La nostalgie de la Grèce à l'aube de l'idéalisme allemand* (The Hague 1967), D. Janicaud, *Hegel et le destin de la Grèce* (Paris 1975), and the thorough investigation by J. Vieillard-Baron, *Platon et l'idéalisme allemand 1770–1830* (Paris 1979). Vieillard-Baron has also edited a transcript of Hegel's lectures on Plato and provided a relevant explanatory introduction: G.W.F. Hegel, *Vorlesungen über Platon 1825–1826* (Paris 1976/ Frankfurt am Main 1979). Further studies concerning the German reception of Plato are gathered in Vieillard-Baron's *Platonisme et interprétation de Platon à l'époque moderne* (Paris 1988).

[20] 'Dialog und Dialektik oder Platon und Hegel', in: R. Bubner, *Antike Themen und ihre moderne Verwandlung* (loc. cit.).

[21] As far as Schleiermacher is concerned, we are principally interested here in his translation of the Platonic dialogues. In this context, I shall ignore Schleiermacher's own later concept of 'dialectic' as the 'skilful art of dialogue in the domain of pure thought'. The most careful and committed study of Schleiermacher's concept of dialectic – one that is even more detailed and elaborately differentiated than the original under examination – is F. Wagner's *Schleiermachers Dialektik* (Gütersloh 1979).

also comprise a previously unknown manuscript that significantly enhances our understanding of the beginnings of idealist philosophy. This well-ploughed field of research could indeed hardly have been expected to promise such an important find at this stage. Yet Schelling's Berlin papers include a bundle of manuscripts comprising around 230 pages[22], which was obviously later given the title *Typical Conceptions of the Ancient World on Sundry Subjects as Gathered from the Works of Homer, Plato and Others.* The piece largely consists of numerous more or less systematically arranged notes and excerpts on Gnosticism and various preparatory materials for Schelling's 1795 dissertation, *De Marcione.*[23]

Right at the beginning of the collection, we discover approximately twenty pages of excerpts that are more synoptically connected in relation to the later material, expressly dated by Schelling himself to 'August 1792' and designated as follows: 'On Poets, Prophets, Poetic Inspiration, Enthusiasm, Theopneumatics and Divine Influence upon Mankind in general as Related by Plato'. As far as I am aware, this textual source has never been seriously examined before.

Schelling begins with a motto from Plato's dialogue *Timaeus*[24] on the subject of necessary and divine causes. It is the latter that require our particular attention if we are ever 'to accede to a blessed life'. And Schelling himself has expressly underlined the passage in the Greek text where Plato exhorts us to follow this path to blessedness. It is also rather surprising to discover that Schelling's exegetical labours are directed towards the dialogue *Ion*, which is centrally concerned with the kind of knowledge ascribed to the rhapsode. This was regarded at that time as an extremely marginal dialogue that hardly belonged amongst the preferred texts as far as the contemporary literature on Plato was concerned.

The dialogue is usually overlooked because it does not seem to represent any of the essential ideas associated with Platonism. Herder quotes it occasionally[25], but the histories of philosophy compiled by Brucker, Tennemann and Tiedemann clearly pay no attention to it whatsoever. The first German translation of the dialogue, by Graf Stolberg,

---

[22] The manuscripts are preserved in the archives of the newly established Berlin-Brandenburg Academy of Sciences.

[23] For detailed clarifications of the text and background, cf. the editorial report provided by J. Jantzen in the new critical edition of Schelling's works (AA II, p. 195 ff.).

[24] *Timaeus* 68c.

[25] *Über die neuere deutsche Literatur* (1767), in: J.G. Herder, *Frühe Schriften*, ed. U. Gaier (Frankfurt am Main 1985), for example, pp. 315, 339 f.

appeared in the *Selected Dialogues of Plato*, which was published four years after the compilation of Schelling's notes.[26] In the context of the first early research into Homer, F.A. Wolf discussed the status of the rhapsode, and touched briefly upon the *Ion* in his influential *Prolegomena ad Homerum* of 1795.[27] Wolf attempts to extract valuable information about the nature of the rhapsode from what he describes, far from any appreciation of Socratic irony, as a highly entertaining dialogue ('ex iucundissimo illo sermone Platonis'). A similar interest will reappear in Schelling later, and thus open a field of research that is far removed from the topic of philosophical 'enthusiasm'. And C.J. Bardili, a relative of Schelling's who was active at the *Stift* until 1790, had also drawn upon the *Ion*, a few years before Schelling's engagement with the text, in order to provide a complementary learned discussion on the Christian conception of the importance of prophecy. Schelling cites this short study by Bardili[28] at the beginning of his own piece, briefly taking up one of its suggestions before proceeding to develop his own ideas. Bardili himself makes only a passing reference to Plato's passage concerning the 'interpreters of the interpreters'.[29]

It is true, however, that the *Ion* actually plays the major role in Goethe's short text *Plato as Partaker of a Christian Revelation*, a piece from 1796 that was occasioned by Stolberg's translation of the dialogue, but only published in 1826 in Goethe's journal *On Art and Antiquity*. Goethe writes as follows[30]: 'How has it come about, for example, that the *Ion* is cited as one of the canonic writings, given that this little dialogue is nothing but a species of pastiche? Probably because there is some talk of divine inspiration at the very end! But unfortunately Socrates expresses himself here, as in several other places, in a merely ironic fashion'. This evaluation, which was unknown to Schelling, is a significant one. It is all the more remarkable, then, with what sureness of purpose the young idealist Schelling seeks out the themes that interest him most amongst these ancient texts, and finds just what he can use in material that was largely ignored or despised in his own time. 'But Plato always regards poetry as a sacred mystery that calls for further clarification' (page 2 of Schelling's original).

---

[26] Vol. 1 (Königsberg 1796).   [27] Cf. chapter 22.

[28] C.G. Bardili, *Significatus primitivus vocis prophḗtēs ex Platone erutus cum novo tentamine interpretandi I. Cor. Cap. XIV* (Göttingen 1786). I am grateful to Dr. M. v. Perger in Freiburg and Dr. M. Franz in Bremen for a number of important suggestions in this regard.

[29] *Ion* 535 a.

[30] J. W. v. Goethe, *Werke* (Hamburger Ausgabe), XII, p. 245.

Undeterred by the highly sceptical irony expressed by Socrates in the *Ion*, Schelling reads the relevant Socratic remarks in an *affirmative* fashion. Socrates is trying to show that the rhapsodes who interpret the great poets do not themselves possess the appropriate art or skill (*technē*) for this task. Hence they do not understand what they are doing, or why they are doing it. The rhapsode Ion is only really familiar with the poetry of Homer, and confesses to a loss of interest and attention where other styles and voices of poetry are concerned. It is the Muse who prompts the rhapsodes in their songs, who lifts them beyond the everyday to the heights of inspiration and possession. Socrates compares the divine power that communicates its influence so mysteriously from the poet through the rhapsode to the listener with the power of the magnet. If the poets are 'messengers of the gods', those through whom the latter find utterance, then the singers who perform their poetry are themselves 'messengers of messengers' (*hermēnēon hermēnēs*)[31], representing thus a doubled hermeneutic with a sublime divine origin.

A 'divine dispensation' (*theia moira*)[32] holds sway in all things, but it remains unclear whether the rhapsode's miraculous inspiration removes the exercise of poetic talent from all rational enquiry, or whether the appeal to divine intervention merely serves to conceal the rhapsode's ignorance and incompetence, to excuse his reluctance or inability to give an account of what he is about. Schelling generalises this ambivalent appeal to inspiration and turns it into a fundamental principle. According to him, Plato is not merely talking here about the art of poetry but about 'all the operations of the understanding'. And Schelling refers in this connection to the famous passage in the *Meno* where it is claimed that the possession of virtue is not something that can be taught or learned since it arises from 'divine dispensation'.[33]

'When Plato describes the prophets and seers who read the future as an example of such divine power, he is not thinking of those later practitioners of deceit, the fantasts and soothsayers of his own time, but rather of those ancient sacred prophets and hierophants of the original world, as these were spoken of by sacred tradition, and of whom those later seers can be regarded only as a degenerate scion – he was thinking upon the very first origin of the prophetic gift in that original world, an origin that tradition has shrouded in holy darkness, and in which *art* actually possessed less share than *divinior quaedam in sapientibus animi vis*, if I may quote here the words of another ancient' (10).

---

[31] *Ion* 535a.
[33] *Meno* 99e.

[32] *Ion* 534c, 535a, 536c, 542 a/b.

Schelling subsequently touches upon the 'mythology of the Greeks' and the 'sensuous philosophy of all peoples' (13), themes that are also familiar from Schelling's other early writings[34] and that would once again come to occupy the centre of his interests during the final phase of his thinking.

But we still have to explain the motivation behind Schelling's essentially affirmative interpretation of the *Ion*. He may have been directly influenced, amongst other things, by the Kantian conception of 'genius'.[35] This was supposed to represent an innate gift, one that could not be rationally explained or technically acquired, and was capable of producing something in accordance with the rules of nature itself. The 'divine dispensation' referred to by Plato corresponds to just this kind of deep insight into nature enjoyed independently of all human theoretical reflection. The aesthetic character ascribed to the origin of those products of the spirit that appear as if they were products of nature is now transferred by Schelling to the secret operations of the understanding itself, which, because it creates in accordance with nature, is never fully transparent to reflective theoretical investigation. We must therefore develop this gift, which is analogous to genius, within the human spirit, and thereby help to bear post-Kantian speculation beyond the limits officially laid down by the Critical Philosophy and towards a philosophy of nature based upon Ideas.

'Genuine poetic power operates according to laws of which the poet himself is not entirely clearly conscious, and which are even less intelligible to other human beings; the product of the poet rather resembles a miraculous effect for which we are quite unable to discover the natural causes – an effect, which of a sudden simply stands there before the eyes of the astonished creator who has called it forth from out the overflowing stream of images and feelings, just like a god who calls forth the world from out of chaos [. . . . .] You may ask as long as you would

---

[34] Schelling, *Über Mythen, historische Sagen und Philosopheme der ältesten Welt* (1793), AA I.

[35] Kant, *Critique of Judgement* §§46 ff.; cf. A 181/2: ' . . . but one cannot learn to write inspired poetry, however elaborate all the precepts of this art may be, and however superb its models. The reason for this is that Newton could show how he took every one of the steps he had to take in order to get from the first elements of geometry to his great and profound discoveries; he could show this not only to himself but also to everyone else as well, in an intuitively clear way, allowing others to follow. But no Homer or Wieland can show his ideas, rich in fancy and yet also in thought, arise and meet in his mind; the reason is that he himself does not know this and hence cannot teach it to anyone else either'.

what genius is, so Rousseau, if I am not mistaken, has said, but if you do not already possess it, you will ask in vain.[36]

'This power at work in the individual human being, incomprehensible as it is to most, is active not only in poetry but also in every accomplishment of the human understanding, active in such a way that precisely the person quite unaware of any such power within himself may be astonished at many of these accomplishments, at all the unanticipated connections and combinations, at the daring turns and conclusions of the human understanding, whereas another may simply cling unmoved to his maxim of 'nihil admirari'. And if every great man were honestly to confess the truth, would we not learn in many respects how many of his powerful thoughts, which exercised the most far-reaching effects in the realm of science, were neither more nor less than such a *hermaion*, which some benevolent spirit had bestowed upon at a fortunate moment' (7/8).

This remarkable text, whose concluding sentence is clearly intended as a rhetorical question concerning such unexpected and fortunate discoveries, is already beginning to efface the strict distinction that Kant had drawn between the *methodical* approach of science and the *poetical* process of invention. Schelling here places the scientific investigator of nature alongside the artist and explicitly recognises the privileged operation of genius at work in the connective and synthetic efforts and accomplishments of the human understanding in general, something that cannot itself be explained in a purely explicit and reflective manner. Schelling thus combines the epistemologically crucial synthesising capacity emphasised in the Kantian theory of knowledge with a creative aesthetic capacity that points beyond the Kantian position, thus suggesting a new source of intellectual and spiritual productivity. Fichte would soon develop Kant's *intuitus originarius* into a new notion of intellectual intuition as the appropriate model for such productivity, a line of thought that Schelling himself was also later glad to follow. But we can already recognise in Schelling's early position, as yet untouched by Fichte's further influence, the source for that systematically fruitful early idealist conception of philosophy in which Kant's third Critique and Plato's vision of the gifts divinely bestowed upon poets and singers enter into a mutually illuminating relationship with one another.

---

[36] The remark in question is to be found in Rousseau's article on 'Génie' in the *Dictionnaire de musique* (Paris 1767).

V. Schelling's Commentary on the *Timaeus*

In the following discussion, I should like to examine another document
from the hand of the young Schelling, one that can be regarded as
the 'preliminary step' towards the published and generally well-known
philosophy of nature that found its first programmatic expression in
his *Ideas towards a Philosophy of Nature* of 1797. It was always previously
assumed that Fichte's identification of the theoretical and practical aspects of reason through the posited principle of original self-activity
directly suggested the project of a philosophy of nature on comparable
principles as the next stage of development. And Schelling has rightly
been credited with following through this project in a deliberate and
consistent fashion. It was thanks to this original achievement in substantially extending the idealist position to incorporate the philosophy
of nature[37] that an academic career in Jena, through Goethe's intervention, was first effectively opened up to Schelling.

Now, there is another manuscript, subsequently given the title of
Commentary on the Timaeus, that also gives evidence of Schelling's early
independent philosophical thinking. The text provides a cursory commentary upon certain passages from Plato's *Timaeus* in the interest of securing the principal aims and intentions of the new idealism. Schelling
is particularly concerned with the passage in which Timaeus speaks
about the beginning of the world and the constitution of the 'elements'
(*Timaeus* 53c). Schelling makes use of this ancient document expressing
a conception of the world compatible with his doctrine of Ideas quite explicitly
in the name of the new idealism and without the slightest concerns
about anachronistic interpretation. He allows no philological doubts
to obstruct his access to the text. This manuscript, which in contrast to
the one we discussed earlier, was published some time ago, has also en-
riched the scholarly labours, already bordering upon the forensic, that
have been so painstakingly dedicated to clarifying the origins of idealism over the last few decades.[38] Schelling's *Commentary on the Timaeus*
itself *predates* the *System Programme* and its explicit call for a philosophy

---

[37] For more on the specific local and general historical background here, cf. M. Durner,
'Die Naturphilosophie im 18. Jahrhundert und der naturwissenschaftliche Unterricht
in Tübingen. Zu den Quellen von Schellings Naturphilosophie' (Arch. Gen. Phil. 73,
1991, especially p. 88 ff.).

[38] Cf. the seminal work by D. Henrich, *Der Grund im Bewusstsein* (Stuttgart 1992), which
represents a major synthesis of his numerous earlier studies in this field, and essentially
interprets the development of German idealist philosophy in terms of a conception
originally formulated, though never fully elaborated, by Hölderlin.

of nature based on Ideas, as cited and discussed earlier. The manuscript reveals that Schelling, about two years after composition of the text documenting his early reception of the *Ion*, was already pursuing the idea of a philosophy of nature *independently* of his intellectual engagement with Fichte.

It was K.J. Windischmann who first published a German translation of the *Timaeus* as an 'authentic original document of true physics' in 1804. He dedicated the work to 'Prof. Schelling, the rediscover of the true and most ancient physics' in the 'firm conviction of the harmonious agreement between two great men': the 'magnificent original document of physics, which the world spirit has preserved in Plato's *Timaeus* for the benefit of all posterity' can only adequately be comprehended and appreciated by contemporary philosophers of nature. The philologist A. Boeckh commented that Windischmann's 'empty and confused phantasies' had merely 'performed an unwelcome service for the world spirit'.39 Schelling himself responded to Windischmann's dedication of the translation in a letter of thanks of 1 February 1804 as follows: 'I am most delighted to read the *Timaeus* in German given that I have read it so often before in the Greek. But what would you say if I were to tell you that the *Timaeus* is not actually a work of Plato's at all. It loses nothing of its true value if it fails to bear this name, but this insight itself provides us with an entirely new perspective of judgement and a new document for our understanding of the difference between the ancient and modern worlds. Despite the fact that Aristotle and other writers cite the *Timaeus* as a genuine Platonic work, I would even be prepared to regard it as a very late Christian work that was intended to make good the loss of the genuine original work, if it did not indeed cause that loss'.40

Just why the sedulous Schleiermacher, so careful in his ordering of the dialogues, so ready to preface each translation with its own specific introduction, should have chosen to omit the *Timaeus* when he came

---

39 *Über die Bildung der Weltseele im Timaeus des Platon*, in Boeckh, *Gesammelte Kleine Schriften*, III (Leipzig 1866), p. 137.

40 In H. Fuhrmans (ed.), *Schelling, Briefe und Dokumente* III (Bonn 1962). For other similar expressions of caution regarding the question of authenticity, cf. Schelling, *Philosophie und Religion* (1804), SW VI, p. 36, and *Über das Wesen der menschlichen Freiheit* (1809), SW VII, p, 374; but cf. *Philosophie der Offenbarung*, SW XIII, p. 100, where Schelling assumes the authenticity of the dialogue and appeals to Schleiermacher in this connection. C.G. Bardili, as mentioned earlier, had wondered (in his *Epochen der vorzüglichsten philosophischen Begriffe*, I, Halle 1788, p. 193) whether the entire dialogue was itself based upon an 'original text' by Timaeus of Locri 'to which Plato had merely added his own elucidations, thoughts and remarks'.

to produce his German version of Plato's writings is difficult to say. There is repeated mention of this dialogue in his correspondence with Schlegel. As late as 5 May 1804, Schlegel reports from Paris in a letter to Schleiermacher that he himself will be offering a translation of the *Timaeus* in one or perhaps two years time.[41] As is well-known, all of these work plans eventually came to nothing, and Schleiermacher was reluctantly compelled to take over the remaining burden of work on his own. In the event, his translations of Plato do not include *The Laws* or the *Timaeus*, although Schleiermacher's general introduction refers repeatedly to both dialogues. It was presumably simply the lack of time that accounts for this omission.

VI. Kant and the Demiurge

Let us now consider Schelling's commentary, written at a time when he still took the *Timaeus* to be an authentic Platonic text. The principal interest that guides Schelling's selective reading of this dialogue, that presents Plato's 'philosophy of nature' in the form of a learned myth, is directed towards the central notion of the 'Demiurge' and the 'presuppositions' of its creative activity in shaping the world. Schelling interprets Plato's remarks as an attempt to explain the unity of the intelligible world, and one that, for all the immediacy of its initial character, nevertheless corresponds to Kant's project of transcendental philosophy.[42] Thus the Ideas, 'which Plato understands to

---

[41] *Aus Schleiermachers Leben in Briefen*, III, ed. W. Dilthey (Berlin 1861), p. 342. Cf. also the relevant notes on Plato, which are thought to date from before 1803, and have now been published in the new critical edition of Schleiermacher's works (I 3, Berlin 1988, p. 359 [No.56] and p. 373 [No. 118]).

[42] This text of Schelling's, which the Munich editors date to 1794, is found in a notebook under the heading: '7) Concerning the spirit of the Platonic philosophy'. For further details, cf. the editorial report provided by H. Buchner: 'Timaeus' (1794), in *Schellingiana* IV, ed. W.E. Ehrhardt (Stuttgart 1994). This edition was produced in the context of the new critical edition of Schelling's works. The manuscript in question, with certain interruptions, numerous insertions, and some marginal emendations and elucidations, discusses parts of Plato's *Timaeus* found between 27d 5 and 53e 1, together with some excerpts from the *Philebus*. Instead of the Stephanus numbering with which we are familiar today, Schelling refers to the text as laid out in the Zweibrücken edition (Bip. IX, p. 301 f.). This edition provides the dialogue with the subtitle *ē peri phuseōs* and adds: 'cum Marsilii Ficini interpretatione'. This refers to the Latin translation, which appears in parallel at the bottom of the page throughout. The subtitle is further explicated as: 'sive de natura vel de universitate'. On a few occasions, Schelling refers explicitly to Ficino's translation. This text is also to be found in the archives of the former East Berlin Academy of Sciences (NL 34). The remarkably difficult circumstances in which

include all the pure concepts belonging to the faculty of representation' (20, note), are directly contrasted with the realm of sensuous intuition. The Platonic distinction between being and becoming[43], which possesses an essentially ontological status, is here interpreted with reference to the world-producing creative God as a direct parallel to Kantian epistemological distinction between the *a priori* forms of the understanding and the sensuous reception of the empirical manifold (the *noēsis meta logou* over against the *doxa met'aisthēseōs alogou*). According to Plato, the ontology of the unalterably self-same in contrast to the changeable character of that which comes to be and passes away provides the appropriate point of orientation for creative activity of the Demiurge. Schelling takes over this idea by interpreting this creative agency in terms of the critical conception of subjectivity.[44]

'For here it is already presupposed, as it were, that the Demiurge should have had a certain ideal before its eyes and in accordance with which it undertook to produce the world. If this ideal was indeed an eternal and ungenerated one, that is, a pure ideal entirely independent of everything sensible, then the creative product that the Demiurge formed in accordance with the former would inevitably itself be perfect, for all perfection is nothing but the harmonious agreement with ideals. If, on the other hand, the world was copied from a sensible image, then it would inevitably become something imperfect and irregular for irregularity is the very character of everything sensible' (20 R). The productive relationship between paradigm and copy is translated here into a transcendental perspective upon the conditions of possibility of experience. [Plato] could not possibly have regarded the form of the world, its regularity and its law-governed character, as a form simply inherent in matter itself or as one that could itself be produced by

---

I tried to get access to the text in the early 1980s not merely provides the stuff of anecdote with regard to conditions at the time, but also provides an exemplary illustration, in miniature, of a certain chapter of modern German history. One can only be grateful that such things now belong to the past.

43 *Timaeus* 27d 6 ff.

44 For the new Munich edition of Schelling's works, H. Krings has provided a detailed interpretation of the manuscript under the programmatic title of 'Genesis and Matter', which the author has kindly made available to me in advance of publication. Krings goes so far as to interpret Schelling's 'Kantian' inspiration as already essentially Platonising in character: 'On closer examination we can see that Schelling guides the critical-transcendental approach of Kant more strongly into the current of Platonic thought than the other way around' (p. 7).

matter. He was compelled to assume that the form of the world resided in something quite different (something distinct in its very essence from matter); accordingly, he located this form in the understanding itself.'[45]

The dualism between regularity and irregularity is immediately linked by Schelling with the passage from the *Philebus* that discusses the dialectic of the limited and the unlimited and the relation between the two.[46] '[Philebus] could discover the cause of this connection between limiting form (*peras*) and indeterminate matter (*apeiron*) neither in the former alone nor in the latter alone, nor indeed in both of them together [....] It seemed to him rather that a third term was required, one that would be able to connect both or to provide "the world with a form that was itself an afterimage of the original and pure form of the understanding"' (21 and 21R). Schelling thus interprets the *relationship of original image and derived afterimage* that underlies the creative activity of the Demiurge as a configuring of the world in accordance with an ideal projection. And here we see the emergence of a central theme of Kant's third Critique, a work that is repeatedly mentioned in Schelling's subsequent marginal notations. The quotation marks in the concluding sentence of the passage are clearly intended to refer us directly to Kant's book.[47]

'The key for explaining the entire philosophy of Plato is to notice that he everywhere translates *the subjective into the objective* (my emphasis, R.B.). That is why we find in Plato the observation (although it was already made long before him) that the visible world is nothing but an image or copy of the invisible world. No philosophy would ever have come upon such an observation if the philosophical reason behind it were not to be found within ourselves. For insofar as the whole of nature, as it appears to us, is not merely a product of our empirical

---

[45] The neo-Platonic commentary by Proclus grounds the argument in the traditional way within an essentially teleological and cosmological context. It was only with the rise of critical philosophy that the dialogue would be interpreted in terms of the theory of knowledge. Cf. *Agathou gar to cosmeín kai tattein*. In *Platonis Timaeum Commentaria* (ed. E. Diehl), Leipzig 1903, p. 285, line 3, on *Timaeus* 30a.

[46] *Philebus* 23c ff. In this connection, the relationship between the *Timaeus* and the *Philebus* is far from obvious. Schelling may well have been influenced by Plessing, who had already drawn a parallel here, and who is often mentioned in Schelling's manuscript (cf. F.V.L. Plessing, *Versuche zur Aufklärung der Philosophie des ältesten Althertums*, 2 vols., Leipzig 1788/90). It was of course only Schelling who first attempted to establish a relevant connection with Kantian lines of thought.

[47] Kant, *Critique of Judgement* (1790), A XXV f.

receptivity, but is properly an effect of our faculty of representation insofar as the latter contains pure, original and self-grounding forms (of nature), then to that extent the world belongs through representation to a higher faculty than that of mere sensibility, and nature is thus presented as the very type of a higher world that expresses the pure laws of this world. By perceiving the legislation of nature that is prescribed by the pure understanding, man could therefore have been led very early to the idea that the visible world is the type of the invisible, a thought that is grounded in man himself insofar as it is referred to the law-like character of nature in general, but one that leads merely to delusion as soon as it is also extended to the realm of sensible intuition (with respect to its matter)' (24 and 25R).[48]

Nature is thought in relation to man, conceived as a totality that is projected out of man himself and his own immanent potentiality. Nature is thus more than the world of phenomenal appearances that are to be grasped as standing collectively under the order of laws prescribed by the understanding. For nature now presents itself to knowledge as an already organised interconnection of parts, as if it represented the externalisation of some inner reality, or as if the human spirit had posited nature over against itself as an after-image or reflection of its own being.[49] Kant's *Critique of Judgement* had defended a comparable perspective with regard to theoretical science as a general maxim for systematic investigation. Of course, this itself tells us nothing about the substantial reality of nature in itself, but merely clarifies the correlation, required by the demands of knowledge, between the appropriate coherence of nature and our own primary *a priori* intellectual purposes. The post-Kantian thinkers grounded all their speculative hopes on the ambiguous status of Kant's third Critique, which, although it certainly went beyond the rigid restrictions of the transcendental aesthetic, never projected a philosophy of nature like that so characteristic of 'objective idealism'. The final masterpiece of the founder of critical philosophy, attempting as it

---

[48] For a similar view, cf. G.G. Fülleborn, *Beiträge zur Geschichte der Philosophie* 9 (Jena/Leipzig 1798), p. 49 ff.: 'Led astray by the false glimmer of all-too vivid and imaginative notions, Plato was driven upon the rocks that should no longer have offered any peril for philosophical wisdom, and adopted the system of the Locrian'.

[49] A few years earlier, D. Tiedemann had already seen such thoughts as an adumbration of the Christian conception of the Trinity that Augustine, certain other Church Fathers, and the Scholastics, had later attempted to interpret in terms of the rational structure of the world itself. Cf. *Dialogorum Platonis argumenta exposita et illustrata* (Zweibrücken 1786), p. 310.

did to produce a kind of systematic synthesis on the basis of reflective judgement without crossing the line and falling into a reckless and irresponsible rationalism, was thus regarded as a profoundly revelatory text whose seals needed only to be broken.[50]

Schelling's study of the *Timaeus*, which probably also involved a direct exchange of views with Hölderlin[51], opened up one possible path of advance here. Schelling's occasional reference to the 'faculty of representation' reveals his familiarity with Reinhold's recent attempts to develop Kantian epistemology in a new direction.[52] But there is as yet no direct or tangible engagement with Reinhold's *Attempt towards a New Theory of the Human Faculty of Representation* of 1789.

Together with the letters[53], the brilliant early pieces that Schelling published in 1794[54] and 1795[55] reveal the epoch-making significance of his encounter with Fichte's philosophical programme, outlined in the *Doctrine of Science*, which was based upon an explicit examination of the structure of the ego. Schelling then takes up the Platonic line of thought again in the introduction to his *Ideas towards a Philosophy of Nature* (1797), which attempts to go beyond the stage represented by the philosophy of reflection by recalling our attention to the tradition of the classical 'metaphysics of substance' from Plato through to

---

[50] Cf. the emphatic public expression of this view in Schelling's slightly later work, *On the Ego as Principle of Philosophy* of 1795 (SW I, p. 232, 242). For the context in which Schelling developed his early concept of philosophy, cf. the thorough dissertation by B. Sandkaulen-Bock, *Ausgang vom Unbedingten* (Göttingen 1990). H. Kuhlmann, in his study *Schellings früher Idealismus* (Stuttgart 1993), acknowledges his unfamiliarity with Schelling's early commentary on the *Timaeus*.

[51] Cf. Hölderlin's allusion, in the earliest *Hyperion* fragment of 1794, to the tale of Solon as recounted in *Timaeus* 22b. (Hölderlin, *Sämtliche Werke*, Stuttgarter Ausgabe III, p. 169).

[52] We would be much clearer on this point if we possessed more than simply the title of one of Schelling's *specimina* from his time at the Tübingen *Stift* (namely, *Über die Möglichkeit einer Philosophie ohne Beinamen, nebst einigen Bemerkungen über die Reinholdsche Elementarphilosophie*). For the 'Reinholdian' line as represented at the *Stift*, cf. J.L. Döderlein, in D. Henrich/J.L. Döderlein, 'C.J. Diez', *Hegel-Studien* 3, 1965, p. 285. In *Das neue philosophische Magazin* of 1790 (edited by J.H. Abicht and F.G. Born with the subtitle 'For the further Clarification and Application of the Kantian System'), an anonymous contributor (actually Tenneman) published an essay entitled 'An Attempt to Explicate a Passage from Plato's *Timaeus* through the Theory of the Faculty of Representation'. The passage in question is Bip. IX 312 (34b 10 ff. in the Stephanus numbering). This otherwise unremarkable essay shows at least how Reinhold's characteristic vocabulary was already being taken up in Kantian circles.

[53] Schelling to Hegel (6.1.1795; cf. also 4.2.1795)

[54] Schelling, *On the Possibility of a Form of Philosophy in General.*

[55] Schelling, *On the Ego as Principle of Philosophy.*

Spinoza and Leibniz. In terms of the historical development of idealist thought, Schelling's turn away from Fichteanism has often been interpreted as a liberating breakthrough in which this, the most gifted of all Fichte's followers, first discovers his authentic intellectual task and then takes the necessary immanent step from subjective to objective idealism. Thus the philosophy of nature comes to complement the original emphasis upon the self-grounding ego, and eventually leads after 1800 to a systematic philosophy of identity that locates the highest point of systematic construction in the point of indifference between the poles of subjectivity and objectivity.

While this standard interpretation is not entirely false, it ignores the genuine inspiration that the encounter with a newly reawakened Plato provided for the entire range of problems bequeathed by Kant. Schelling's spontaneous and intuitive engagement with a philosophy of nature modelled on the powers of ideal creation, pursued as it was in the spirit of intellectual clarification, immediately brought him onto the right path that allowed him to formulate his own contribution to the achievements of the idealist movement.

VII. Schelling's Approach to Mythology

Apart from the substantive interpretation of the Platonic myth in the *Timaeus*, the remarks concerning the *literary form* of the work that Schelling inserts by way of marginal annotation are also highly instructive. He projects the complex situation in which the younger minds now found themselves at the *Stift* back onto the ancient sources. For the new generation was embroiled in the struggle between the enthusiastic reception of Kant and the new philosophy and an orthodoxy that emphatically insisted it was also speaking in the name of reason.[56] On the one hand, Schelling expressed the common Enlightenment theme that the prevailing political powers naturally conspired to obscure the truth and that the crucial task was therefore that of deciphering the inevitably concealed message of liberation. On the other hand, he voiced clear hostility to the kind of inadequate contemporary defences of Christian

---

[56] In addition to Schelling's aforementioned letters to Hegel, cf. his own queries and replies (24 December 1794 and the end of January 1795) in *Briefe von und an Hegel* I, ed. J. Hoffmeister, (Hamburg 1952); for a partial English translation of the correspondence, cf. G.W.F. Hegel, *The Letters*, tr. Clark Butler and Christiane Seiler (Bloomington, Indiana University Press 1984).

revelation that were mounted by his teachers at the *Stift* (by Storr and others).

The way in which Schelling writes so directly out of his own situation, as he and his like-minded contemporaries themselves perceived it, means that he avoids the two ways of interpreting mythical presentation that we are most likely to consider appropriate today.[57] On the one hand, deliberate recourse to myth is frequently justified on the grounds that our finite human understanding is incapable of grasping on its own a truth that is only fully revealed to the gods, an approach that is well exemplified in the Platonic dialogues, and especially in relation to the central analogies employed in the *Republic*.[58] On the other hand, mythical presentation in the dialogues sometimes performs the strategic function of identifying still obscure problems and suggesting further perspectives that have not yet been explored, thus expressing the need to formulate further arguments for the systematic intellectual position that lies behind the dialogues themselves. The interpretation of Plato articulated by the contemporary 'Tübingen School' (Krämer and Gaiser) appeals to all of these various literary features in defence of the view that it is necessary to look beyond the text of the dialogues for the 'unwritten doctrine' that underlies them.[59] But Schelling adopts neither of these approaches, which are now so familiar to us. For Schelling, the whole problem is not essentially a *hermeneutic enigma* at all, as it was for his contemporary Schleiermacher, who would soon base his entire translation of Plato on this assumption (see Section XIII).

According to Schelling's view of the matter, Plato is actually expressing himself here in an apprehensive, cautious and obscure manner. 'He speaks precisely in the tone which the persecuted friend of truth must still assume even now. [. . . . .] For see how alike is the language of truth in all times!' (21 R). And in a marginal remark he adds 'c'est tout comme chez nous'. And as far as the presumptuous claims of

---

[57] In the short essay of 1793, *Concerning the Myths, Historical Legends and Philosophemes of the Most Ancient World*, Schelling still defends this view, which was widespread at the time: 'Plato too, it would seem, was often enough compelled to present his philosophy in purely sensuous terms. One must often tread paths that wander in a kind of half-light...' (AA I, p. 227).

[58] For example, *Republic* 504d and 506d ff.

[59] This line of interpretation is further developed in Th. Szlezák, *Platon und die Schriftlichkeit der Philosophie* (Berlin 1985); and more recently the same author's *Platon lesen* (Stuttgart 1993).

revelation are concerned, Schelling writes, 'This entire procedure represents nothing but the exaltation of revelation at the expense of reason, something which can never prove to be advantageous to either of them, an act of injustice that is utterly incompatible with the honest methods of the unprejudiced historian, an act of injustice which utterly forgets something that it beholds every single day before its very eyes, namely how often it is not conviction supported by proper reasons but rather superior political power which has privileged a certain view of things, which has put the voice of opposition to silence, or forced it to speak in a lowered and almost imperceptible tone . . . '

The 'unbiased historian' will not yield to dogmatism, even if the strongest battalions are all on the other side. For it would be intrinsically unjust, and a violation of autonomous reason and hallowed revelation alike, to attempt to force the two together. For his own part, Plato was expressing his own monotheistic convictions in his account of the Demiurge, even if he refrained from presenting a strictly demonstrative theory out of consideration of the circumstances. Schelling's excited rhetoric here suggests that the resolute defence of a truly rational theology is required to counter the discredited behaviour of a 'priesthood that has recently feigned its attachment to reason'.[60] The struggle between reason and revelation, which so animated Schelling's young contemporaries, can only be decided by someone who can advance the cause of the new idealism with a theory of the absolute as the rational subject intrinsically related to the world as a totality. It is precisely in this direction that Schelling obviously wishes to develop Kant's own suggestions for a theology framed in the context of the third Critique.[61]

VIII. The World as a Living Being

'For we must further remember that Plato regarded the whole world as a *zōon* – that is, as an organised living being – and thus as a being whose parts are only possible in relation to the whole, whose parts relate reciprocally to one another as ends and means and thus reciprocally produce one another with regard to both their form and their

---

[60] As formulated in the *Earliest System Programme of German Idealism*; English translation in H.S. Harris, *Hegel's Development. Towards the Sunlight 1770–1801* (Oxford 1972, p. 511).

[61] Kant, *Critique of Judgement* §§71 f. (especially A 331 ff.). Kant's decisive verdict on physico-theology (§ 85), on the other hand, is avoided or ignored.

interconnection with one another'. And here Schelling adds a note, 'See Kant's *Critique of Judgement* §65'. The text then continues: 'We must bear in mind that, in accordance with the subjective constitution of our faculty of knowledge, we cannot possibly conceive of the emergence of an organised being except through the causality of a concept, an idea [*Idee*] that must determine *a priori* everything contained in the being in question, that just as the individual parts of the organised being reciprocally produce one another and thus produce the whole as well, so too the idea of the whole must in turn be conceived as already determining *a priori* the form and harmoniously related parts. (note ibid.)

'To this extent, Plato was able, or rather even found himself compelled, to assume ideas underlying the natural being, but precisely only ideas, only *zoa noeta*, only the original paradigms of natural beings insofar as reason can conceive of their form as destined to cohere harmoniously into a whole, into a purpose.

'This was an elevated idea of Plato's that could easily inspire him to spiritual intoxication. For he wished to pursue the harmony that characterised natural beings not merely in their relation to one another but also within each individual itself, and to do so not along the paths of an empirical science of nature but by investigation of the pure form of the faculty of representation itself. It is no miracle, therefore, if Plato expressed himself concerning this sublime idea in a language that soars uncommonly beyond the usual speech of philosophy, if his very language is itself the expression of a philosophical intoxication that inevitably seizes hold of us once we discover the super-sensible principle of the form and harmony of the world within ourselves.

'But it was just this intoxicating vision of a principle sublimely enthroned beyond the entire realm of the sensible that led Plato to express himself so powerfully and compellingly concerning the nature of this principle, and the purity that removed it so utterly from the realm of the material. It is therefore almost impossible to understand why the belief in the physical existence of these ideas has so often been attributed to him, since he explicitly presented the form of their existence as directly opposed to the form of all physical existence' (25 R and 26).

The first thing that strikes us here is Schelling's positive remarks about the unusual *language*, which fittingly expresses the philosopher's intoxication with his sublime discovery. The discovery directs us to an ideal principle for the form of the world, both with respect to its individual members as immanently organised and purposive beings and with respect to the overall harmonious arrangement of the cosmos itself. That the origin of this principle actually lies 'within ourselves' is not what is written in Plato, but rather something that naturally suggests itself to his later commentator by virtue of an essentially trans-historical parallel with Kant's transcendental re-formulation of the classical conception of teleology.[62]

The inspired and enthusiastic language of Plato, the praises of which we have often seen Schelling so ready to sing, would certainly also have appealed to the author of the *Oldest System Programme* who readily invoked the aesthetic spirit against the arid 'philosophers of the letter'.[63] But Schelling emphasises here, and indeed repeatedly throughout his commentary, that Plato's doctrine of ideas is not to be interpreted in a vulgar sense as a claim concerning *physical* existence. The term 'physical', with its Kantian connotation of empirical intuition, is somewhat misleading. The *a priori* character of the ideas certainly cannot belong to the sphere of *doxa* and the irrational domain of sensible intuition, as Schelling stressed at the beginning of his discussion. Yet the ideas do enjoy the status of something actual, do signify more than simply the orderly forms of the human understanding that are dependent upon the *a posteriori* deliverances of sense. The classical position in the debate concerning the reality of the ideas begins to waver when confronted with the merely 'probable' myth of the Demiurge who created the world as a living being.[64]

---

[62] Just before the paragraph we have quoted, Kant himself writes: 'Plato, himself a master of this science [sc. geometry], was overcome by enthusiasm when he saw that the original character of things is such that it can be discovered independently of any experience, and that the mind is able to derive the harmony of beings from their supersensible principle; (to these beings we must add the properties of numbers, with which the mind plays in music). It was this enthusiasm that lifted Plato above empirical concepts to ideas that he thought could be explained only by an intellectual community existing between ourselves and the origin of all beings' (*Critique of Judgement* §62. A 269).

[63] This point is surely worth bearing in mind given the still disputed authorship of the *System Programme*.

[64] In his *Commentary on Plato's Timaeus* (Oxford 1928, p. 75 ff.), A.E. Taylor takes great pains to play down the idea of the relation between God and the world as expressed in the middle period dialogues (the *Phaedo* and the *Republic*) and the theology formulated in the *Laws*, and to exclude the later neo-Platonic and Christian notions (Dante). Although it naturally does not occur to him to consider neo-Kantian or idealist parallels in this connection, he does cite Lotze's writings on metaphysics. Taylor's perceptive and erudite commentary itself indicates, in a secondary and indirect manner, how Schelling's original insight can shed sudden light upon an important problem from a very unexpected quarter.

IX. The Problem of Organisation

The explicit allusion to §65 of the *Critique of Judgement*, which Schelling
makes twice in the course of his discussion, refers us directly to Kant's
complicated analysis of 'organised beings'. The organised being is not
merely determined by virtue of the fact that the interrelationship of
parts and whole here resembles that of a work of art that is dependent
upon the maker or designer as its external cause. The cause of the
constitutive relationship between parts and whole is rather to be sought
in the fact 'that the parts (of the natural product) only combine to
form a whole insofar as they are reciprocally both cause and effect
of that form'.[65] The example that Kant provides clearly reveals the
difference involved here. In a watch, every little wheel forms part of
that functional unity that the watchmaker has designed in advance and
that he may well have to restore in the future. But no single wheel in the
watch produces any other wheel, any more than any watch is capable of
producing another watch, or of repairing and adjusting the defective
mechanism by its own means, 'yet this is precisely what we can expect
of the organised products of nature. – An organised being is therefore
not merely a machine [...] but rather a self-perpetuating formative
power.

'In considering nature and the ability it displays in organised products, we say far too little if we call this an *analogue of art*, for in that case
we think of an artist (a rational being) apart from nature. Rather, nature organises itself, and it does so within each species of its organised
products; for although the pattern that nature follows is the same overall, that pattern also includes deviations useful for self-preservation as
required by circumstances. We might be closer if we call this inscrutable
property of nature an *analogue of life*. But in that case, we must either
endow matter, as mere matter, with a kind of property (as hylozoism
does) that conflicts with its own nature. Or else we must supplement
matter with an alien principle (a soul) *conjoined* to it. But if an organised product is to be a natural product, then we cannot make this soul
the artificer that constructed it since that would simply remove the
product from (corporeal) nature. And yet the only alternative would
be to say that this soul uses as its instrument organised matter; but if we
presuppose organised matter, we do not thereby make it a whit more

---

[65] A 287.

intelligible. Strictly speaking, therefore, the organisation of nature has nothing analogous to any causality known to us.'[66]

The paradoxical character that Kant expounds here leads him to ascribe to nature a certain *inscrutable capacity* of its own. All the known analogies seem to fail us in this connection, for whether we appeal to the agency of the artist or that of life itself, we end up either demanding more of mere matter than it can deliver, or of arguing in a circle, or of indulging in purely metaphorical comparisons with the 'soul'. Unable as he is to explain the inner formative powers of nature, Kant surprisingly turns instead, in a footnote to the section in question, to the field of contemporary politics: 'On the other hand, the analogy of these distinct natural purposes can serve to elucidate a certain kind of human association, though it is one found more often as an idea than in actuality: in speaking of the complete transformation of a large people into a state, as took place only recently, the word *organisation* was frequently and very aptly applied to the establishment of legal authorities etc., and even to the entire body politic. For each member in such a whole should indeed be not merely a means, but also an end or purpose; and while each member contributes to making the whole possible, the idea of that whole should in turn determine the member's position and function'.

Kant's immediate turn from the problems of natural teleology to the political constitution of the state, precisely in the contemporary context of the *French Revolution*, must have electrified his readers in the Tübingen *Stift*. The new social forms currently being created by appeal to reason also illuminate the rational productions of nature. Since we can have no definite knowledge about Kant's own thoughts here, given his principled scepticism concerning metaphysics, we must look to further points of comparison. Such a strategy unwittingly suggests recourse to ancient mythology, which could only express the idea that the world owed its existence to the free production of reason in essentially pictorial images. In the new post-revolutionary situation, the body politic was no longer to be regarded as a piece of mechanical clockwork, a sort of a Leviathan that could only be kept in motion externally or artificially. Rather the body politic now takes on the appearance of an ethical totality of society, together with all the authentic roles played by the parts of that society, that is united in mutual purpose.

[66] A 289 f.

If the inscrutable organising capacity of nature is to be explained in some such way as this, then strictly speaking, the Demiurge would appear to be a superfluous hypothesis. And this is clearly how Schelling himself understood the Platonic story of the ideally created 'living being' that is itself the world.[67] Here once again he reveals his interpretative tendency to penetrate the literary discretion of the text in order to explicate his own systematic theses. He assumes that Plato was only able to express through indirect mythical narrative what Schelling's philosophy of nature was soon destined to proclaim without the garments of mythology – namely, that the world as a whole maintains itself through the harmony of its respective parts, which are themselves purposive totalities and thus not merely so many elements of a further transcendent functional context. For on the latter supposition, the ultimate guiding cause would have to be located externally beyond the complex totality itself, a thought that would fundamentally contradict the principal maxim of all Schelling's philosophising up to and including his later systematic 'philosophy of identity'.

According to that maxim, it is quite impossible to conceive any possible transition from the unconditioned to the conditioned.[68] This is because the opposition thereby presupposed between the conditioned and the unconditioned would unwittingly turn the latter itself into something finite, thus transforming it back into something conditioned. And then it would lack that superiority over everything conditioned that lends it the authentic status of the unconditioned in the first place. Thus the necessary differentiation must proceed in an entirely immanent manner insofar as the intrinsically indifferent absolute must express itself both in the shapes of nature and spirit, shapes that thus represent the conditioned forms of the absolute itself.

If any transition from the unconditioned to the conditioned is inconceivable, then the conceptual grounds for all conditioned relationships must be sought in a more complex conception of an absolute that

---

[67] I shall not discuss the question of the 'world soul', which Schelling's commentary later mentions in passing. Vieillard-Baron, in the study already cited (cf. note 19), has provided a lucid examination of Schelling's own essay on the subject, *On the World Soul, a Hypothesis of Higher Physics for the Elucidation of the Universal Organism* (1794). In this context, Vieillard-Baron naturally wonders about Schelling's possible knowledge of the *Timaeus* (p. 147 ff.) because the commentary under discussion here had not then been published.

[68] Cf., for example, *Philosophical Letters on Dogmatism and Criticism* (1795), SW I, p. 294, 313 f.; *Elucidations of the Idealism Propounded in the Doctrine of Science* (1796/97), SW I, p. 367.

stands in an essential relationship to itself. Such an absolute would no longer merely represent a principle, such as Spinoza's single substance or Fichte's conception of the ego, which was modelled on the former. The concept of a self-relating absolute thus suggests, at least in outline, the idea of a self-constructing system, and an idea with which mature idealist thought breaks with the paradigmatic approach of the classical metaphysical tradition. This argument leads to Hegel's speculative panlogism and eventually to the later Schelling's 'positive philosophy', which attempted to overcome the former by demoting it to the status of a purely 'negative' philosophy. But this takes us far beyond the original philosophical impulse that post-Kantian thought received from the encounter with Plato.

x. Schlegel's Romantic Insight

We have already discussed the transitional achievement of the young Schelling in developing the post-Kantian philosophical position in relation to Plato's concept of enthusiasm and his cosmological use of myth. I would now like to draw attention to a *second innovation* of early idealist thought that reflects a different aspect of the rediscovery of Plato's philosophy in this period. This aspect is well expressed in the aesthetic appeal that the *System Programme* directs specifically to those who are capable of uniting intellectual thought and creative imagination, in contrast to mere 'philosophers of the letter'. The notion of *philosophy itself as a work of art* is an original idea that found a lively echo amongst the early romantic and idealist thinkers of the period. Kant, of course, would have contemptuously dismissed this idea as an expression of the very kind of unbridled and irresponsible 'enthusiasm' that his critical philosophy had struggled, and with initially evident success, to control and contain. But the rediscovery of Plato, the obvious literary artist amongst philosophers, offered a shining example for a whole new dimension of thinking over and beyond the habitual scholastic conflicts of philosophy, one that had nothing to do with traditional dogmas and the criticisms mounted against them, with argumentational proof, reliable conceptual foundations and logical demonstration.

On the contrary, the new philosophy demanded by the times essentially required quasi-artistic gifts insofar as it could never be articulated without the kind of 'spirit' and 'aesthetic sense' explicitly emphasised by the *System Programme*. But spiritual attunement and a sense for the beautiful have never been regarded as conventional accomplishments that could be taught by rule, but only as essentially inexplicable gifts of genius that cannot be externally acquired at will. This general train of thought testifies to the apocryphal continuity between the 'enthusiastic' Platonisms of Shaftesbury and Hemsterhuis, even if we cannot speak of any expressly identifiable 'influence' at work here.[69]

Friedrich Schlegel was certainly the first to introduce the idea of philosophy as an all-embracing work of art into the intellectual world at the close of the eighteenth century. He had no difficulty in appealing directly to the example of Plato in this connection since, according to his own testimony, he had himself grown up with the writings of Winckelmann and Plato. And Schlegel's own pioneering early work of 1795–97, *On the Study of Greek Poetry*, already discusses whether the Platonic dialogues should be regarded as 'poetical philosophemes or philosophical poems'.[70] And thus around 1798, we find Schlegel considering the idea of translating Plato's Dialogues into German, something that indeed later came to pass with the direct influence and express collaboration of his friend Schleiermacher.

Schlegel was so enthusiastic about promoting such a project of 'symphilosophein', or collaborative philosophical reflection, precisely because he expected the literary and aesthetic *critic* to supply autonomous contributions of his own that would live up to the standards and demands of the original creative works to be transmitted and discussed. 'Perhaps an entirely new epoch in the arts and sciences would commence if such collaborative work in philosophy and such collaborative work in poetry became so widespread and so intimate that it would no longer be so singular a thing to behold several mutually enhancing kinds of people joining together to produce essentially shared works'.[71] From the governing romantic perspective of a 'progressive universal poetry', this process would gradually lead to the dissolution of all distinctions of genre, to the unification of art and philosophy, and to the intensification of social communication, all by virtue of the ongoing

---

[69] In a piece entitled 'Simon ou des facultés de l'âme' that is occasionally mentioned by Schlegel, Hemsterhuis imitates a kind of Socratic dialogue centred upon the problem of the soul. Posing as the 'editor' of the text in question, the author presents his own views ironically in the context of the prevailing Enlightenment culture: 'l'inutilité d'une pareille doctrine dans notre siècle de perfection ne me laisse que le triste avantage de vous avoir offert une antiquité' (*Oeuvres* II, Paris 1809, p. 222).

[70] F. Schlegel, *Kritische Ausgabe* I, p. 332.   [71] Athenäum Fragment 125 (KA II, p. 185)

and never-ending transformation of the contingent and particular in the light of the universal.

Thus, both the critics and the original authors involved would exercise and reveal their own powers in ever new ways precisely through the continuing process of commentary and interpretation. The relevant model, therefore, is not a godlike creation of a system *ex nihilo*, as it was for the early idealists, but rather an actively sympathetic response on the part of the critic and the philologist to the significant creative works of the past. As far as the aspirations of the early romantics were concerned, this would constitute the culminating achievement of modernity itself. In spite of the fact that both these programmes – that of the idealists and that of the early romantics – were formulated at the same historical moment, towards the end of the last decade of the eighteenth century, they nonetheless represented quite different perspectives with regard to the question concerning the relevant contemporary interpretation of Plato.

'In a dialogue, in a dialogical work of art, for example, it is properly speaking the mutual communication of thoughts accomplished by the participants that is itself the object of representation [*Darstellung*]. What is represented is the indeterminate, which is precisely why every representation is something infinite. But it is only the determinate that can be communicated as such. And it is not the indeterminate but the determinate that all sciences seek. In the highest of all sciences, however, which is not supposed to teach us anything determinate but must rather determine what it is to determine anything at all, it is precisely therefore insufficient simply to supply what is thought as something that is already finished and concluded. This science is not designed to teach us this or that conclusion of thought, but rather thinking as such. And that is why the relevant communications here also necessarily assume the form of representations; for one cannot teach thinking itself except by act and example, by actually thinking in the presence of someone, and not by simply communicating what has already been thought, but rather by representing to the other the process of thinking as it arises and comes to be. And that is precisely why the spirit of this science can only be rendered completely clear in and through a work of art'.

Schlegel's implicit reference here to Plato's masterpieces of philosophical art, which embody the living process of thinking and thereby invite the reader to participate actively in that very process, occurs in a work devoted expressly to Lessing, critic par excellence and much praised model in Schlegel's eyes. The passage in question is dedicated 'To Fichte', and Schlegel is clearly referring to Fichte's *Doctrine of Science* ('*Wissenschaftslehre*'). Philosophical 'Science' for Fichte teaches nothing determinate to which it might be bound, but simply represents thinking itself as act and example, as something that each individual must actively perform in an essentially autonomous fashion.[72]

'Representation' here is the name for the communication of the indeterminate in the determinate, something that can only properly be grasped as process and movement. It is reflection upon this problem of representation [*Darstellung*] that gradually reveals the aesthetic moment of philosophising itself. Plato presents the original paradigm of such a philosophising, a kind of thinking that was revived and calls to be deciphered in Lessing's critical contributions to the 'Fragmentenstreit', and that now finds its most topical and promising incarnation in the work of Fichte. Thus it is that Schlegel can effectively regard the epoch-making *Doctrine of Science*, despite its systematic philosophical intentions, as a breakthrough in the proper task of presenting the wavering play of the indeterminate in the determinate.[73] 'It is only there where the first principles of the true, for the discovery or rediscovery of which the age is pre-eminently indebted to You [sc. Fichte], are also taught in accordance with a strictly rigorous method of philosophy, that the freer productions and achievements of the purely natural philosophical spirit likewise find their proper place'.[74]

Since Schlegel characterises the *modern age* that transforms the traditional 'querelle des anciens et des modernes' as one of dynamic change, the task is precisely to encourage active participation in order to strengthen and consolidate this process.[75] The parallel with the early idealist expectations for a specifically modern kind of metaphysics that responds to the needs of the time lies here in the idea of an aesthetic re-articulation and reinterpretation of the tradition rather than in the autonomous creation of a new system of thought. For the early romantics, this would simply perpetuate the old struggle of competing systems that Kant had already diagnosed as the fundamental failing

---

[72] F. Schlegel, *Lessings Geist aus seinen Schriften* (KA III, p. 48).

[73] I have pursued the way in which Fichte's *Doctrine of Science* was adopted and interpreted in terms of Romantic thought in the essay 'From Fichte to Schlegel' (included in the present volume).

[74] F. Schlegel, KA III, p. 47.

[75] Cf. H.R. Jauss, 'Schlegels und Schillers Replik auf die "Querelle des anciens et des modernes"' in his book, *Literaturgeschichte als Provokation* (Frankfurt am Main 1970).

of dogmatic metaphysics. It was precisely this post-Kantian rebirth of interest in system-building, on the other hand, that prompted the young Hegel, in his critical writings of the Jena period, to a systematic engagement with the problem of effectively mediating between system and history, a project that came to completion in the *Phenomenology of Spirit*.

According to the early romantics, the contemporary philosophical relevance of Plato did not lie in any substantive return to his theory of ideas, but rather in providing a self-reflective response to the classical tradition in terms of a new image of Plato. This new image of Plato is embodied in the translation of his works as undertaken in the spirit of contemporary romanticism. Schlegel himself announced the relevant terms of this approach, and left a number of suggestions for others to pursue. The greater share of the real work fell to his friend Schleiermacher. The correspondence between Schlegel and Schleiermacher reflects the inevitable disappointment that ensued, but in which it is nonetheless possible to see something like the 'cunning of reason' at work. For the project effectively gave Schleiermacher's versatile rather than original natural talents the opportunity of providing the Germans with a new Plato of their own, although it demanded truly Herculean labours and all the renunciation involved in occupying a clerical position while he performed them. The still highly valuable result of these labours can certainly be compared with the equally vivid and effective German renderings of Shakespeare at the hands of August Wilhelm Schelegel and Ludwig Tieck. Both of these projects are indeed great romantic achievements in their own right.

XI. Schleiermacher's Plato

Quite apart from this decisive service in making available for the first time the entire oeuvre of an ancient philosophical authority that was still largely untapped, Schleiermacher also provided an unparalleled interpretation of it, which, from a *hermeneutical* perspective, represented an entirely new level of engagement. Schleiermacher's Plato is both the replica of an ancient philosophical work and a specifically modern reflective work of an increasingly aesthetic character. The paradigmatic significance of Schleiermacher's Plato lies in the claim that philosophy itself must now assume artistic form, or at least productively respond to that ancient rivalry between creative poetry and philosophical thought that Plato himself had been the first to identify as such. This naturally

evokes the question concerning Plato's 'unwritten doctrine' as handed
down through an indirect tradition that certainly changes the image
of the author modelled solely on the dialogues. This question has
long been the subject of heated controversy that I do not wish to become involved in here. It seems to me that everything relevant has
already been said, and there is a consequent danger of simply repeating prior positions.[76] I shall return to the problem solely in connection
with Schleiermacher's own introduction to his Plato translations (in
Section XII).

H. Krämer has recently claimed that Schlegel's 'infinitising' concept of reflection has falsified the authentic Plato, who was actually, as
can be inferred from the 'unwritten doctrine', a *systematic* thinker. At
the same time, Krämer is more sympathetic to Schleiermacher, who has
long been criticised for his reading of Plato.[77] According to Krämer's account, Schleiermacher's reading is dependent not so much on Schlegel
as upon the philosophy of art that Schelling developed after 1800.[78]
I do not think that either of these claims are convincing. The problem does not lie, to use Hegel's terms, in the 'bad infinity' that derives from Fichte, which extends the path of knowledge *ad infinitum*
and thereby prevents the required construction of a proper system.
Nor does Schleiermacher actually defend, as I attempt to show later,

---

[76] For the sake of brevity, I would refer the reader to my remarks in *Antike Themen und ihre
moderne Verwandlung*, p. 29 ff., 168 ff. Tigerstedt is quite right, in criticism of Krämer,
in wondering how Schleiermacher's short and substantively modest introduction to his
translation could possibly have proved so damaging as to obscure the formerly well-
established image of Plato as an essentially systematic thinker. On this view, proper historical justice has only been done during the last few decades through the new Tübingen
interpretation of Plato in terms of the 'unwritten doctrine'. In truth, however, we must
concede that it is precisely the aesthetic dimension of Plato that has secured a kind
of unofficial continuity in the reception of his work. The extremely erudite study by
Tigerstedt, *Decline and Fall of the Neoplatonic Interpretation of Plato* (Comment. Hum. Litt.
52, Helsinki 1974), clearly demonstrates that the original connection between Platonism and neo-Platonism had already dissolved long before Schleiermacher's intervention.
Krämer actually concedes as much in his otherwise highly critical response to Tigerstedt
(*Philosophische Rundschau* 27, 1980, p. 22).
[77] H. Krämer, 'Fichte, Schlegel und der Infinitismus in der Platondeutung', *Deutsche Vierteljahrsschrift* 62, 1988.
[78] Krämer has provided a masterly synthesis of the line defended by the Tübingen School
in his English book, *Plato and the Foundations of Metaphysics* (New York 1990). And he pays
particular attention to the roots of Schleiermacher's image of Plato in early romantic
and idealist thought (cf. especially chapter 2). 'The myth of the self-sufficient artistic
dialogue, the comprehension of which is indispensable to the understanding of the
philosophy of Plato, arose not only from the protoromantic program of the unity of
philosophy and poetry but is itself part of a metaphysics of art' (p. 27).

a metaphysics of art as conceived within the ambitious framework of Schelling's 'philosophy of identity'. The real stone of offence in this connection is rather the conception of *philosophy as a comprehensive work of art.* The real *skandalon* that underlies the continuing debate about Plato as a systematic philosopher concerns not the protreptic but the aesthetic character of philosophy. One may or may not particularly welcome this approach. But the 'romantic' reading of philosophy in this connection has never claimed that the task is infallibly and precisely to reproduce the meaning of a historical author irrespective of the intervening temporal distance. The relevant task is rather to disclose the spirit, and not simply the letter, of the author with respect to our own contemporary consciousness.

Even the questions concerning the genuineness of the dialogues, their proper sequence, their sometimes fragmentary character, and so on, all of which are frequently discussed in the correspondence between Schlegel and Schleiermacher, taken along with the overall philological aim of historical authenticity, do not of themselves determine the governing approach to interpretation. Thus we find Schlegel writing on one occasion: 'I must actually confess to you something that you will perhaps find quite heretical; the whole concept of *completeness* seems to me a superstition as far as this undertaking is concerned. For this cannot be found unless it be in the spirit of Plato himself and the one who understands him; for there are important works of his which are lost, or never completed, and the two people who best understand Plato (namely you and I) are in such disagreement in this connection that what one of us regards as belonging essentially to the Platonic corpus, the other regards as quite destructive of overall coherence in the latter'.[79]

A similar thought is also echoed in a later letter of Schleiermacher's (18 July 1808) that was addressed to the philologist Boeckh, who had written a most enthusiastic review of the Plato translations. 'We [Schlegel and Schleiermacher] were soon quite clear that the whole demanded some kind of ordering; but insofar as I remember, we wavered between choosing a chronological one and one that was more designed to disclose Plato's work to the present age in the best and

---

[79] Schlegel's letter from Paris of 5.5.1803, in: *Schleiermachers Leben in Briefen*, p. 342. This thought also finds a perfect parallel in Schlegel's brilliant essay 'On Unintelligibility', which was published in the *Athenäum*. In a tone of romantic irony, Schlegel here presents the hermeneutic task as something that can only be fulfilled in the course of the entire history of our human attempts at understanding.

speediest manner possible. I do not know whether Schlegel at that time was already possessed of the insight which dawned upon me only later – namely, that both must come to one and the same thing'.[80]

The general *conclusion* to be drawn from our foregoing reflections can be expressed as follows. Plato is the ancient author who appeals most particularly to the modern consciousness insofar as he represents the status of philosophy prior to the dissolution of the unified mythological world-picture produced by the negative power of the reflective understanding. That is why he speaks so strongly to the contemporary needs that find expression once the path of transcendental philosophy, as opened up by Kant, has been taken to its end. For the task now is precisely to try and articulate a form of thought that is designed to integrate the activity of reflection within itself. This form of thought is not the simple extension of reflection *ad infinitum*, but rather a teleological anticipation of closure that acknowledges the indispensable temporal dimension of history. Hence the process, and the continual labour, of hermeneutic interpretation necessarily comes into play here, not indeed as the empty repetition of an eternal relativism, but as an 'anticipatory orientation towards perfection', as Gadamer expresses it.

In one of his fragments, Schlegel writes as follows: 'Everything that can be achieved as long as philosophy and poetry remain separate from one another has already been achieved and completed. The time has now therefore come when they should be united'.[81] The early romantics desired to assume this historically conditioned task, which had itself been brought forth by the exercise of self-conscious reflection. And they saw Plato as a remote forerunner in this regard. 'Perhaps Plato's *Republic* represents an intimation of the absolutely romantic in its style'.[82] The historically unencumbered appeal to the canonic ancient thinker simultaneously serves to mediate the past, to bridge the intervening distance, by revealing its abiding significance for the present tasks of thought. And it is this *romantic dialectic of the old and the new* that leads to the positive re-evaluation of Plato as a specifically literary figure. Hence it is not the methodically controlled search for demonstrable truth that motivates the work of Schlegel and Schleiermacher. The fact that Plato, as rendered intelligible from a contemporary perspective, now assumes

---

[80] Reprinted in W. Dilthey, *Gesammelte Schriften* XIII, 2, Göttingen 1970.
[81] F. Schlegel, KA II, p. 267.
[82] F. Schlegel, *Literary Notebooks 1797–1801*, ed. H. Eichner, Frankfurt am Main 1980, nr. 894; cf. also nrs. 871, 965, 1800, 1809.

a form that facilitates and encourages familiarity with the relevant texts, that allows the tradition to speak anew, is a desirable and welcome side-effect of their labours. To express the matter briefly and paradoxically: it is precisely through the indirect engagement with Plato that the self-imposed concerns of philosophy around 1800 first come to a clearer understanding.

XII. Philosophy as a Work of Art

Schleiermacher's 'Introduction' to his translation of Plato (1804) has always rightly been celebrated as a masterpiece of hermeneutic thought.[83] It dispenses with all metaphysical exaggerations and succeeds in getting straight to the heart of the matter precisely by virtue of its explicit technical and professional reflections upon the relevant problems. And the heart of the matter is Plato's philosophy as presented to us in the various dialogues. The appropriate access to this philosophy therefore can only be found through consideration of the form of its self-presentation. The dialogue form imitates the active conversation between teacher and learner in which both sides come together and interact in reference to a shared theme that binds them to one another. This dialectical co-operation in the effort of thinking has a decisive advantage in comparison with the systematic written treatment of a particular question. For the former approach allows us to proceed actively step by step, unfolding the nature of the relevant problem and returning constantly to see if it has been genuinely understood. The broadly systematic written treatment of philosophical claims has nonetheless generally become the norm ever since Aristotle's lectures were transcribed for posterity. Plato himself deliberately counter-posed the dialogue form to the imposing but exaggerated bluster and bewitching eloquence of the Sophists. All those who subsequently followed Plato's example, however, tended to employ the dialogue form simply as an external vehicle for saying things that they could just as well have expressed quite differently. In that case, avoidance of something like the systematic form of a treatise amounts to little more than a kind of embellishment that contributes nothing to promoting real insight into the issues.

The truly mysterious and profound element that Schleiermacher hopes to reveal in explaining and justifying the peculiar literary

---

[83] Cf. H.-G. Gadamer, 'Schleiermacher als Platoniker', in Gadamer, *Kleine Schriften* III, Tübingen 1972.

form of the Platonic dialogues is what he calls 'interrelationship' [*Zusammenhang*]. It is this idea that defines the fundamental category of all 'understanding' [*Verstehen*]. Understanding in general only emerges by constructing a whole out of its relevant parts and permitting, in turn, the analysis of the parts through a prior grasp of their inter-related character. In this connection, Schleiermacher appeals to the organic metaphor of the living body and its parts[84], which Plato him-self had already employed to represent the authentic *logos*.[85] What Schleiermacher here describes as 'interrelationship' will later become the influential concept of the 'hermeneutic circle'. The concept aims to capture the establishment of an inner relationship between differen-tiated details and the complex whole that is constituted through such details. To establish the relevant 'interrelationship', however, is pre-cisely to renew this dynamic configuration explicitly for oneself, and this can only be accomplished through an active rethinking of the mat-ter at hand. The one who 'understands' must therefore produce the relevant question itself anew in his own mind. That is why the dialogues can never properly be grasped without the active participation and pro-ductive response of the reader. One cannot really know, and one cannot legitimately claim, what is effectively contained in the dialogues if one fails to pay due attention to this principle of 'interrelationship'.

But the interrelationship in question is ultimately that of the overall *coherence of the various dialogues* in relation to one another. The dialogical principle of all genuine philosophical expression is thereby extended to the entire corpus. No one step along the path of thought, no one part of any single dialogue, can be understood in independence of the whole dialogue. But this also implies that no single dialogue can itself be isolated without taking account of the criss-crossing themes that connect the various dialogues. The Platonic philosophy – a work of thought constituted in and through the dialogues – thus reveals an intrinsic similarity to the work of art in general, and the hermeneu-tic effort of interpretation should properly be directed to this crucial analogy.

This approach legitimates the 'early romantic' idea of drawing sub-stantive insights from the *living activity of reflection itself*. To interrogate a text is therefore to institute certain relationships through the active participation of the recipient qua reader, critic, philologist or co-author. For the role of the recipient is uniquely and specifically determined by

---

[84] Reprinted in K. Gaiser (ed.), *Das Platonbild* (Hildesheim 1969), pp. 1–32; here p. 9 f.
[85] *Phaedrus* 264c.

the autonomous and dynamic character of the thinking, which arises in encounter with the text and which in each case participates in producing the meaning it harbours. The task is thus not passively to register the meaning that has been directly expressed and objectified in the text, but rather to respond subjectively to the matter of thinking, which has not already been entirely exhausted in the work before us. This is the appropriate attitude of the one who would really 'understand' what is said.

Schleiermacher himself expresses this thought as follows: 'Every investigation [of a text] should, from the beginning, be conducted and designed in such a way that the reader should either succeed in generating the intended thought inwardly for himself, or have to surrender to the feeling that he has actually found nothing and understood nothing here. This demands that the final conclusion of the investigation should not explicitly be expressed or formulated as such in the text, something which might easily strike those who are only happy as long as they reach the final conclusion as a kind of deception, but which actually compels the soul itself to seek out the conclusion and guides it along the only path where it can discover the latter'.[86] No dialogue expresses everything fully, and no investigation of a text fixes a final end or definitive conclusion, for the production of the 'interrelationship' involved in meaning is a kind of aesthetic act on the part of the original author and the intellectually responsive reader.

In accordance with these considerations, Schleiermacher sees the principal value of his own work to lie in disclosing the 'natural interrelationship' within the Platonic texts that have come down to us. And this is why he renounces the traditional division of the corpus in terms of tetralogies, trilogies, syzygies and so forth. Schleiermacher's constant concern, expressed in the exchanges with Schlegel, about determining the correct order of the dialogues and excluding the spurious texts, is essentially governed by the need to present an *intelligible* rather than a purely *historical* Plato. For we cannot even establish any historical relation to something that we cannot in some sense already 'understand'. In Schleiermacher's printed announcement of the forthcoming translation, we therefore find him writing: 'These efforts are such that, even if they should contain certain errors, they cannot fail to encourage those who are capable of it to undertake new and better investigations of their own'.[87]

---

[86] Schleiermacher, loc. cit., p.12.   [87] Reprinted in Dilthey, loc. cit.

The 'natural' character of the sought-after 'interrelationship' does not therefore simply mirror the past intellectual biography of an individual. We should be concerned not with the psychological or developmental issues involved, but rather with providing a subsequent and well-rounded presentation of a philosophical oeuvre in accordance with its dialogical form. The original author has left many things open or still unclear in order to encourage and enliven the thinking of the reader. The 'interrelationship' of ideas that is the crucial element here is itself constituted within *the interaction between author and reader*, irrespective of the intervening historical distance. That is why the early romantic model of the philosopher as artist here becomes the appropriate symbol of the hermeneutic task in general.

This is immediately reflected in the pre-eminent status accorded to the *Phaedrus*[88], the dialogue that always stood at the forefront of discussions between Schlegel and Schleiermacher and would also cost the latter years of effort as translator. For it is in this dialogue that the relationship between written and oral approach to philosophy is directly thematised as such. That is why it would inevitably form the propylaeum at the entrance to the properly apportioned structure of the entire Platonic corpus. The fact that there has long been general agreement that the *Phaedrus* should probably be ascribed to the later phase of Plato's thought cannot fundamentally 'refute' the justice of this earlier perspective. However remarkable it may sound, we cannot deny that the 'natural interrelationship' here takes a certain precedence over the date of historical composition. For all of its legitimate demands, therefore, the historical criticism of sources is still powerless to challenge the ideal of the philosopher-artist. For these different approaches simply represent two quite different interests. We have to concede that historical knowledge is directed towards a different goal than that envisaged by an aesthetically motivated form of active thought.

XIII. The Hermeneutic Solution

This approach also determines Schleiermacher's judgement with respect to the still much debated question concerning the precise relationship between Plato's exoteric writings and his esoteric 'unwritten

---

[88] For more on this, cf. the extremely informative study by Y. Lafrance, 'Schleiermacher, Lecteur de Phèdre de Platon' in *Revue de Philosophie Ancienne* 8, 1990.

doctrine'. It is striking that he only accepts Aristotle as a reliable witness with regard to matters that are already documented in the Platonic dialogues themselves.[89] As well-informed student and first serious critic of his own philosophical teacher, Aristotle 'could not possibly have struggled, against his better knowledge, with little but a shade'. The neo-Platonists are rather to be credited as the first thinkers to give systematic form to Plato's work. Now the claim that one can simply relate all of Aristotle's philosophical objections directly to the dialogues is one that is very difficult to defend. To that extent, the criticisms that have been mounted against Schleiermacher's tendency to *absolutise* the hermeneutical principle by those who insist upon the systematic character of Plato's thought are quite justified. For that is what he does insofar as he emphasises the inter-referential character of the dialogues while interpreting the sense and direction of such references in an entirely immanent manner.

The basic controversy between Schleiermacher and the proponents of an 'esoteric' Platonic doctrine can be simplified in terms of the following question: what is the best *direction* for our research to take if we all actually agree upon the fact that the dialogues do often harbour intimations of what is deliberately unsaid? Can we properly explain the dialogues themselves *in terms of one another* as long as we are sufficiently careful to pay attention to their subtly wrought character and the complex structure of the entire oeuvre? Or must we also acknowledge a certain cognitive dimension that effectively lies *beyond* the works as we have them, a dimension to which all the relevant allusions and references point without distinction? The defenders of the esoteric interpretation[90] appeal to that 'succour' that, according to Plato himself, we must bring to the *logos*.[91] This succour is to be found either in the synthetic intellectual labour of the reader who reconstructs the work as a subtly designed interrelationship of moments, or, should that prove insufficient, in the unavoidable recourse to a separate set of special doctrines that are not stated as such in the dialogues themselves. The very idea of an intimating allusion demands that it be identified and interpreted precisely as an allusion. But of itself this

---

[89] Schleiermacher, 'Introduction', loc. cit., p. 8 f. This is a view that had already disturbed A. Boeckh in his otherwise extremely positive review of Schleiermacher's translation (Boeckh, *Gesammelte Kleine Schriften* VII, Leipzig 1872, p. 8; first published in 1808).

[90] Cf. Th. Szlezák, Platon und die Schriftlichkeit der Philosophie (cf. note 59).

[91] *Phaedrus* 275c.

decides nothing about the proper direction in which our thought should turn.

And that is why the continuing controversy over the significance of an esoteric Platonic doctrine can never definitively be resolved by appeal to uncontested facts or compelling demonstrations of one kind or another. Everything here depends upon whether an interpretation that remains entirely *immanent* to the work can properly meet the needs of interpretation in general. Every interpreter brings needs that are shaped by the framework of the age to the task of explicating historical documents. To declare oneself dissatisfied with a certain interpretation is, at the very least, to say as much about the original material under investigation as about the intentions of the interpreter in question. For the historically conditioned reasons we have already indicated, the early romantics were essentially seeking the philosopher as artist, and were grateful to find such a philosopher in Plato. The representatives of the age of science, on the other hand, were looking for an essentially scientific thinker, and since they could not find the latter in Plato the author of dialogues, they imagined they might discover one at the systematic level of an 'unwritten doctrine'. And what Plato will an emerging age that is so sceptical of science eventually present to us? Jacques Derrida has long since begun to address in his own way the question concerning the textuality of philosophy.

Emphasising the dependence of all interpreters upon the specific *premises* they bring with them to the texts they wish to elucidate should serve to relativise the struggle of competing convictions and to dampen the militant cries of Enlightenment in its supposed conquest of persisting ignorance. For we have always been seeking to discover and proclaim the 'true' Plato. And this too was Schleiermacher's most important aim and concern. The true Plato is always a projection insofar as a given age effectively recognises itself in the interpretation it provides and thus confirms the truth it proclaims, even while a different age in turn will challenge that interpretation on the basis of a different set of interests. That is why we must acknowledge the intrinsically finite character of all our effective knowledge, and accept this limitation, which is grounded in the specific nature of the cognitive interest itself. One can interpret this 'relativising' insight in transcendental terms by regarding this condition of the possibility of knowledge as a historical category. This would imply a hermeneutic perspective elaborated far beyond Schleiermacher's original intuitive insight and a methodologically grounded recognition that all our efforts of knowledge transpire within the unpredictable and uncontrollable horizon of tasks that history has in each case already bequeathed to us.

As far as the search for the 'true' Plato is concerned, this means we must refuse the *distinction between interpretation and historical fact.* The historical Plato is also the Plato that is most intelligible with regard to further efforts of interpretation. Interpretation and historical research are not alternatives. At most, it is merely a question of differently articulated and plausible approaches that are more or less convincing in relation to the relevant material as a whole. There is no unsurpassable or incontestable reality in itself existing over and beyond our interpretations. And if there were some such reality in itself beyond all interpretations, we should still have to describe it as intrinsically intelligible, and thus as falling potentially within the framework of what we can interpret.

Schleiermacher clearly identified the central problem in the already cited letter to Boeckh when he says that it only later dawned on him that his effort to determine the chronological order of the dialogues and his effort to make Plato available to the contemporary age ultimately came to one and the same thing. For it would actually be impossible to establish any chronology, whatever the arguments, demonstrations and empirical data produced in its favour, that effectively served to rob Plato's work of its intrinsic intelligibility.

In conclusion, I should merely like to cite a couple of remarks that clearly reveal the original hermeneutic impulse that is always haunted by a certain ambiguity insofar as every attempt to decipher obscurity necessarily runs the risk of failure or possible over-interpretation. In a letter to Henriette Herz of 10 August 1802, when he was still immersed in the labours of translation, Schleiermacher wrote the following: 'I often understood so little of Plato as a whole, when I first came to read him in the context of university study, that I possessed nothing but an obscurely glimmering presentiment of his meaning, but even then I could not fail to love and admire him'. And in a moment of weakness and despair when confronted by the magnitude of his task, he confessed: 'This was my most cherished literary aspiration. But let it now consort with the others. Fifty years hence, another will certainly do it better than I could ever have done'.[92] Two hundred years later, we must concede that no one has ever produced a better version of Plato, from the literary point of view, than this profoundly conscientious and

---

[92] Schleiermacher to Reimer (undated). (*Aus Schleiermachers Leben in Briefen*, p. 349).

versatile thinker who remained true to the brilliant insight of his friend
even when the latter had long since abandoned himself to a plethora
of other projects.[93]

---

[93] In 1808, Boeckh noted with reference to Schleiermacher: 'Only ten tears ago hardly any
great desire to work upon the writings of Plato had yet been stirred, and the latter was
a far more isolated figure in German lands than he is today' (*Gesammelte Kleine Schriften*
VII, p. 46).

ARISTOTLE AND SCHELLING ON THE QUESTION OF GOD

I

It is generally acknowledged that the later Schelling, in the context of his untiring efforts to provide the final expression of his philosophy, developed a *new reading of Aristotle* to aid him precisely in this task. The long years of Schelling's withdrawal from prominent academic life were marked by a continuous struggle to articulate a philosophical position that could finally present itself as the consummation of his own intellectually productive beginnings. At the same time, success in this would also serve to curb the influence of his older rival Hegel, whom Schelling occasionally liked to characterise philosophically speaking as something of a 'later arrival'. For in his final Berlin years, Hegel had effectively become the pre-eminent figure in German philosophy, and indeed retained this position at the summit of contemporary significance for some time even after his death when the Hegelian school had split into rival orthodox and progressive factions.

In this situation, Schelling was necessarily concerned to present Hegel's speculative dialectic, with its encyclopaedic exposition of spirit, essentially as an extreme and one-sided development of the systematic philosophical discoveries that Schelling had made in his early years. In Schelling's eyes, therefore, Hegel had come up against the intrinsic limits of the original idealist approach without being able to overcome them himself. From the perspective of his mature philosophy, the later Schelling classified Hegel's position as that of a 'negative philosophy' that would need to be succeeded by a new 'positive philosophy'. And in this connection, the recourse to Aristotle plays a significant role *in formulating the distinction between positive and negative philosophy*. Thus Hegel's eventual successor to the chair of philosophy in the University of Berlin could explicitly confess of himself: 'the original author of the philosophy of identity at that time knew little about Aristotle'.[1] One may plausibly suppose, therefore, that it was Schelling's argument with Hegel, who considered himself as the modern Aristotle, that effectively motivated his own return to this exemplary philosopher of antiquity.

In the relevant secondary literature, commentators such as Fuhrmans, Schulz, and even Tilliette, have not always paid sufficient attention to the parallels between Schelling and Aristotle. In more recent years, however, J.F. Courtine has subjected the relevant connections to close and careful examination[2], and the following discussion will therefore also touch upon the results of his research. Nonetheless I am interested here in a rather different problem than that which concerns Courtine. I am not primarily concerned with the *express content* of the later Schelling's 'positive philosophy'. The latter has been significantly clarified by the labour of specialists in spite of the complexity, partial obscurity and considerable terminological inconsistency of the relevant material. I am interested rather in the *strategy*, if one may express it this way, that animates the later Schelling's philosophical discourse.

I wish to ask what significance a theological construction can possess for a comprehensive philosophical concept of reality. And in this respect, the comparison and contrast between Aristotle and Schelling proves to be particularly instructive. For it is not merely that both philosophers belong within the broad frame of European ontotheology, which Heidegger has defined as the innermost core of metaphysics in general. It is rather that both thinkers, in their distinctive and respective treatments of 'ultimate questions', serve to reveal fundamental and different approaches that are clearly not further reducible in any way.

II

First, I should like to recall, in brief outline, the reasoning by which Aristotle prepares a philosophical pathway towards theology. From early on, it was accepted that philosophers were called upon to say something on the question of the 'gods'. But Aristotle claimed that he was the first

---

[1] Schelling, *Philosophie der Offenbarung* 1841/2 (the Paulus transcript), edited by M. Frank, Frankfurt am Main 1977, p. 142.

[2] 'La critique schellingienne de l'ontothéologie', in: *La question de Dieu selon Aristote et Hegel*, edited by Th. De Koningk and G. Planty-Bonjour, Paris 1991, particularly pp. 245 ff.

thinker who had successfully provided a basis for rational speech about God or the divine – namely, one that went beyond the narratives of myth without losing itself in the 'enthusiastic' speculations of Plato. The approach adopted by Aristotle here proceeds more or less as follows.

The central problem of Aristotle's entire philosophy is that of conceptualising the phenomenon of *change* or movement. It is essentially for this purpose that Aristotle introduces the principal distinction, a novelty in relation to Plato, between the theoretical, practical and poetic domains of philosophy. These rubrics concern the nature of knowledge, of orientation in human action, and the technical principles governing the production of artefacts in general. The concise retrospective summary of previous philosophies that Aristotle provides in the first book of the *Metaphysics* serves to explain the *origin* of Aristotle's general philosophical problematic in a very plausible manner. Thus Heraclitus' insight into 'change' as a fundamental and irreducible feature of the world led Plato to attempt to master the experience of transience by recourse to an absolute conceptual determination of reality. The Platonic assumption of stably subsisting 'ideas' above and beyond the multiple appearances of the sensuous world signifies a major philosophical advance. But the precise relationship between the ideas and the phenomenal world through the disturbing notion of 'participation' (*methexis*) nonetheless remained unclear.

Aristotle sees Plato's use of the term 'participation' more as a symptom of the difficulty than a genuine solution for it. For Aristotle, therefore, knowledge must be grounded instead upon *principles* that do not, unlike Plato's 'ideas', subsist purely in their own eternal right so that everything else appears merely as a sort of pale ontological copy of authentic reality. It is these principles that genuinely serve to ground the character of reality in its concrete being. By means of his canonical distinction between the four aspects involved in such grounding (the matter, the form, the whence and the whither of motion and change), Aristotle attempts to do full conceptual justice to the essentially teleological nature of reality. It is this developed conceptual apparatus that allows us to explain the existence of things in the world in accordance with their fundamental structure as changeable entities.

This approach naturally gives rise to the further question concerning *the overall interconnection* that obtains within this world of movement. The fundamental structure of all movement cannot itself have 'come into being'. For in that case, there would be an original movement from which all further movement would arise. We would thus be confronted with an infinite regress, and would be quite unable to understand the original state from which movement ultimately emerges, or to explain how this sudden emergence itself is possible.[3] Reflection upon this paradox leads Aristotle to assume that movement as such must be eternal. But in that case, there must be a sufficient reason for such movement. And this requires recourse to the idea of an unmoved mover, which allows us to explain the everlasting persistence of movement in a unique fashion.

Such a *principle* must intrinsically and necessarily be capable of maintaining the overall teleological process of the world in being. It follows that this active accomplishment cannot simply represent a power or capacity that might never actually be realised, or one that may indeed be realised in fact, but not in any essential or necessary way. In the first case – whereby we could speak, as it were, of a 'slumbering god'[4] – we could find no genuine explanation since the decisive function of producing movement without simply being part of the process itself would then subsist in a state of mere possibility. In the second case, we would lack an ultimate explanation precisely because everything could just as well have transpired otherwise. But from the contingent fact that something actually gives rise to movement, while it also need not have done, we can derive no reliable theoretical certainty.[5] But this latter is precisely what we require of an ultimate explanation that would satisfy our intellectual needs here.

The ultimate principle that we are seeking in the domain of metaphysics cannot possibly fail its intrinsic task of providing a foundation for the entire structure of reality. It is inconceivable that this active principle should ever permanently cease as such – that is, that it could ever fail to constitute, with an unchangeable necessity of its own, the ultimate ground of the ontological structure for everything other than itself that is in a state of change and motion. This is why Aristotle describes his ultimate principle as 'cause for itself and for what is other than itself'.[6] The principle that sustains everything else can therefore

---

[3] There is a comparable paradox in Kant's cosmological doctrine of the antinomies that can only be resolved by recourse to the idea of the freedom of the will – that is, by a transition from the domain of theoretical to that of practical philosophy.

[4] Cf. *Metaphysics* XII 6, 1074b 18 and *Nichomachean Ethics* 1178b 19 f.; cf. also Plato, *Republic* 533b–534d and *Laws* 808b–c.

[5] *Metaphysics* XII 6, 1071b 5 ff.; for this entire question, cf. also *Physics* VIII.

[6] *Metaphysics* 1072a 15.

only exist in a state of continuous *realisation* or *actuality* (*energeia*) that is without alternative possibility. It is precisely this superior ontological status of the ultimate principle, as compared with all other kinds of being, which essentially constitutes its 'goodness' or 'bounty' and makes it into an object of 'love' for everything else that it affects. These celebrated metaphorical expressions serve to characterise the cosmological role of a being, which, since it can itself exist only in a state of highest actualised power, is also responsible for the fact that all other beings actually are as they are. For otherwise, as Aristotle says, 'there would be no beings'.[7]

Aristotle therefore claims to have developed a rational concept of *God* or the divine as a result of analysing the ultimate cosmological ground of all change and movement. It is this intrinsically intelligible thought that grounds the conceptual approach to all of reality that Aristotle presents explicitly in the first book of the *Metaphysics*. In this context, it is important to recognise that the successful advance of knowledge constitutes the path through which one can develop a proper doctrine of God. But there is no attempt here to elucidate or demonstrate a conception of God, already characterised as something absolute, in a purely philosophical way, as is the case with the medieval 'proofs' for the existence of God.

III

Aristotle presents a *rationalisation* of a fundamental kind in which the successful pursuit and analysis of grounds and causes serves to disclose the authentic core of a philosophical problem. But that the human being intrinsically desires to understand the world in general is the unconditional premise classically articulated in the opening statement of Aristotle's *Metaphysics*: 'All human beings strive by nature after knowledge'. This immediately reveals the intimate connection between the *theological principle* on the one hand and the *cognitive impulse* of theology on the other. The concept of God and the being of God would seem to converge here. In contrast with Plato's concern with the highest idea of 'the Good', Aristotle primarily wished to avoid introducing essentially 'practical' considerations into the domain of theoretical speculation in an arbitrary or illegitimate manner. Nonetheless he was inevitably

---

7 *Metaphysics* XII 6, 1071a 25.

compelled to speak of the 'life' of God (*diagōgē, zōē*) and, in analogy
with it, of the life of the philosopher who is driven to undertake metaphysical enquiry.[8] For the life of God and the life of the philosopher
alike are modes of being that are characterised by an experience of
ultimate and intense fulfilment. God does not merely subsist in its own
right as a pure principle, but only fulfils its essential function as a principle because the divine simultaneously represents the most perfect
reality there is, one that appears undisturbed by alternative possibilities or any threat of non-being. This ultimate actuality, in this its highest form of intensity and concentration, can only be grasped as pure
and unalloyed activity to the extent that reason itself here concerns
itself with nothing alien or foreign to itself, is dependent upon nothing other than itself – that is, that it is free and actual entirely in and
through itself.[9] That is why the philosopher, in the exercise of his characteristic and absolute 'virtue' (*aretē*), comes to approach the life of
God.[10]

Aristotle speaks of a certain 'sought after science' (*epistēmē zētou-
menē*)[11] that was formerly described as 'wisdom' (*sophia*), and that as
a result of the textual decisions of later editors has come to be called
meta-physics (that is, the treatise following after the *Physics*). The sought-
for discipline that is yet to be developed is certainly not as useful as
other sciences[12] but it can well be considered as the most noble there is
on account of its subject-matter and its 'method'.[13] But would the creation of such a 'science' enter into *rivalry with the Gods*? Insofar as such
a thing would seem to transcend our human powers, it might indeed
incite the envy of the Gods, as many of the poets fear. But following
here in the wake of Plato's critique of the poets, Aristotle objects that
for the most part, poets 'lie', and observes that those who are universally acknowledged as 'wise', far from incurring the envy of the Gods,
may rather be called the 'favourites of the Gods' (*theophilestatos*).[14] It
is thus that Aristotle would legitimate his own programme of metaphysical enquiry, in a way that can properly be regarded as a kind of
rationalisation.

[8] *Metaphysics* 1072b 14–30; *De Caelo* 292a 21 ff.
[9] *Metaphysics* XII 9.
[10] *Metaphysics* I 2; cf. *Nichomachean Ethics* 1177b 16–1178a 8, 1178b 7–32.
[11] *Metaphysics* XII 6, 983a 21.   [12] *Metaphysics* 983a 10 f.
[13] *Metaphysics* 983a 23.
[14] *Metaphysics* 982b 25 ff. and *Nichomachean Ethics* 1179a 24 ff.

IV

Schelling essentially employs Aristotle's theology as a foil and contrast to Hegel's *Science of Logic*.[15] According to Schelling, the Stagirite had emphatically turned away from the purely conceptual method of Platonic 'dialectic', and his celebrated 'empiricism' consisted precisely in the fact that he refused to thematise the character of reality solely in the light of the 'logoi'. Schelling attempts to interpret the Aristotelian approach here as a venerable insight into the perennial relationship that obtains between what he calls positive and negative philosophy. From this perspective, Hegel the supposedly Aristotelian thinker comes rather to stand alongside Plato, and it is now Schelling who first properly and fully articulates what Aristotle's turn from mere conceptuality to actual reality had originally intended to accomplish. For Schelling, positive philosophy itself could never emerge without the prior realisation of negative philosophy. But the necessary step beyond negative philosophy is oriented towards a kind of 'transcendence' that no logical conceptual system can ever recuperate.

Hegel's *Science of Logic* had taken the place of the former metaphysics after the traditional metaphysical doctrines of 'first philosophy' had been repudiated through the most radical sceptical developments of early modern thought and the impact of Kant's critical philosophy. The revolutionary attempt to clarify the character of reason definitively and entirely from within its own resources can be said to have reached its ultimate and consistent expression in Hegel's speculative logic. Of course, the fatal error here, in Schelling's view, was that Hegelian logic was boldly attempting, despite the insights of Kant's critical philosophy, to accomplish the ultimate goal of classical metaphysics by recourse to conceptual means alone. According to Schelling, the result of this approach could only be a fundamental failure to grasp that ultimate

---

[15] In the following discussion, I refer to the Paulus transcript of Schelling's Berlin lectures on the *Philosophy of Revelation* of 1841/2 (edited by Manfred Frank, pp. 139 ff. Cf. also the text of the *Philosophie der Offenbarung* printed in Schelling's *Sämtliche Werke*, vol. XIII, Vorlesung 8). Without being able to enter here into detailed philological questions, I regard the relevant passages on Aristotle contained in the Paulus transcript to be particularly significant and illuminating. In general, the transcript clearly represents a very careful and precise record of Schelling's words. The corresponding texts for Schelling's published 'works', as presented by the philosopher's son, cannot themselves be regarded as entirely authentic since they were edited specifically in the light of publication. Generally speaking, we still know much less about the precise textual basis of Schelling's later philosophy than we do about that of Hegel's published lectures.

dimension of reality that can never be demonstrated from the concept alone. For what ultimately engages us over and beyond the power of the concept is nothing less than being itself. Schelling describes this as 'existing being' [*das Existierende*], the actual existence of which cannot rest upon any prior conception we may have of it: it is the pure 'that' without a 'what'. Since in the wake of the reflective Kantian turn, concepts were thematised before actuality itself, then as far as the highest and ultimate problem of all philosophy is concerned, we must give up trying to ground an original 'prius' and turn instead to an unconditional acceptance of an actual 'posterius'.

In Schelling's eyes, Aristotle had already effectively brought philosophy to this point, and this is why he appeals to his example precisely in opposition to Hegel. For the latter had not even grasped the paradox that we can never reach real being simply on the basis of the concept, any more than we can do so by presenting the systematic interconnection and reciprocal generation of all possible concepts and categories in the manner of a dialectical logic. 'This ultimate principle is thus to be found in Aristotle precisely as actually existing being; but this is only because his entire science is grounded upon experience. He already has before him the entire world as the actual world, but he is not concerned as such with the actual [*das Wirkliche*], but only with the *what*; and thus the ultimate principle for him is only being that is *actus purus* merely according to its nature (but not according to its existence). That is why Aristotle makes no use of his ultimate principle as something that actually exists'.[16]

Whereas the 'most consistently developed perspective of negative philosophy' in the modern age maintains that 'the actual God possesses its own life solely in the development of the human spirit'[17], Aristotle's original programme for his 'sought for science' reveals an authentic sense for the path that philosophy should properly pursue. Philosophy is therefore still *seeking* its genuine object. This seeking tendency of metaphysics with respect to God as the ultimate principle and dimension of all philosophy finally culminates in the Unmoved Mover, but also with an essentially conceptual determination. It is the *what* of God that is determined here as thinking, as the highest *energeia*, as pure act qua act. And it is not the fact of existence, underivable from anything else, that the ancient empiricist effectively ascribed to God.

---

[16] Paulus transcript, ed. M. Frank, p. 142.   [17] Ibid., p. 153.

'Even now, this path of Aristotle, of advancing from existing being to the logical domain, should constitute the only proper path for philosophy. But the God of Aristotle cannot entirely satisfy us. We possess a profound awareness of God, and this not merely on account of Christianity, but also on account of mythology. Mythology did not have real value for Aristotle.'[18] It is true that in one important passage at the beginning of the *Metaphysics*.[19] Aristotle equates the *philo-sophos* with the *philo-mythos* insofar as both experience the sense of 'wonder'. But in fact, Aristotle fails to exploit the mythological dimension any further as he pursues his philosophical path of theological 'rationalisation'. If we are to pursue the path from negative to positive philosophy, it is the *revelation* provided by Christianity that must surely serve as a decisive point of orientation here. The most profound difference between Schelling's approach and that of classical metaphysics consequently lies in the unique nature of a *Creator God* who already transcends the world.

Aristotle sought to identify a *world-principle* that would render the entire structure of given reality conceptually transparent. Over and beyond this, Schelling still seeks to clarify the fact that reality is *given* to us in the first place. And this would be equivalent to providing a philosophical articulation of the Christian message of a God who stands outside of and free in relation to the world that we can grasp conceptually. Nothing that we understand about what actually is can possibly guarantee the primordial givenness [*Urgegebensein*] of reality itself. What would philosophy amount to if it merely spoke cleverly of what does not actually exist? No amount of sophisticated philosophical discourse is capable of transforming possibility into actuality. Thus Schelling writes: 'There is being not because there is thinking, but there is thinking because there is being'.[20]

We can clearly see, therefore, that the Aristotelian turn against Hegel's panlogism in Schelling's later philosophy once more resumes the original motivation behind the development of post-Kantian idealism in general. The first post-Kantian thinkers grasped that reflection cannot begin from itself as the absolutely prior principle. For precisely as reflection, it always presupposes something else from which to detach and separate itself. This insight into the status of Kantian transcendental philosophy as an enquiry that necessarily commences at a meta-level of thought led in turn to the demand for a metaphysics of the 'beginning'.

---

[18] Ibid., p. 143.   [19] *Metaphysics* 982b 18 f.
[20] Schelling, *Sämtliche Werke* XIII, p. 161, footnote.

Jacobi had referred in this connection to Spinoza's fundamental claim that philosophy must simply begin with the absolute itself. It was this constellation of issues and problems that set the intellectual movement of early German idealist thought upon its original path. And there also arose, together with the problem of beginning, the ingenious idea of a mythology that might support and sustain the nakedness of abstract thought, might nourish it with some already understood content and mediate it with the collective views and intuitions of people in general.[21] These embryonic notions of a necessary primordial givenness and of a kind of collective intuition of truth only come to full maturity in Schelling's last lectures on the *Philosophy of Revelation* and the *Philosophy of Mythology.*

V

The comparison with Schelling's classical forebear clearly reveals that in fact Aristotle does precede from an ultimate givenness that cannot itself be deduced from prior concepts. What is at issue here is the *structure* of all reality as intrinsically dynamic. This was self-evident for Aristotle because the intellectual efforts of his predecessors had already essentially revolved around this problem. Aristotle has no desire to produce a revolutionary philosophy, but simply attempts to bring the previous achievements of reason to a definitive and appropriate conceptual articulation. That philosophy is related and oriented to a real cosmos, that we do not indiscriminately employ concepts to which no actuality corresponds, that in short we have no need to *demonstrate the existence of the world* before we think about that world – none of this represented an issue for Aristotle any more than it did for ancient philosophy as a whole!

The idea of trying to penetrate behind the givenness of the actual world as a process of change and movement, of attempting to ask after this very givenness any further, itself presupposes the long secularisation process of the Christian certainties of a faith monotheistically oriented towards the notion of an absolute personal divinity. What remains once the entire theological context of this faith is removed or ignored is

---

[21] Cf. the much quoted *Earliest System Programme of German Idealism*, which emerged from the close intellectual collaboration between Hegel, Hölderlin and Schelling in the mid-1790s. There is an English translation of this text in H.S. Harris, *Hegel's Development. Towards the Sunlight 1770–1801* (Oxford 1972), pp. 510–12.

simply *the bare enigma of being*, which utterly presents itself as such without further determinability or conceptual approachability. How is it that there is anything at all rather than nothing, if we no longer presuppose God as the creator? Being is thus given to us in an ultimately inexplicable fashion. The appropriate response of philosophy is not the attempt to master this enigma through the concept, but rather a silent and serene acknowledgement of that enigma. It is no accident that Heidegger, during the middle period of his thought, was fond of defining his own approach with specific reference to Schelling.

It is nonetheless true that it is the full development of rational philosophy and its conceptual resources that must lead us in the first instance to this crucial point where *all purely conceptual labour is broken off*. To categorise rational philosophy as 'negative' means precisely to step back from such philosophy and all its possible achievements. There is as yet no appropriate terminology that 'positive' philosophy can employ in this connection since it is stepping out beyond the previous mode of philosophising. Quotations thus begin to take the place of authentic concepts: we are confronted here, in Spinoza's words, with what is 'blindly existent'. If expressed in Aristotelian terms, the usual philosophical fronts will now have to be reversed: by no means is God the 'necessary' being that we know already cannot fail to exist. God rather becomes 'the contingent' that is to be accepted and acknowledged because it cannot possibly be deduced in any way. Alluding implicitly to Aristotle's *Metaphysics*, Schelling writes: 'The task was to reveal the contingent in that which exists prior to all thought. The contingent precedes what exists, precedes actually existing being, so that the latter is not posited as essence [*Wesen*] at all, but in being posited, quite ecstatically, as beyond itself is precisely what exists. Essence has not externalised itself before it thinks itself as such. It contains the antipode of everything that is Idea, but in this opposition it is itself Idea, on account of this total reversal [*Umkehr*]'.[22]

Finally, two questions emerge here that, closely considered, simply reveal themselves as two ways of describing the same philosophical dilemma. If authentic philosophising of this kind must renounce all dialectical procedures, then it is impossible properly to conceptualise the relation of ultimate intensification and reversal that leads from negative to positive philosophy. One cannot simply explain what transpires when all thinking is focussed upon the ultimate principle if one then

---

[22] Paulus transcript, ed. M. Frank, p. 167.

proceeds seriously to claim that this ultimate principle can itself never possibly be derived from thought. The familiar schema of *determinate negation* with which Hegel constantly operates in his conception of the 'dialectic of the limit' offers us no assistance here. For this approach merely served to sustain the illusion that one could pass *beyond* the concept *through* the concept itself – namely, to the point of its own absolute negation. But the being that must simply be accepted and acknowledged in an attitude of philosophical empiricism is not the negation of the concept. A conceptually elaborated 'leap' of this kind leads us nowhere. That is why Schelling spoke so contemptuously of Hegel's *Logic*: 'Once the system has to take the difficult step into actual reality, the thread of the dialectical development is utterly broken'. The Idea would have to be induced by 'boredom', as it were, to rupture its purely logical existence. This is how Schelling, in alluding to Hegel in his preface to a work by Victor Cousin[23], effectively describes the hopeless predicament of the philosopher's hall of mirrors.

The other version of this difficulty – namely, of being unable to explain the transition from negative to positive philosophy – consists in the fact that both Aristotle and Hegel were able to locate theology in a precise relationship to the *position of the philosopher*. For according to Aristotle, he who pursues what is 'most properly knowable' (*malista epistēton*) transcends the usual condition of finite man and comes to approach the Gods themselves. And according to Hegel, anyone who has studied the entire *Science of Logic* can grasp there the intrinsic coincidence between absolute knowledge and the absolute itself, which latter is indeed nothing other than the total self-mediation of spirit. Schelling re-describes what Aristotle calls 'the most properly knowable' precisely as 'the unknowable'[24], and insists: 'the merely, the simply existing being [*das nur Existierende*] is exactly what defeats everything that would be derived from thought, it is that before which thought finds itself struck dumb, before which reason itself bows down' – for here 'thought is bereft of power'.

In relation to the function that Aristotle essentially ascribed to God – namely, that of thinking his own being – Schelling takes refuge in a surprising paradox that is partly reminiscent of *existential philosophy*. 'But this necessity of thinking himself there would also harbour a monstrous limitation; no mortal could ever take such a thing upon himself. To think always upon oneself would surely be the most terrible of states

[23] Schelling, *Sämtliche Werke* X, p. 212 f.   [24] Paulus transcript, ed. M. Frank, p. 151.

for any healthy nature. Goethe said:"I think only when I produce"'.[25]
We cannot ascribe to God what would never even satisfy a mortal man.
Any healthy nature strives to go beyond itself and occupies itself only in
active relation to something other than itself, as the Goethe quotation
thrown in here is intended to suggest. And precisely as creator God
pre-eminently must also go *out beyond himself.*

The Aristotelian deification of man through philosophy, which im-
perfectly and temporarily vouchsafes to us what God performs eternally, is here reversed with the process that renders the absolute finite
and denies the limitation involved in the thought of utterly exclusive
self-relation. It is precisely *not* appropriate to God to be permanently
engaged in thinking only himself and nothing else. This transformation of theological perspective, in the light of the conditions of our
human existence, is another way of avoiding the temptation to offer
an internally consistent and progressive dialectical exposition within
the entirely conceptual realm. In other words, the new positive philosophy does not itself relate to negative philosophy as a 'negation of the
negation'.

Aristotle says that without God, everything would actually be nothing, because the world-process requires an ultimate ground. Schelling
maintains, on the other hand, that without God, it is simply the conceptual system itself that collapses into nothing. The appropriate response
of rationalism to the nugatory character of a purely negative philosophy
is thus supposed to drive us ineluctably towards that original and inconceivable [*unvordenklichen*] God that is the absolute precisely because it
is itself no ground, and requires no ground for itself. But this absolute
can only represent an *abyss* [*Abgrund*] for thought, and more than this
we cannot know about it. Thus it has been possible to place Schelling's
thought in close proximity to the critique of idealism that was mounted
alike from both the practical and political perspectives of existentialism
and materialism. And both these interpretations are entirely plausible
in the case of this profound and Protean thinker because in the last
analysis they actually prove to be indistinguishable from one another.

[25] Ibid., p. 176.

HEGEL'S *SCIENCE OF LOGIC*: THE COMPLETION OR SUBLATION OF METAPHYSICS?

I. Logic as Metaphysics

Hegel has proved influential by virtue of the *method* rather than the system of his philosophy. He has been regarded above all as a subtle exponent of dialectic, and his work has found considerable resonance, particularly in Marxist thought and social philosophy in general, because of the claim that all states of affairs should ultimately be interpreted 'dialectically'. But the approval accorded this approach has actually served rather to obscure a general understanding of his principal work, the *Science of Logic*. The 'dialectic' is a procedure of thinking – but how can such a procedure give rise to content? For every science must first be able to present a content that it is specifically competent to treat. And more to the point: if dialectic is indeed a procedure of thinking, then it must advance by means of contradictions – but how could a system ever arise out of contradictions?

Readers and exegetes of Hegel, when they are not prepared simply to parrot his words, have generally capitulated before these claims. They have turned their attention instead to those of his writings that do not essentially contain the key to the system, but rather try and apply the dialectical method to the tangible themes of *history, society* or *art*. Thus the most influential writings of Hegel have been, originally, the *Philosophy of Right*, and in the twentieth century, first, the *Phenomenology of Spirit* and, later, the lectures on *Aesthetics*. It is here that the dialectical method seems capable of operating in a particularly plausible way. For in the structures of law and politics, in the history of human consciousness or in the encounter with works of art, we are not simply presented with unmediated or naked facts and phenomena, as it were, but rather with conceptions of the latter, with interpretations of reality, with objective expressions of spirit. Intellectual reflection here encounters so many forms in which it can recognise itself, and it is precisely this that provokes and encourages the movement of dialectical thought.

As far as these specific fields of Hegelian thought are concerned, we see that the following presuppositions obtain in each case: (1) the relevant domain is *limited* – that is, one can always count on finding certain existing conceptions and representations about the subject matter in question; (2) the source of this limitation is not itself *thematic* – that is, we are not explicitly concerned here with the connections between the issues in question and all other issues that might ultimately be relevant; (3) intellectual reflection here encounters and recognises itself without *fundamentally* having to explain or clarify this fact – that is, the various shapes and forms of reflection can all be investigated straightforwardly without resolving the relevant material content into pure reflection as such. But none of these presuppositions is valid for the *Science of Logic*: no already secure stock of conceptual tasks and problems can be assumed here, nor can the relationship that obtains between the *Logic* and the rest of the System be ignored, and nor again can thought simply appropriate the relevant logical content without explicitly clarifying its own nature and function.

One could even say that the status of the *Logic* can be defined precisely by the fact that all the presuppositions that specifically characterise the other parts of the system are here invalid. And that is why the *Science of Logic* inevitably appears so enigmatic. For there is obviously no simple answer to the three questions we might pose here by analogy with the aforementioned presuppositions: (1) What precisely is the particular *content* of the *Logic* in comparison with the other substantively defined parts of philosophy? (2) What is the *connection* between pure logic and the domains of 'real philosophy' that are themselves saturated with material content? (3) How does reflection explicitly 'come to itself', as Hegel says, within the *Logic*, and what precisely is it that is conceptually grasped and accomplished through the ultimate self-clarification and self-encounter of thought? The difficulty lies in understanding the *Logic*, the vital heart of the system, as itself a part of the whole system, and in elucidating in turn its specific character from the perspective of its own place in the system.

There is one simple response to this problem that the interpreter of Hegel is spontaneously tempted to give: that is, the *Logic* is generally explained as Hegel's version of 'metaphysics'. But this explanation does not take us very far because it merely replaces one enigma with another.

For precisely the discipline of 'logic', which since Aristotle's *Organon* had essentially performed the task of organising the formal procedures and instruments of thought, could never claim to represent the highest science of all in the original classical sense of 'First Philosophy'. The reference to classical models cannot help us therefore to answer the question concerning the specific status of Hegel's *Logic*. Nor indeed is it self-evident from the perspective of the philosophical tradition that the domain of first principles should be specifically integrated as part of the system, rather than separated from the rest in accordance with its general grounding function. It is quite true that Hegel, particularly in the original *Preface* to the *Science of Logic*, did not fail to indicate his desire to restore the vanquished discipline of metaphysics to some new status of honour in the present. But is it really possible simply to revive the relinquished claims of metaphysics? Is the metaphysical impulse, the will to metaphysics, really sufficient to renew a ruptured tradition of thought? Is not precisely the loss of metaphysics the very problem that thought must now seriously address?

Hegel's invocation of a restored metaphysics, and one definitively completed as a science, is by no means an intellectually naive attempt to continue the traditional concerns of a pure science of reason as if nothing had transpired in the intervening period. Hegel is rather reacting explicitly against a *specific situation in the history of philosophy*, and one that is essentially influenced and determined by Kant's transcendental critique of reason. For according to Hegel, the prevailing philosophy of the age had contributed to the 'remarkable spectacle' in which we now 'behold an educated people without a metaphysics – like some otherwise richly embellished temple that nonetheless still lacks a Holy of Holies'.[1] The situation of an educated people without a metaphysics represents a historical observation to which one might readily assent without wishing to draw any further conclusions. The situation in question only appears paradoxical upon a certain premise that Hegel tacitly assumes but which is surely far from self-evident. This premise implies that the cultural level of development of the age itself intrinsically demands its ultimate fulfilment in and through the science of philosophy. The public victory of enlightenment would inevitably remain incomplete without a new sanctuary of metaphysics in the richly embellished temple of culture.

---

[1] Hegel, *Wissenschaft der Logik*, *Preface* to the first edition. G.W.F Hegel, *Werke in zwanzig Bänden* 5, p. 14 (Suhrkamp, Frankfurt am Main 1969).

Now the systematic task of constructing an edifice of unshakeable knowledge is quite conceivable without having to ascribe any crucial role to the increasingly problematic discipline of metaphysics. Throughout the early modern period, thinkers had worked away at building up our knowledge of the world without any appeal to metaphysics in the hope of finally producing a truly comprehensive understanding of reality as a whole. In the philosophical tradition, on the other hand, the highest knowledge exemplified by metaphysics had concerned itself essentially with the eternal truths about the immutable nature of things, and appealed to the powers of a reason that sublimely transcended the merely empirical realm. But the eventual *historicising of metaphysics* necessarily encouraged a new perspective that no longer properly fits with the traditional concept of the discipline.

In fact, the historical approach to metaphysics, which would have been entirely alien to its classical self-understanding, ultimately results from the effective destruction of this formerly canonic discipline, and of which Kant's *transcendental philosophy* is the most eloquent document. The 'critical revolution of our mode of thinking' imposed itself as a necessity once Kant showed that the actual condition of metaphysics as a pure science of reason was entirely inconsistent with its essential character. In spite of its claims to supra-temporal knowledge, the views of the different metaphysical schools are all too variable and inconstant, nothing is actually certain, and everything is as contested as it ever was. It is this scandal of historical decadence that motivated Kant's critical enterprise. And the ensuing dissolution of metaphysical dogmatism is the principal event with which philosophy must now effectively come to terms.

But the historical influence of the critical philosophy had also served to render the situation even more acute. For while Kant had indeed provided decisive arguments against the philosophical ambitions of traditional metaphysics, he had not himself succeeded in systematically establishing the new form of metaphysics that he originally wished to develop on a secure 'critical' basis. In Hegel's judgement, the followers of Kant had also failed to articulate a metaphysics 'that would be able to step forth as a science' because they remained too beholden to his transcendental philosophy, although they were all indeed attempting to develop an appropriate metaphysical supplement to Kantian criticism.

What would be the character, then, of a metaphysics that truly corresponded to this historical situation? Obviously not every inner sanctum will serve to fit the finished temple of knowledge. It is quite clear that such a new metaphysics cannot fall back into a pre-Kantian position and simply continue the Aristotelian philosophy of the eighteenth-century schools in the same manner as before. Nor should it fall victim to the belief that Kant's systematic programme can still successfully be accomplished despite all previous experiences of failure. Hegel rightly perceives that Kant's critical approach, which makes the structural clarification of the subject-object relationship itself into the principal question for philosophy, does not permit the construction of metaphysics at all. And finally we must also draw the appropriate lessons from the false trails of post-Kantian thought as represented in early idealist philosophy, or what Hegel describes in this connection as the 'philosophy of reflection'.

In their own fashion, Fichte and Schelling both demonstrated that the bold and decisive advance from transcendental criticism towards a new metaphysics was bound to fail unless the critical view of the fundamental synthetic structure of self-consciousness were thoroughly revised. Hegel in turn was especially percipient in grasping why the unconditional and absolute transformation of the principle of finite cognition based upon the subject-object relationship into the pure ego – which opposes the non-ego to itself according to Fichte, or into an empty identity, where all opposition between subjectivity and objectivity vanishes according to Schelling – inevitably frustrates the development of those systematic conclusions that were originally intended.

If one takes Hegel's explicit engagement with his predecessors and contemporaries seriously, then his ultimate appeal to the venerable title of metaphysics appears even *more remarkable*. Those interpreters of Hegel who simply repeat such talk of the *Logic* as a metaphysics would thus appear to be overly naive in their approach. Marx, as is well known, expressed profound scepticism with respect to the speculative hypertrophy of Hegelian thought, and wielded his analytical dissecting knife precisely in order to separate Hegel's solid theoretical insights into society from the grandiose claims of his system. For, according to a much-quoted dictum of Marx, the logic of the subject matter had here been confused with the subject matter of logic. And neo-Marxist interpreters, up to and including those of the Frankfurt School, have essentially concurred with this verdict without further hesitation. In the meantime, it has become necessary to look again at Hegel himself in order to revise this tradition of Hegel critique. Not so very long ago, this proved to be a burning issue, whereas nothing but ashen clouds now seem to hang over these rapidly abandoned intellectual positions.

Heidegger, on the other hand, interprets the concept of spirit presupposed in Hegel's *Logic* in terms of much earlier conceptions of metaphysics as part of his strong claim that all of European philosophical thought has led increasingly to the onto-theological obscuring of the fundamental question concerning being. Insofar as Heidegger rather emblematically presents Hegel as a particularly extreme example of metaphysics compared with others, Heidegger has made it rather too easy for himself in relation to a philosopher who truly is a kind of antipode to his own position. In terms of conceptualising the internal tension between 'history' and 'metaphysics', Hegel and Heidegger actually stand much closer to one another than the latter is willing to admit. And at least within the philosophical tradition, Hegel is a plausible candidate for the thinker who has reacted most sensitively to the historically conditioned character of the enigmatic metaphysical enterprise itself.[2]

If we really wish to enquire after the metaphysical significance of Hegel's *Logic*, therefore, we must stop trying to employ the traditional terminology to do so. We must recognise the novel idea that Hegelian metaphysics explicitly includes the previous *history of thought* within itself, and that the supra-historical truths of purely rational philosophical knowledge are not derived here in abstract opposition to the experience of historical change, but rather with a full conscious awareness of such change. And it is this consideration that should decide whether we wish to describe Hegel's *Logic* as the *completion* or as the *sublation* of metaphysics. Obviously there is no question of interpreting the history of philosophy here as a purely external chronology of different conceptions and systems. The history of philosophy is implicitly present in the *Logic* rather in the sense that the latter takes up *all* the relevant concepts that previous metaphysics has produced and simultaneously subjects them to conceptual *reconstruction*, as the second Preface expressly indicates.

The *Logic* brings in no special concepts to add to the already existing conceptual stock of philosophy as if to claim that its own were the only true and definitive ones, and superior to all other competing

---

[2] The penetrating interpretation of Hegel presented by Michael Theunissen (*Sein und Schein*, Frankfurt 1978) seems in some respects to avoid confronting this problem. While Theunissen recognises that the *Logic*, as Hegel's principal work, possesses an intrinsically 'critical' function over against every form of scientistic positivism, he also attempts to decipher it as a conclusive theory of the ideal society that is supposed to replace traditional metaphysics.

concepts. Hegel had often enough encountered just such claims to definitive completeness in the work of his own contemporaries and seen them all soon overtaken by successive programmes for philosophical systems that boasted very similar pretensions. His *Logic* is not designed to perform this role, but rather to provide an intrinsically coherent and interconnected articulation of the totality of all previously generated concepts. Hegel's *Logic* thus *methodologically reinterprets the entire history of metaphysics*. Hegel shows total confidence in the conceptual resources available for this methodical task and fully shares the typically modern conviction concerning the 'scientific' character of philosophy. It never enters Hegel's mind even for a moment that metaphysics might not actually permit such total methodical reconstruction and might therefore resist incorporation as part of any philosophical system, or that metaphysics might essentially be concerned with something quite different from this, something that fundamentally eludes any such methodological approach.

II. The Project of Methodological Reconstruction

This methodical approach to constructing a viable contemporary metaphysics naturally presupposes that all of the relevant fundamental concepts have actually emerged and that there will be no need to supplement the *entirety* of such concepts with any new examples in the future. With respect to the metaphorical conception of the temple that lacks its inner sanctum, therefore, history plays the essential role of supplying all the necessary materials for its completion. Indeed, the bold enterprise itself can only properly be contemplated at the historical point that effectively marks an end, from the substantive point of view, of metaphysics.

If history were in fact to lead our philosophical thought in further and quite unpredictable directions, such an attempt at comprehensive reconstruction would inevitably fail. Now the conviction that we already possess all the required concepts in question is not based upon an extravagant philosophy of history illegitimately introduced to govern the domain of metaphysics, but depends entirely upon the success of the attempted reconstruction itself. For if all our concepts can be brought together in a unity that obviates the need for infinite progress in future, the interconnected structure we are seeking will have been established. But as long as new concepts continue to arise, the intended unity will remain incomplete. Whether this unity can be reconstructively established can only be determined through the actual execution of the task. This cannot be decided externally because no grounds for such a decision can possibly exist independently of the internally grounded structure itself.

Hegel would oppose this approach to the *romantic* position as represented by the early Schlegel, for example. For Schlegel had paradoxically concluded, on the basis of Fichte's systematically developed *Doctrine of Science*, that we must hope for an ultimate convergence of philosophical truth, one that is not yet possible today but that will inevitably come to pass at the end of time. The utopian reflections upon a metaphysics of the 'wholly Other' that we find in Benjamin and Adorno work in a very similar way by appealing to the immanent power of some intrinsic historical tendency that has yet to reach fulfilment. And the later Heidegger's notion of 'releasement', in acknowledging the unmasterable 'sending' of being, would likewise attune genuine thinking to an independent historical process that will only reach its goal once we learn to curb our hasty methodological attempts to impose order upon the world. Hegel was never seriously confronted by the alternative of an unarticulated, and perhaps inarticulable, metaphysics whose future path has been consigned to the autonomous course of history itself. For Hegel fundamentally mistrusted the thought that the ordering character of reason should withdraw before the unpredictable turnings of history in order to open up a space where it could supposedly be liberated into its own opposite. And in this he remained a true protagonist of modern *rationalism*, even though he attempted to counter the *reified form* of such rationalism by means of his own carefully developed dialectic of the limit.

It follows from this perspective that while history does perform an indispensable preliminary role in the establishment of a definitive modern metaphysics, it cannot and should not be made responsible for the success or failure of the ultimate project of rational philosophical 'science'. And to delegate this task to history would in truth precisely prevent the construction of the temple of philosophy. To the extent that history can effectively be integrated within a theory claiming eternal validity, then its power to hinder the completion of metaphysics would seem to be broken. It is the programme of methodical reconstruction that must save the construction of Hegel's 'temple' from the perils of historical relativism.

If we carefully consider Hegel's intention to reconstruct all the relevant concepts of metaphysics by recourse to the very history of the discipline, it is possible to explain the difference between Hegel's approach and that of traditional metaphysics that we mentioned at the beginning. The questions that initially appeared so enigmatic were those concerning (1) the substantive content of the *Logic* itself, (2) the place of the *Logic* within the entire system of philosophical disciplines, and (3) the self-reflexive character of the concept. Above all, it was extremely unclear why it was necessary for the *Logic* to forgo the special position classically ascribed to metaphysics and be fully integrated within the dialectical system instead. The special position of metaphysics was formerly justified precisely in contrast to the domains of finite or imperfect knowledge. Thus Parmenides had segregated philosophical truth from the world of mere opinion, Plato had opposed the ideas to the realm of appearances, and Aristotle had defined the highest science of being as such in contrast to the particular sciences that investigated the specific aspects of existing things.

The first two questions are directly connected, since the disappearance of the special realm of first principles also dissolves the formerly unproblematic identification of its specific *contents*. Concerning the latter, one always knew one thing at least – namely, that they had to be able to ground whatever it was that required grounding. The basic problem of ground, of the grounding principle and grounded content, constituted the self-evident background here.

Even the metaphysics of early modern philosophy, however sophisticated in its innermost structure, continued to depend upon an elementary appeal to the abstract difference between the grounding principle and the conclusions drawn from the latter. This is an unquestioned assumption for Spinoza in his arguments against Descartes, for example, and in the context of early idealist thought, both Fichte and Schelling still build upon Spinoza's example in this respect. And Reinhold's *Elementarphilosophie*, specifically designed to set Kantian Criticism upon secure foundations, was the first work to announce those demands for effective grounding that would soon become definitive within the context of transcendental philosophy.

But in Hegel's *Logic*, this persisting remnant of immediacy in the metaphysical appeal to supposedly pure substantive principles of reason is finally dissolved, and yields to a progressive development of conceptual content through the methodical clarification and overcoming of immediacy. The category of 'ground' is thus transformed into one concept amongst many others that serve to disclose actuality, and thereby finds its proper place within the overall development of the *Logic*. Hegel expressly introduced the expression 'determinate negation' to elucidate the way in which he undertakes to transform, resolve and re-articulate traditional metaphysics. The entire procedure of 'methodical clarification' culminates in the concept of determinate negation. And this is also where we shall find the answer to our third question concerning the self-reflexive character of the Hegelian concept.

III. Excursus on Determinate Negation

Determinate negation signifies that a given concept only acquires specifiable content if the concept in question can be delimited over against a concept that it is not. This delimitation is a negation, and arises in direct relation to an initially anonymous 'other' that is implicitly presupposed. Whatever this 'other' may be in any specific case, it constitutes an entirely formal opposition over against the articulated concept in the process of negation. The next step of the exposition then clearly reveals that the 'other' that was immediately employed for the purpose of conceptual determination is in turn not indeterminate at all, but is itself determined through the initial act of determination. For it is determined precisely as *other-being* relative to what was originally to be determined. Reflection upon the act of determining thus sublates the original appearance of immediacy and explicitly mediates both sides with one another qua the determinate moment and its own other. This internal relationship, which binds the 'one' and the 'other' together serves, *ipso facto*, to enrich the determination under consideration.

A much discussed example of the process we have sketched here is the *initial sequence of concepts* in the *Logic*: those of 'being', 'nothing' and 'becoming', which in the accompanying 'Remarks' are also clearly referred back to the early positions of pre-Socratic philosophy. The ancient thinkers had never considered that the fundamental concepts they had immediately employed stand in an intrinsic relationship to one another. But once they are explicitly reconstructed in terms of this relationship, they lose the purely exclusive character that originally marked their historical opposition to one another. They do not become false, but rather present themselves in a different manner once they are brought, *ex post facto*, into a logical connection with one another.

I cannot address here the question raised by Gadamer[3] as to whether the reversal from 'being' into 'nothing' should be read merely as an 'inauthentic' transition, in which case we encounter the first genuine

---

3 H.-G. Gadamer, *Hegels Dialektik* (Tübingen 1971), p. 60. This idea would seem to derive from Heidegger: *Gesamtausgabe* 68 (Frankfurt am Main, 1993, p. 52).

mediation only with the concept of 'becoming'. The important point is that the step from the pre-conceptual domain into the first position in the *Logic* – namely, the 'indeterminate immediate', designated with the traditional basic term of ontology as '*being*' – results from the deliberate elimination of any other intervening determinations, and thus from an *act of negation* explicitly undertaken by philosophical reflection. The initial position is built up, therefore, by recourse to what first presents itself as conceptually other – namely, mediation and determinacy in general. This process is repeated structurally at all subsequent levels of the logical determination of the concept. Reflection upon the unavoidable act of determining in relation to some conceptual other expressly includes the supposition that renders such determination possible. Reflection retrospectively limits negation, which as the denial of anything and everything would otherwise evaporate entirely into the indeterminate, as a negation of the preceding determinacy. And by means of this retrospective incorporation of previously unacknowledged presuppositions, reflection in each case enriches the next step as a negation that awaits further determination in turn. This generates an increasing level of complexity that itself gives rise to the succeeding concept.

Hegel's most elaborate application of this methodological approach, presenting the self-explication of the concept as determinate negation, is probably to be found at the *beginning of the logic of essence*.[4] If the beginning of the logic of being referred us to the pre-Socratics, the beginning of the logic of essence is concerned directly with the central issue of modern philosophy – namely, with *reflection*. Through recourse to the logic of being as a whole, the logic of essence commences with a conceptual difference that initially simply indicates the formal distance between this second part and the preceding development, already presented as complete in its own terms. In the light of the now central theme of essence, this difference is interpreted as the difference between the 'essential' and the 'inessential'. The step thus presents itself as an effortless translation of the entire conceptual constellation that has arisen in the previous course of development.

The inessential that continues to cling to the essential acquires greater weight once it is invested with the venerable opposition of *essence* and *appearance* that has accompanied metaphysics like a shadow ever

---

[4] On this question, cf. M. Wölfle's Tübingen dissertation *Die Wesenslogik in Hegels 'Wissenschaft der Logik'* (2 vols., Stuttgart 1993), which is without doubt the most detailed commentary on a Hegelian text that has ever been produced.

since Parmenides and Plato. From the time of the ancient Greeks onwards, to grasp the essence of things was to avoid falling victim to appearance, was to see through the latter as such and thereby to break its
power over us. In accordance with Hegel's dictum from the lectures on
Aesthetics – that appearance is essential to essence – the relationship in
question is now grasped as internal to essence itself, instead of essence
first triumphantly distinguishing itself from mere appearance. From the
dialectical perspective, essence and appearance thus belong together.

The classical terminology of the philosophical tradition is methodically integrated within the logical development insofar as the relevant
substantive concepts are now articulated in their proper respective positions, and thereby expressly connected with one another. But inasmuch as the traditional disparity between essence and appearance is
interpreted precisely as the conceptual constellation in which essence
originally posits itself as such, a certain parity between both dimensions
also emerges here. In a brilliant and elaborate series of moves, Hegel
then identifies the peculiar character of the problem of reflection that
had served as the foundation for early modern philosophy even though
it had never properly been clarified upon the path leading from Kant
through Reinhold to Fichte and Schelling. For two equally valid sides
are here related to one another in such a way that we can no longer
decide which side ultimately presupposes which, and which therefore
takes priority over the other. This relationship, which can never be
stabilised because it only exists precisely in the equally valid reciprocal sublation of both *relata*, explains the constantly restless oscillation,
which is what reflection simply *is*.

'Transition or becoming sublates itself in its transition; the Other that
becomes as such in this transition is not the non-being of a being, but
the nothing of a nothing, and this, the fact of being the negation of a
nothing, constitutes being'.[5] The immediately following subsections on
'positing', 'external' and 'determining' reflection in the first instance
harbour an extremely subtle debate with Fichte, whose primordial act
of 'positing', according to Hegel, is actually a form of 'presupposing',
and is therefore incompatible with the original pathos of the Fichtean
enterprise. It is likewise incompatible with Kant's appeal to reflective
judgement, which turns absolute reflection into something essentially
external. For Hegel, therefore, positing and external reflection are

---

[5] Hegel, *Wissenschaft der Logik* II 1, 1 C; *Hegel's Science of Logic*, trans. A. V. Miller (London
1969), p. 400.

finally sublated to constitute the form of self-determination, in which
the process of reflection differentiates itself out of its own unimpeded
and self-mediated movement. Thus the classical logical principles of
identity, difference and contradiction all find their appropriate place
here under the rubric of the 'essentialities and determinations of reflection'.

IV. A Treatise on Method

It is through this consistent development of purely formal conceptual
acts that the *Logic* is able to move forward in a rationally intelligible
fashion. Without depending upon alien material, it generates its own
content insofar as any concept, if its exact determination can only be
properly grasped, will already refer us to its neighbouring concept and
its exact determination in turn. This forward movement successively
grasps all the concepts that have previously shown themselves to be
significant within the metaphysical tradition. But with respect to this
question of significance, and that means the role each concept plays
within the totality of concepts, no further external considerations are
introduced. The relevance of a concept and its specific place within the
structure of the *Logic* are thus generated together.

Utterly ignoring all *chronological* sequence, we begin with the sim-
plest conceptual forms, pass through various levels of further complexity, and finally arrive at the richest structures of all. After traversing the
three substantial parts dedicated to 'being', 'essence' and the 'concept',
which are rather surprisingly divided into 'objective' and 'subjective'
logic in contrast to the usual triadic organisation favoured by Hegel,
the path finally ends where there are no further concepts to be thematised, and the entire procedure itself is made the object of conscious
reflection. The *Logic* thus concludes by reflecting upon its own *method*,
the only theme that remains once all the relevant concepts have been
reconstructed and thus all possible conceptual content has been articulated. Since the radical formality of the procedure itself is presented for
analysis, the circle can close because the content-generating method of
the *Logic* now suddenly becomes its own immediate object. The conclusion of the work reveals how it was the self-reflection of the concept
that sustained the entire process of development.

Now it is usually the case in philosophy for a *treatise on method* to precede the actual substantive philosophical labour. And that is what the editors of the Aristotelian corpus described as the *Organon* of philosophy.

Bacon in the seventeenth century and Lambert in the eighteenth responded to this by proposing a *New Organon*. Descartes's *Discours de la Méthode* clearly articulates the new position in this respect. Those proposals concerning method clearly correspond to different conceptions of philosophy. But the independent status of the abstract discussion of method as such still remains untouched. The transformation of this distinction between prior methodology and subsequent substantive reflection expresses a completely new conception of 'logic'. All well-intentioned approaches, rare though they are, that attempt to derive something from Hegel's *Logic* remotely resembling modern ideas concerning formal logic would therefore seem to be misguided in principle.[6]

The fact that the 'method' appears at the very end of the *Science of Logic* throws very significant light upon the primacy of what Hegel calls the 'authentic content' [*die Sache selbst*] of the work. The autonomous development of this content can be brought to explicit conscious awareness once that development has been accomplished, and indeed definitively so insofar as it is grasped as a final result.[7] The entire potential of Western metaphysics can thus gradually be drawn out along the 'self-constructing path'[8] of progressive conceptual explication, a process that is essentially governed by 'determinate negation', as we indicated earlier. This potential is already implicitly provided through the historical experience of philosophy, although it has never before been methodically articulated and has thus always sought in vain to attain the status of a genuine 'science'. The convincing realisation of metaphysics can only consist in its exhaustive conceptual reconstruction in the present. The fact that the entirety of 'authentic content' returns to itself at the end of its own developmental path ensures that there are no further methodical considerations that still remain to be addressed. This ultimate self-clarification of the concept allows for the

---

[6] See, for example, P. Stekeler-Weithofer, *Hegels Analytische Philosophie. Die Wissenschaft der Logik als kritische Theorie der Bedeutung* (Paderborn 1992). The author employs the conceptual resources of a special group of modern logicians, but he quite fails to do justice to the dialectic proper. Cf. also the collectively authored volume of essays from a similar perspective that does include some more stimulating contributions in this respect: *Vernunftkritik nach Hegel. Analytisch-kritische Interpretationen zur Dialektik*, eds. Ch. Demmerling and F. Kambartel (Frankfurt am Main 1992).

[7] Cf. my essay, 'Die "Sache selbst" in Hegels System', in R. Bubner, *Zur Sache der Dialektik* (Stuttgart 1980).

[8] Hegel, *Wissenschaft der Logik*, *Preface* to the first edition.

method which, *ipso facto*, concludes the enterprise of such a *Science of Logic.*

In the introduction to the work, where he presents the 'general concept of logic', Hegel contrasts the procedure of the 'former metaphysics' with that of Kantian Criticism, and makes a passing reference to *language* in this connection. 'Such metaphysics did not therefore regard thought and the determinations of thought as something alien to the object, but rather as the essence of the latter, thus claiming that things and the thinking of things – just as our language also expresses an affinity between the two – correspond with one another in and for themselves'. Hegel returns to this point in the *Preface* to the new edition of the *Logic*, which he was about to undertake shortly before his death. And referring back to the original sense of the word *logos*, he describes language as the very domain of investigation for 'logic'. Since the human spirit has externalised itself in language, it is here that we should seek to identify the substantive content of our concepts and it is here that the philosophical labour of conceptual clarification should begin. For language already ubiquitously contains the relevant categories, though still obscurely mixed up together with one another: 'The logical dimension [*das Logische*] is so natural to human beings, or is indeed rather their distinctive nature. But if one contrasts nature in general, as the physical domain, over against the spiritual domain, we should have to say that the logical dimension is rather the supra-natural element that permeates all natural behaviour of the human being and thereby turns it precisely into something human'.

Language as an index of the supra-natural within the sphere of anthropology, as a *metaphysics of the everyday*, as it were, implies the spiritual saturation of our entire relationship to the world. I shall return to this thought in the final part of my essay in order to free the continuing controversy concerning the metaphysical significance of the *Logic* from the horns of a dilemma, according to which we must interpret the work either as the end or as the sublation of traditional metaphysics, either as its completion or as its overcoming. But however we try and turn and twist the matter, a metaphysics that finally absorbs its own history remains a quite unprecedented philosophical undertaking. It seems to me that Hegel's invocation of metaphysics as the exemplary form of the 'highest science' was little more than a pedagogic formula for his own project of a comprehensive dialectical system of philosophy. After the historically identifiable collapse of the traditional metaphysics of the Schools, there is no longer any reliable foundation upon which one could possibly construct a new system. But the model of language can direct us, through and beyond a historically ruptured consciousness, towards certain theoretical claims that cannot be repeated in an unreflective manner, but must rather be legitimated in an entirely new way.

v. The *Logic* as Philosophy of Language?

The following considerations may strike convinced defenders of Hegel as unorthodox. But any source that provides a theoretical means of shedding some light upon this complex area should be welcome, especially in view of the extremely difficult hermeneutic situation involved here. We shall have to decide at the end whether an interpretation of the *Logic* in terms of a *philosophy of language* can provide the required, if problematic, legitimation for the idea of an ultimate theory of the world such as Hegel appeals to under the name of metaphysics.

The contemporary discussion that I take up revolves around the problem of the historical transformation of concepts. The debate, familiar in the anglophone philosophical literature under the title of 'conceptual change', concerns description of the logical comparability of different linguistic contexts, categorial systems or conceptual paradigms. A few indications concerning the origin of this problem must suffice here. A first step in this connection was the overcoming of nominalism, which had correlated semantic meanings with certain objects in an atomistic fashion without adequately considering the inner structural relationships of language itself. It was now understood that it is only within some larger framework that a semantic unit can properly function – that is, intrinsically intelligible and communicable in the first place. And this in turn led to further intensive engagement with the question concerning the reciprocal dependence between the semantic unit, whether the individual word or proposition, and the totality of a spoken language.

With the repudiation of the nominalistically inspired project for constructing an 'ideal language', it soon became evident that there is no single categorial framework that would be valid for all semantic units. On the contrary, one has to recognise the variety of historically evolved languages, linguistically articulated world-views, scientific bodies of theory, cultural paradigms and conventional language games. Here I ignore all the linguistic, sociological and historical implications that follow from this simply in order to emphasise the very *plurality of semantic systems*.

This immediately prompts the question concerning the possibility of intelligibly comparing one system with others, the possibility of grasping a transition from one system to another or to the 'next' system. For all these systems claim equally to relate in some way to reality. Various answers have been suggested to this question, ranging from Wittgenstein's insistence upon mere description of the family resemblance between language games, through the kind of hermeneutics of cultures that is associated with Winch or Geertz, to Quine's very strong thesis concerning ontological relativity.

And in a parallel development to this, we can also observe the modern claims of conceptual relativity in the theory of science. Thus the remaining core of traditional empiricism in Popper's principle concerning the radical falsifiability of empirical hypotheses has itself been dissolved in the light of Kuhn's theory of paradigm shifts. It is no longer possible to grasp science as a direct confrontation with reality, but only as something that is already mediated in terms of more general orientation or paradigm that serves as an organising perspective for ongoing research. The paradigms succeed one another in the course of history as effectively self-contained structures in a way that renders genuine comparison between one paradigm and another impossible. Feyerabend has finally drawn the relevant scientific moral from Kuhn's reflections upon the history of science. Thus *paradigm change* is not merely a fateful fact that has to be accepted. The actual development of a plurality of alternatives rather represents a task that must consciously be undertaken for the sake of strengthening rationality in the face of the ever-present threat of dogmatism, and especially that of philosophers. Insisting on the unity of any given paradigm merely serves to narrow down our intellectual perspectives, whereas the open examination of other possibilities can only enrich our scientific understanding of the world. This propagation of an anarchism of alternatives takes a further provocative step over and beyond the semantic analysis of conceptual change.

The fruitful perspective here implies due emphasis upon the necessary mediation of the empirical material through processes of interpretation. As long as the practitioners of science believed that it was possible to grasp reality by means of direct and undistorted experience, then it seemed permissible to neglect the conceptual fluctuations of potential meaning within different scientific theories. For experience itself was always deemed capable of ultimately correcting the instability of our particular conceptual approaches. But once the empirical material is included within and related to the conceptual framework of a given prevailing paradigm, the former must be regarded as itself dependent upon theoretical presuppositions. Instead of experience simply being in a position to correct theory, we have to acknowledge the 'theory-laden' character of all possible experience. This need for requisite interpretation thus plays down the critical role formerly ascribed to direct experience.[9]

And now a further parallel immediately suggests itself: the overcoming of the *Kantian theory of knowledge* in Hegel's *Logic*. The Kant who insisted that concepts without intuitions are empty clearly confessed his allegiance to empiricism in this decisive respect. Without this ineliminable dependence upon the givens of experience, the entire system of transcendental philosophy would revolve fruitlessly in a void. Hegel's principal objection to the Kantian dualism of concept and experience, which serves to mirror the modern separation of subject and object, is directed towards the element of reflection that underlies this separation. To regard the concept as mere form, and to make sensuous experience responsible for material content, is to posit a relation of reflection in which one side necessarily presupposes the other. The reciprocal relationship of these two sides is not something that is simply found as given, but is an assumption that precedes all empirical experience and one that must properly be recognised as an accomplishment of reflection itself.

Hegel's *Logic* makes constant appeal to precisely such forms of *reflection of reflection* under the general heading of the 'speculative'. Hegel thereby points out the accomplishments that are constitutive for certain structures even though the former, implicitly involved as they are, are not themselves explicitly thematised along with the structures they serve to constitute. The structures in question are immediately regarded as characterising the matter at hand, whereas the real task is to decipher them as structures that have been generated in a certain way, as results of prior accomplishments, as forgotten products of reflection. We could also express this fundamental thought in non-Hegelian terminology and say that nothing generally intelligible to us is simply 'given', as something that has to be accepted as such, but is rather always already something 'interpreted'. In the Hegelian terminology we have been using here, this thought is expressed in the claim that language, as

9 Here I resume my earlier reflections in the essay 'Dialektische Elemente einer Forschungslogik', in R. Bubner, *Dialektik und Wissenschaft* (Frankfurt am Main 1973).

the representative embodiment of spirit, penetrates and permeates the entirety of our relationship and comportment to the world.

One needs only apply this fundamental principle to a plurality of cases in order to gain access to what Hegel calls the 'movement of the concept'. The expression has acquired such common currency through the Hegelians that no one now enquires more closely into the nature of this remarkable dynamic in which all of our concepts are caught up, or asks after the requisite nature of concepts that could be subject to the principles of such a dynamic in the first place. The plurality of logical situations where this reflection of reflection, as we have described it, is required itself demands articulation of its inner structural context. Such situations confront us whenever their own inherent limitations can be demonstrated step by step by appeal to the same criterion. The crucial connecting thread here is the progressive discovery of the unreflective presuppositions upon which the particular conceptual forms in each case depend. In the light of this criterion, they will all reveal some constitutive deficiency with respect to rationality.

Such a *deficiency* will present itself whenever a specific conceptual form is incapable of fully integrating some element that makes an essential contribution to its original self-articulation. Philosophical logic explicitly reveals these deficiencies in relation to the various forms by explicating the essential but unclarified presuppositions that belong unnoticed to each form in turn. Subsequent philosophical reflection upon the reflection already implicit in the form of knowledge under consideration sublates – that is, cancels and transcends – the relevant limitation, and thus represents a further step in correcting the defective rationality in question. It is obviously only through recourse to this speculative activity of reflection that we can grasp the 'movement' of the concept that expresses the necessary and immanent character of the subject matter itself. Naturally there is no question of understanding such reflection in the phenomenological or psychological sense as an activity of consciousness, but only in the logical sense of contributing to the production of a system of interconnected concepts.

The analogy to the aforementioned notions of conceptual change in the more recent philosophical discussion of *semantics* may now have presented itself more clearly. For semantics essentially locates the individual bearer of meaning – the relevant expressions or propositions – within the broader framework of some categorial system, language or paradigm. The concrete and specifically determinate units of meaning fulfil their function of referring to something determinate, which is thereby rendered communicable and intelligible, without simultaneously and directly referring to that total framework. They refer to a specific 'something' by virtue of the environing context of a language or schema that is implicitly presupposed. The expressions in question only possess their meaning within a language, but their meaning is not identical with that language. For one must already be familiar with the language as a whole in order to understand such expressions as bearers of meaning in the first place.

Although this relationship between the semantic unit and the total framework is constitutive for the semantic function in general, it never itself explicitly finds expression in words. The conditions of meaning themselves cannot meaningfully be expressed in the same way as the content that they effectively enable us to express. The relationship between the unit and the whole that is presupposed here itself remains shrouded in obscurity. It is only the encounter with alternative possibilities in the form of other languages or other paradigms that brings this forgotten dimension to light. Once we observe that other ways of speaking and communicating are also quite possible, however unusual or unfamiliar they may appear to us, we suddenly recognise this relationship, which is constitutive for every use of language though necessarily concealed within the successful act of speech. We may not be able to understand the new language right away, and the alien paradigm in question might well remain closed to us, but it is precisely through the confrontation with alternative possibilities that we realise that they are as unproblematic to others as our own languages and paradigms are to us.

VI. Semantic Change and Dialectics

The challenging questions arise in each case through the transition from one language to another. Those that are important for our central problem here should not simply be conflated with the social, linguistic, or historical difficulties of adjustment or reorientation generally involved in moving from one language to another. It is not so much the process of acquiring new vocabulary, of practising previously unknown rules, or of familiarising oneself with alien forms of life that appears so enigmatic here. The enigmatic question is rather this: how can it be that language, something we have spontaneously at our command, without knowing why, can also present itself in a different manner, and that we do not need to know why this is so in order ultimately to make ourselves at home in another language. In other words: *the reliable use of semantic functions does not presuppose a semantic theory.* And that is precisely what any semantic theory itself must explain. We can appreciate just how little progress semantic theory has hitherto made in this direction if we consider the rather extreme solutions that have been proposed for this interesting philosophical question. They range from Chomsky's rationalist flight to 'ideae innatae' to Quine's pragmatist appeal to learning processes based upon the model of stimulus/response.

Hegel's dialectical logic permits an illuminating comparison to be made with respect to these semantic questions. For it is quite possible to situate the conceptual structures of the *Logic* in a 'third realm' that possesses a certain autonomous character of its own over against the physical world of experienced nature and the psychological domain of consciousness with all its images and representations. Gottlob Frege, the inaugurator of modern semantics, had expressly demanded the recognition of just such a 'third realm' in his important essay entitled 'Thought' in 1918.

If one understands 'thoughts' to signify all semantic contents that cannot be interpreted psychologistically but must be subjected to logical analysis – that is, all linguistic elements that meaningfully refer to the world, then it would appear necessary for us to organise this plurality of thoughts within a specific realm of its own. In his later writings, Karl Popper has expressly pursued this Fregean demand by appeal to Tarski's semantic definition of truth. Much in the style of Hegel's concept of spirit, Popper has constructed a logically connected sequence of such conceptual structures with the ultimate purpose of articulating a comprehensive and true theory of reality.[10]

But there is an essential difference between Hegel's dialectic and these semantic conceptions. For the constitutive relationship between the entire framework of a language and the individual semantic details *itself remains indeterminate* unless and until the encounter with conceptual alternatives calls our attention back to the framework ultimately presupposed in all discourse. Even the change from one language to another, or from one categorial system to the succeeding one, makes no difference to the fundamental indeterminacy of the connection in question. Since it is essential for the successful command of a language, as it is for unimpeded movement within a given paradigm, that the framework be unproblematically accepted and never becomes thematic as

---

[10] K. Popper, *Objective Knowledge* (Oxford 1972).

such, then any newly arising change merely reveals the fact that there is such a framework in the first place.

Mere change on its own does not facilitate determination of the specific relation between the transformed framework and the newly determined semantic details within it. It looks as though semantic theory has simply reconciled itself to the thought that no further or precise determination is possible in this respect. Obviously we seem to be satisfied with the comforting observation that the relationships remain much the same before and after the change in question insofar as the process of change has not affected the actual use of language. The processes of radical change, the 'revolutions' as Kuhn calls them, constitute the only really disturbing factors since it is only during such changes that normal practice cannot successfully be sustained. Once the normal situation is restored, the challenge that might have led to a more precise determination of the relationship between framework and detailed content simply disappears.

Davidson, for example, makes the following consoling suggestion: 'In giving up dependence on the concept of an uninterpreted reality, standing outside all schemes and science, we do not relinquish the notion of objective truth – quite the contrary. [. . . .] Of course truth of sentences remains relative to language, but that is as objective as can be. In giving up the dualism of scheme and world, we do not give up the world, but re-establish unmediated touch with the familiar objects whose antics make our sentences true or false'.[11]

Such pragmatic consolation is quite unacceptable as far as the Hegelian *dialectic* is concerned. Every concrete transition raises the question concerning the problematic relationship between the individual case and the framework as a whole. The 'movement of the concept' consists precisely in the sequence of these transitions. Since the totality of the *Logic*, within which every individual concept finds its appropriate place and determinate character, is essentially produced through nothing but the complete movement of the concept, every single step of this movement is relevant to the whole structure. That is why the question concerning the constitutive interconnection of our concepts does not simply fall back into oblivion once some significant conceptual change has been recognised. Every step from one concept to the next makes a genuine contribution to *determining the formerly unclarified relationship*

---

[11] 'On the Very Idea of a Conceptual Scheme' (1974), in D. Davidson, *Enquiries into Truth and Interpretation* (Oxford 1984).

between the whole and its parts. The methodical construction of the *Logic* as a whole, which derives its own determinate character from the determinate character of the individual moments it embraces, also simultaneously elucidates the determinate relationship between both of the dimensions involved.

Hegel describes this process as follows: 'It is only along this self-constructing path that philosophy is capable of becoming an objective and demonstrable science'. The individual concepts are determined step by step through the transition from one to the next, and the path as a whole is determined through the totality of such steps. But the relationship between the whole and the individual moments is not for its part simply left open and thus abandoned to the fateful event of some suddenly unexpected conceptual transformation. It rather continues to determine itself as this 'self-constructing path', where the sequence of steps unfolds in a way that is neither blind, nor disorganised, nor wavering in vague anticipation of some completed whole. What the semantic analysis of conceptual change simply presupposes appears here as thematic object for the task of conceptual determination. The connection between the whole and the individual parts, the overall context of a language that sustains semantic determinacy without being conceptualised as such, presents itself here explicitly as something that is be grasped conceptually – that is, to be determined internally. Since the determination of this connection with the whole is also at issue in every transition between specifically determined individual concepts, dialectical logic possesses a means of conceptualising these otherwise inexplicable transitions. The irrational character of paradigm shifts, where systems that are 'incommensurable' on the semantic perspective simply clash with another, can be eliminated by recourse to the totality implicit in every particular act of determination.

VII. Concluding Summary

If one is prepared to follow modern semantics in understanding the notion of conceptual framework or governing paradigm as a total perspective upon the world, then we have the prospect of reformulating the approach of traditional metaphysics in terms of the philosophy of language. But the plurality of such frameworks only effectively presents itself in the course of a *historical process*. The philosophy of language itself has no appropriate theoretical means at its disposal for conceptualising such a sequence of positions. The perspective of semantic holism coincides with that of hermeneutics in acknowledging the necessity of simply living with the historicity of language. Hegel's *Logic*, on the other hand, attempts to provide a conceptual model capable of grasping the historically conditioned character of our concepts. To that extent, Hegel can plausibly claim that the science of philosophy, as a completely self-comprehending theory, has first properly conquered the dangerous challenge of history.

This approach provides specific *legitimation* for the claim that the classical task of metaphysics, as 'first philosophy' and as the 'highest science', has now truly been accomplished. The Aristotle who is cited without further commentary at the end of Hegel's *Encyclopaedia of the Philosophical Sciences* had merely promised such a thing. In the subsequent development of philosophy, metaphysics was gradually undermined by the growing recognition of its intrinsically historical character. Kant eventually called for its reformation and renewal, although he was unable to accomplish this himself through his continuing but unacknowledged dependence upon the modern principle of 'reflection'. In the context of this debate between metaphysics and history, which secretly pervades the development of German Idealism, Hegel had good arguments to support his own position.

But the *aspect of closure* that marks his thought remains, of course, notoriously problematic. Hegel's *Logic* deviates so far from the traditional paths of metaphysics as the demonstrative science of ultimate grounds that it is very difficult to provide a decisive answer to our original question: does Hegel represent the 'completion' or the 'sublation' of metaphysics? For the Hegelian confrontation between philosophy as the highest science and the realm of history contains both elements that serve to overcome classical dogmatism and elements that encourage the claim to finality. But Hegel's general approach, as we saw, can also be plausibly understood in a quite different way. Thus the interpretation of the *Logic* in terms of the philosophy of language can accommodate history in an unforced manner within the appeal to the *logos*. And the reconstruction of all those forms of the *logos* through which we attempt fundamentally to understand the world no longer relates to the historical dimension in such an external way that this reconstruction comes to constitute the immanent *telos* of history or effect its definitive conclusion. Such an interpretation of the *Logic* in the light of the idea of semantic change allows us therefore simply to dissolve the alternative as formulated in our original question.

4

HEGEL'S POLITICAL ANTHROPOLOGY

I

Hegel himself would never have welcomed my introduction of the expression 'political anthropology'. In the systematic outline supplied by his *Encyclopaedia of the Philosophical Sciences*, the section entitled 'Anthropology', the doctrine of the natural determinations of the soul, assumes its carefully delineated place under the rubric of 'subjective spirit', whereas the *political dimension* belongs firmly within the domain of 'objective spirit' under the title of 'right'. I should like, therefore, with the help of a few general points, to locate and identify the theme of the following discussion more precisely. This will require us to make a number of distinctions that might otherwise, without detailed examination of the relevant context, merely cause unnecessary confusion. But I draw these distinctions only in order to press on to the heart of the matter at issue.

Ignoring Hegel's specific terminology, it should immediately be obvious to the contemporary reader that my title intends to refer to Hegel's theory of man as a political animal. This expression so emphatically recalls Aristotle that some differentiation of terms is required. Aristotle's claim concerning man as the political animal plausibly emerges from the broader teleological development of his fundamental *concept of action*. From the original analysis of action and its characteristic structures, we pass to the consideration of political institutions, which themselves provide the necessary context and condition for our collective praxis. The 'anthropological' dimension of Aristotle's approach is based upon his ontology, with the governing concept of 'end' or 'purpose' providing the necessary bridge between the two levels of analysis.

Hegel's doctrine of man, on the other hand, is essentially conceived *historically*, so that his political anthropology is intimately bound up with his general philosophy of history. But why precisely do we have to enter into the philosophy of history here? Hegel's answer directs us to the *concept of spirit* that supports the encyclopaedic system in its entirety. This brings us directly to the central category of Hegel's thought, one that in turn requires further differentiation in its own right.

It is true that *spirit* in its very essence is not *historical*, but the development of the historical process, insofar as it is open to human understanding at all, must be re-constructible with respect to its spiritual aspects according to Hegel. Spirit reveals itself therefore primarily from an essentially historical perspective. This is why Hegel came to be celebrated as one of the leading exponents of the great new age of truly historical thought. Dilthey took this view, and consequently repudiated the metaphysics that effectively underlies Hegel's concept of spirit as a useless excrescence.

Expressed in the most general terms, spirit for Hegel is the dynamic process of *self-mediation*, which reconnects original self-distantiation and the subsequent reconciliation of separated moments. These two sides of dissolving separation and re-established unity come together in spirit. The concept of spirit proves so appropriate for deciphering the logic of historical processes precisely because it permits us to connect up all the various paths and detours involved in these processes. But spirit is ultimately the all-comprehensive metaphysical category that grounds everything else, the one provided by Hegel's system precisely in order to meet the fundamental task that animates all post-Kantian philosophy.[1] What then is this fundamental task?

It is that of moving forward on the basis of the contemporary transcendental approach, while simultaneously overcoming the various restrictions it has posed, in order to construct a *system* of philosophy capable of explaining all relevant theoretical and practical content from a *single* centre. Kant had rightly accomplished the turn to transcendental philosophy, so it was claimed, had repudiated the classical tradition of metaphysics, and turned instead to clarifying the constitution of the world through the structural accomplishments of subjectivity. But he had merely remained at the halfway stage of the process insofar as he

---

[1] For more detailed discussion of this, cf. Chapter 3 in this book, 'Hegel's *Science of Logic*: the Completion or Sublation of Metaphysics?'

had failed to supplement the critical achievement of reason with a properly constructive one. It is this issue that essentially forms the point of departure for all the post-Kantian innovations of philosophy.[2]

It is well-known, of course, that Hegel intervened in this debate only towards the very end, after Reinhold, then Fichte and finally Schelling had developed their own increasingly differentiated proposals for grounding the requisite system in terms of an appropriate principle. In his period of productive engagement with his contemporaries, the young Hegel had effectively reacted by criticising all these attempts. Thus he had denied that the *principle* proposed for the purpose could actually perform the role of grounding systematic thought, as in the case of Reinhold; he had admitted that the suggested principle itself was indeed convincing, but nonetheless rejected the theoretical *grounding* developed on its basis, as with Fichte; or finally he had claimed that systematic construction had only been achieved at the cost of losing sight of relevant internal distinctions and thus producing an empty *formalism*, as in the case of Schelling.

In the course of this important critical engagement with his contemporaries, Hegel had clearly grasped the essential character that any philosophical principle suitable for systematic construction must possess. It would have to be a principle capable of establishing the unity of different moments on the one hand, and of permitting the differentiation of unity into its relevant parts on the other. Such a principle could only be that of spirit. For in accordance with its theological origins in the idea of *pneuma*, this concept combines divergent moments in a living process of unification, but is also capable of enduring positivity, diremption and laceration. The solution to the enigma of system would therefore be to *think unity and diremption together*.

On the other hand, and in close parallel to this development, Hegel was from the very beginning an essentially *critical observer* of his times. In his early writings, he provides an acutely perceptive diagnosis of the way in which *diremption* characterised the present condition of the age. The social institutions, the forms of life, the historical constellation of culture had lost that experience of substantial unity that formerly sustained the actuality of political life. The end of the Enlightenment period brought conditions that were self-created insofar as they were the work of arbitrary and uncontrolled reflection, but were also obviously

---

[2] I have attempted to clarify Plato's original role in this respect in the first essay of this volume, 'Schelling's Discovery and Schleiermacher's Appropriation of Plato'.

incapable of meeting the relevant needs of human beings. Hence the widespread sense that some form of intellectual and cultural renewal was required.

It is important to understand how Hegel simultaneously transformed this *diagnosis* into a kind of *therapy*. The central conceptual instrument he employed was the concept of *reflection*. If it is the arbitrary and uncontrolled work of reflection that has produced diremption, then the task is obviously to exercise the appropriate *control over the conceptual resources of reflection*. Genuine insight into the cause of the contemporary condition thus also procures the relevant cure. For the diremption from which the age is suffering represents only one side, the negative one, of the self-mediating character of spirit. It can in principle therefore be taken up, sublated, into a new unity where the historically alert and self-conscious spirit is able to reanimate the substantive content confronting it, and exercise a positive effect of its own.

It may now have become clearer how the *historical* dimension of Hegel's philosophy of spirit must be explained precisely on the basis of his *principled metaphysical approach*. Whenever Hegel is interpreted essentially as a remarkably insightful historical thinker, he is simply ignored as a metaphysical one. In opposition to the aforementioned judgement of Dilthey and others, I believe that Hegel's philosophy is capable of casting such illuminating light upon historical phenomena only because it operates with a principle that is not itself ultimately historical in character. It is a principle of logical mediation that is superior to the more abstract principles of his immediate predecessors as far as systematic philosophical construction is concerned. And Hegel's observation of their failures, from an informed historical perspective upon the problems of philosophy, was not the least of the considerations that led him to believe that his own epoch urgently required a philosophical principle that, far from repressing the historical dimension of philosophy, was fully capable of doing it justice. For the process whereby one system of philosophy was so rapidly superseded by the next was all too obvious to everyone contemplating the contemporary scene. And this only demonstrated just how vulnerable systematic philosophical construction really was to the power of historical change. What was precisely required, therefore, was a principle that was capable of interpreting historical experience without being effectively destroyed by it.

On the basis of these general and rather involved preliminary considerations, I would propose my *initial thesis* that Hegel, thanks to his insight into the structural conditions of his own time, became the first philosopher to *connect metaphysics and history* in a self-conscious and deliberate manner. To establish such a connection is a remarkable project since, in clear contradiction to the philosophical tradition, it effectively brings the eternal domain of the changeless into a delicately balanced and fruitful relationship with the domain of the changeable. This approach neither compromises the metaphysics of absolute spirit, by preserving its insights in a purely historical fashion, nor does it simply transcend real history in an extravagant and purely speculative manner in order to satisfy certain *a priori* assumptions adopted in advance. For Hegel, therefore, one can only properly understand the time by recourse to the conceptual resources of metaphysics, and one can only pursue metaphysics in the light of the highest achievements of the epoch. For our own part, today, we can neither uncritically endorse nor easily reactivate the extraordinary idea of connecting the metaphysical and historical dimensions in this way. It is an idea that can probably best be understood by us in relation to philosophical questions concerning the domain of right and law.

II

This leads directly to the *second* part of my considerations. After attempting to locate the proper site for a 'political anthropology' in Hegel's work, we must now address the substantive question itself. I shall pursue this issue from three perspectives. Firstly, we need to understand Hegel's doctrine as a theory of *institutions*. Secondly, we need to elucidate the *formation* of such institutions. And thirdly, we must recognise that the decisive question at issue concerns the *legitimation* of these institutions. I shall begin with the first point.

As we indicated at the very beginning, our theme is ultimately bound up with the concept of *right*. One might of course want to dispute this claim. For the thematics of anthropology does not appear automatically to coincide with that of jurisprudence. But there is certainly good reason to regard the essential human potentiality for historical existence as embedded within organised social forms that preserve their validity beyond the passing moment and thereby ground the very possibility of collective human action. With this idea in view, the early Hegel had already produced some penetrating studies of the constitutive forms of social life. In early sketches dating from 1799/1800, he had expressed himself vividly and concretely in this respect: 'The ever-growing contradiction between the unknown life that men are unconsciously seeking and the life that is actually offered and permitted to them, and which they had formerly made their own, and the yearning for this life on the part of those who have worked to develop Nature into the form of the Idea within themselves, all of this harbours a striving for the mutual approach of both. The need of the former to become conscious of what still holds them captive, and of the unknown world that they desire, comes to meet the need of those who would pass from their Idea into life [....] The condition of the individual whom the time itself has driven into an inner world of his own and who would preserve himself therein can only represent an everlasting death. But if nature drives him back into life he can only desire to eliminate the negative features of the existing world precisely in order to find and satisfy himself in the world, in order to live at all.'[3]

Hegel here describes the diremption of the time as a felt divorce between the *forms of life* currently available to human beings and the *need* that leads and guides the latter. The need in question is the natural one of finding or creating forms of life in which living human beings can nourish and recognise themselves. In other words: the actual historical life of human beings announces the demand for adequate institutional shapes and forms. Hegel expresses this as the felt dissatisfaction with existing reality and a desire for something else that is still unknown. And equally, on the other hand, the reflective minds of the age themselves strive to transcend their purely inner world in the direction of genuine praxis. This is a condition of diremption insofar as we are unable, under such conditions, to live in harmony with ourselves. If this condition is perpetuated, we are threatened by a kind of death in life within the existing world. If it is effectively removed, on the other hand, we can enjoy the prospect of happiness in the sense of *eudaimonia*, which may be translated here as 'the fulfilled life'.

The historical epoch would seem to be particularly favourable to this project since the ancient remnants of traditional institutions now appear on the very brink of collapse, like the Empire that Napoleon will shortly destroy. The task is to eliminate the negative features of the existing world and thus allow the developed Idea and the felt need to converge at last. One side of society has already raised itself to the level of the Idea, but the philosophers and the educated classes are

---

[3] The fragment is generally known as 'Freedom and Fate' after the title supplied by its first editor. Cf. *Hegel, Politische Schriften*, ed. J. Habermas (Frankfurt am Main 1967), p. 16.

no longer content to concern themselves merely with their own purely scholarly and intellectual realm. And the others, who have hitherto felt obscurely oppressed by the existing conditions, themselves begin to recognise and cast off the fetters that bind them. Such a period of transition tangibly reveals, on both sides, what all were sorely lacking and long desiring. It is here that philosophy assumes the liberating task of interpreting the characteristic tendencies of both sides, and thereby bring their aspirations together.

On the basis of this analysis, we must recognise that human life, as far as real collective and historical action is concerned, requires certain forms within which to actualise itself. These forms are the *institutions* that assume a supporting and sustaining role for the concrete action of the individual. Without institutions, in the broadest sense of the word, human beings are unable to realise their characteristic form of life at all. And if these institutions fail to perform their proper role, existence becomes unbearable for us. This marks the hour for a philosophy that would actively participate in the historical process. For the appropriate forms of human life are clearly not guaranteed by the supra-temporal nature of man, but rather constantly find themselves in a state of historical transformation. The unarticulated feelings and needs of human beings themselves serve to indicate what we mean by 'true' and 'false' at this level of experience. But such manifestations are properly grasped and articulated only through the intellectual labour of philosophical thought.

With this strong emphasis upon institutions, Hegel is primarily setting himself in opposition to *Kantian moral philosophy*, which focusses rather upon the inwardly achieved autonomy of the subject. For in obeying the Categorical Imperative, the individual subject emancipates itself from all empirical restrictions and rises by its own resources to a level of utter universality where without conflict it may coexist with all other rational beings – including even God and the angels. The uniquely individual status here ascribed to rational subjects standing alone before the Categorical Imperative, and the concomitant doctrine of the two realms of the empirically acting self and his intelligible character, seemed deeply unsatisfactory both to Hegel and many others.

Hegel's alternative model assumes the idea of forms of life into which we have always already been introduced. Every acting individual presupposes a process of socialisation that has made that individual familiar with rights and duties within the framework of concrete social existence. The modern emphasis upon the principle of subjectivity is itself the result of a certain abstraction that has dissolved the political forms of life that were rightly regarded as absolutely indispensable in antiquity. If one really wishes to understand the human being as an agent, one must explicitly consider the contextual conditions that are implied here. In the 'Introduction' to the *Philosophy of Right*, Hegel unfolds, in close relation to the concept of will that derives from Kant, the requisite categories in accordance with his own principle of spirit. In fact, Hegel's reworking of this fundamental Kantian concept poses some quite specific problems of interpretation, which I shall have to ignore here. But in the following discussion, I shall assume that the concept of will, understood in terms of the idea of spirit, effectively provides a central practical point of departure for the theory of law and right.

III

I turn now to the second aspect that is so important for our original question: the historical formation of institutions and their development through history. It is obviously the ancient *polis*, already invoked in this respect by Rousseau, that provides the initial paradigm of non-dirempted political life in properly functioning institutions. Rousseau's critique of civilisation and the ensuing appeal for a renewal of political unity were decisive influences upon the young Hegel. It was simply the artificial way in which Rousseau attempted in the *Contrat Social* to unite the plurality of individual wills that Hegel definitely repudiated. Later on, in the *Philosophy of Right*, Hegel even explains the confusions of the French Revolution that culminated in the Terror in terms of this defective principle.[4]

Of course, it was also recognised that the ancient ideal was dead and gone – Rousseau and Hegel were of the same mind in that regard. But the crucial exemplary role of such a politically organised form of human togetherness was still accepted by both thinkers. It was to describe this favoured conception of the social domain that Hegel introduced the term 'ethical life' [*Sittlichkeit*], in deliberate contrast to the Kantian conception of an interior morality of conscience essentially entertained by individual subjects. In my previous remarks, I have rephrased the old-fashioned sounding expression 'ethical life' in terms of 'forms of life', not least because of the substantive and etymological similarity between

---

4 Cf. Chapter 7 in this volume, 'Rousseau, Hegel and the Dialectic of Enlightenment'.

the words 'Sittlichkeit' and 'Moralität' in relation to their respective
roots 'Sitten' and 'mores'.[5]

The problem, of course, is how something like this vanished form of
'ethical life' can possibly be restored in the *modern age* without postu-
lating an abstract social contract that, as an institution of right prior to
all right, cannot but remain a fictional construct. The solution Hegel
proposes here is connected with his aforementioned diagnosis of the
age. The historical period in question is characterised equally by Kant's
intellectual revolution and by the political events that had recently transpired beyond the Rhine. Both phenomena point towards a fundamental transformation of life and thought, but neither can properly fulfil
the hopes and expectations that have thereby been aroused. Kant's
enterprise seems to have halted at the halfway stage, and its systematic completion would now have to overcome, in particular, the reduction of morality to the alleged autonomy of the subject in which each
individual is united with all other rational beings in a transcendent
realm of ends. For there is evidently a fundamental rupture between
Kant's moral philosophy of *inwardness* and his *a priori* philosophy of
law, which specifically governs the *external* relations of free subjects to
one another. The conception of a new ethical life would have to bridge
this division in a way that shows how the authentic self-relation of the
subject and the concrete existence of the subject in the community
properly belong together and can only be explained in terms of one
another.

Running in parallel with this philosophical development, we also
witness the great political transformation that, after an initial period
of euphoria, soon terrified its European onlookers with the bloody
spectacle that ensued. In England, Edmund Burke quickly provided the
kind of conservative political analysis to which all critics of uncontrolled
change have been able to appeal ever since. In Germany, Schiller sought
refuge in the aesthetic solution of a collective pedagogy that might bring
men to freedom without the use of force and effectively prepare them
for it by encouraging the play-impulse at the heart of artistic activity.

---

[5] The old debate concerning 'morality and ethical life' has inevitably been revived in the
wake of contemporary discourse ethics, as we can see from the volume of essays edited by
W. Kuhlmann under this very title (*Moralität und Sittlichkeit*, Frankfurt am Main 1986). The
parallel American 'communitarian' critique of 'liberalism', as exemplified by John Rawls,
for example, has found a certain resonance in Germany. The volume of essays collected by
Axel Honneth provides a good introduction to the debate (*Kommunitarismus*, Frankfurt
am Main 1992).

It was obvious, at least, that any reorientation of society on the basis of 'Reason' that actually led only to further oppression, and eventually even to Napoleonic imperialism, could hardly redeem the hopes and aspirations embodied in the idea of 'ethical life'.

Hegel drew a radical conclusion from his close observation of the philosophical and political situation of the time. Tentatively in his early writings, more clearly in his Jena period, and most clearly of all in the *Phenomenology of Spirit* of 1806, Hegel committed the idea of a new form of ethical life to the freshly inspired powers of *philosophy*. It is philosophy that must first conceptualise, at the theoretical level, what the time demands and events have so far failed to accomplish. And it is this effort to comprehend the time in thought, as a famous dictum of the later Hegel puts it, that prompts the attempt to develop a universally binding order of right through appeal to reason alone and one that would not fall victim to the fatally one-sided character already observed in previous attempts. To accomplish this, philosophy must be able conceptually to penetrate the substantial features of the historical situation and thereby preserve a constant point of contact between the constructive intentions of its own conceptual labour and the needs and demands of the time. Only if we refuse to philosophise in a merely external relationship to history, or in simple independence of it, can we find the authentic possibility in turn of shaping history through reason. For only such an approach can methodically ensure that our theoretical conceptions are capable of intervening in the particular situation of the time. A philosophy of this kind thus also inevitably presses forward for its own historical realisation.

Hegel's *Philosophy of Right*, controversial as it has remained ever since its publication in 1820/21, deliberately continues to pursue the aim we have expressly outlined here. There is no question of simply restoring or perpetuating an older conception of right – like that of Roman law – or of organising some new system of right – like that of the *Code Napoléon*, for example. This is the source of Hegel's conflict with the Historical School of law associated with Savigny and his followers. Hegel's intention is rather to articulate the ethical life that is already present, and ensure that philosophy alone brings its binding principles and convictions to organised expression in an appropriately systematic and conceptual fashion. Ethical life must exist within society because human beings would not be able to live without it – unless, of course, purely utopian fantasies or abstract Enlightenment reasoning were to prevail over the authentic significance of our political existence.

Thus Hegel can declare in the important 'Preface' to the *Philosophy of Right*: 'The truth concerning right, ethics and the state is at any rate as old as its clear expression and promulgation in public laws and in public morality and religion. What more does this truth require, inasmuch as the thinking mind is not content to possess it in this proximate manner? What it needs is to be *comprehended* as well, so that the content which is already rational in itself may acquire a rational *form* and thereby appear *justified to free thinking*. For such thinking does not stop at what is given, whether supported by the external *positive authority* of the state or of the *mutual agreement between human beings*, or by the authority of *inner feelings* and the heart and by the testimony of the spirit which immediately concurs here, but starts out from itself and thereby demands to know itself united in its innermost being with the truth' (my emphases – R.B.).

What is Hegel trying to say here? The truth of ethical life as expressed in public laws and practices has long been known to every citizen of the state, and so evidently known that no philosophy is specifically required to invent or proclaim that truth. To be a citizen is precisely to know one's way about in the public sphere of life. If we wish to go beyond the spontaneous attitude of the citizen who acts within the accepted institutions of society and grasp the substantive content of such action conceptually, then we turn to an explicit philosophical consideration of the principles of right. We thereby bestow a rational form upon the already implicitly rational content in order *to justify the political domain for the free exercise of thought*. Legitimation of this kind supersedes any other form of authority, whether it be the positive character of the existing codes of law, or the possible consensus of the parties involved, or, in particular, any corroboration by appeal to personal feeling and the inner voice.

We should observe two things here: the *content* is already *rational*, but its legitimation can only be accomplished through the *free exercise of thought*. We must initially assume that reason or objective spirit does indeed express itself in the institutions of society if there is to be an appropriate object for any further enquiry. What lies behind this view is Hegel's conviction that social forms that resulted simply from the play of chance or arbitrary compulsions would never really be able to satisfy, for long, the demands of collective action. For human action – Hegel speaks of the 'will' – possesses a fundamentally rational structure of its own. This structure is so deeply rooted that we cannot ignore it if we would properly understand the significance of action as the actualisation of practical subjectivity. This approach has certain unavoidable consequences with respect to social institutions. For human action and its institutional forms must correspond with one another. When that is not the case, we experience a troubling sense of diremption that cannot long be endured.

But what then is the situation, one will naturally ask, where *irrational content* is concerned? Is not the wisest course to adopt a fundamental scepticism in the face of the Leviathan? Hegel responds by claiming that the private reason of the *critic*, once split off from the public realm in this way, will never be in a position adequately to grasp the rationality objectively sedimented in institutions. For the superior content of the social order that has been unhesitatingly accepted and has served to guide collective action hitherto can never acquire plausibility in the eyes of the individual who has resolutely embraced the sceptical perspective. No shape of objective spirit can possibly satisfy a criterion that has been derived from the domain of personal preferences.

On the other hand, we may suppose that senseless public laws that serve merely to obstruct the path of communal action are irrational legal forms that are themselves incapable of conceptual justification. A common spiritual thread thus connects the objective content of right with the subjective interests of agents. In other words: irrationality pure and simple cannot permanently establish itself politically.

There is of course a theory, much cited until recently, that explicitly rejects this position – namely, the Marxist form of ideology critique, which specifically arose through opposition to Hegel's *Philosophy of Right*. I shall merely mention the more recent version based upon the idea of a 'universal context of delusion'. Adorno has argued in this connection that our general delusion concerning the true character of reality has reached the point where irrational social structures can no longer be recognised as such, and are even effectively applauded by a bewitched public. In this case, the assumption that existing forms of social life are binding upon us essentially by virtue of their rational character naturally appears quite groundless. It is only the free reflection of the critical subject that might still dispel the prevailing illusion, and represents therefore the last remaining glimmer of reason and truth.

But what is this reflection other than of the *freely thinking subject* to which Hegel himself appeals in order to examine the rationality of the existing world? If there were no existing site of undistorted reason on account of an all-pervading *delusion*, then critique would lose all significance because there would no longer be anyone to speak on its behalf. If the social-political realm really lay under the prevailing spell of an evil demon, like the 'genius malignus' of sceptical Cartesian epistemology, then no critic could ever claim – except by mere assertion, the appeal to personal feeling, or the testimony of the inner voice – to be anything other than another victim of the same universal delusion. But Hegel denied any legitimate right to all such non-rational authorities. Whether we follow Adorno and reduce the number of freely thinking autonomous subjects to a small critical elite, or whether we appeal to the theory of communicative ethics and its democratised concept of universal dialogue, we cannot properly legitimate the political order without presupposing the criterion of implicit rationality.

IV

We have thereby already begun to address the third aforementioned aspect of our original question – namely, the problem of legitimation. Obviously this is intimately connected with the idea of 'free thinking' invoked in relation to the rational examination of existing laws and customary practices. Philosophy has to recognise reason's right to that free exercise of thought through which public ethical life is justified and an implicitly rational content is articulated in an appropriate rational form. But that is precisely the task of a 'philosophy of right' as Hegel understands it. We must therefore reject anything that cannot stand up to examination before a clear-sighted and impartial forum of thought that is neither secretly in league with the existing world nor intrinsically beholden to any irrational authorities. But what philosophy does recognise in this connection possesses doubtless *validity*. The right in question is thus acknowledged, rightfully, in the light of reason, and is thereby legitimated as such.

Hegel endorses the principle that no law has any real chance of commanding obedience unless it is intrinsically *accepted by those involved*. No customary practice is immune to challenge, no form of life acquires continuous historical validity, unless and until those involved at a naive and pre-philosophical, though by no means necessarily irrational, level are prepared to participate in this interaction. In this respect, they find themselves addressed precisely as citizens of the state, as members of an organised community. The system of law and right is there to serve their interests insofar as the latter are properly understood. They must therefore evaluate that system in the light of what it is they wish to accomplish in the realm of praxis. As agents, they must be convinced that they fulfil their ends more effectively within the domain of law and the state than if they concentrated upon an essentially egoistic practical perspective. As acting subjects, they are then able to *recognise* themselves substantially within the social order presented to them.

Now the possibility of this self-legitimating recognition presupposes a certain *process of education* [*Bildungsprozess*] that progressively reduces private idiosyncrasy, purely individual inclinations and animosities, and aspects of natural contingency. To some extent this has already been accomplished in the course of socialisation, which first introduces the practically-oriented subject into a political community of action. There is therefore no danger here from the kind of frivolous subjectivism that would evacuate the substance of the concept of right itself. The free examination of the world through thought refers rather to a capacity for developed subjectivity that ultimately forms the link between the enlightened agent and the theoretical perspective of the philosopher.

There is no way in which we could properly ignore this effective process of social education in general, which first raises the individual subject from the original level of particularity into that of *universality*. For it is not the case that just anyone, in his immediate circumstances, dependent perhaps upon collective moods of the moment, or subject to the deliberate devices of propaganda or agitation, could simply represent an ultimate judge of the rationality of the existing social order. Ever since Rousseau attempted to distinguish the 'volonté générale' from the 'volonté de tous' this paradoxical predicament has revealed itself in every modern constitutional state.

It is quite true that *intellectuals* in Adorno's sense can function as a sort of corrective. But they must take great care precisely not to adopt the superior role of a secular priesthood or supposed avant-garde in possession of the true and undefiled will of the people. The cultural process that gradually develops binding universal perspectives out of multiple and particular ones is painfully but indissolubly bound up with people's individual lives. It cannot be technically arranged in advance, replaced by ritualised performance, or delegated to leading sages like those whom the Greeks called 'sophists'. Nor can this enigmatic question possibly be resolved by verbally invoking the philosophical *a priori*, definitive transcendental groundings, or allegedly normative presuppositions. This problem lies like a shadow over the attempt to ground the idea of democracy by appeal to discourse ethics. No citizen has any privileged access to the rational character of social institutions. It is subjects who have learnt to comport themselves self-consciously at the level of political universality that effectively bestow recognition within already historically developed forms of life secured by rights. No political theory can ignore or transcend this irreducible socio-cultural threshold.

In paragraph 260 of the *Philosophy of Right*, Hegel elucidates the significance of *subjectivity* in the following way: 'The principle of modern states has enormous strength and depth precisely because it allows the principle of subjectivity to attain fulfilment in the self-sufficient extreme of personal particularity, while at the same time bringing it back to substantial unity and thus preserving this unity in the principle of subjectivity itself'. Modern states do not merely allow the explicit development of the subject as such, but could even be said actively to encourage it therein. But this is only one extreme, and the other extreme the modern state equally preserves in equilibrium with it is precisely that of institutionally embodied social unity. In truth, this *unity* is effectively sustained and ultimately confirmed by all the subjects who owe their own developed subjectivity to that unity.

If the state did lead an independent life of its own at the expense of the individual, it would represent nothing but the dominant self-maintaining power of a system conceived in purely functionalist terms. In this situation, the subject would simply feel excluded from it, and accordingly refuse to participate in it. The modern state survives precisely because it overcomes the traditional tension between the *individual and the whole*. The social whole continues to live as long as the individuals can properly fulfil their claims and aspirations within it. For in the final analysis, social institutions constitute one and the same spirit with that of the subjects themselves, they derive from the same principle as the latter, and consequently avoid the traditional opposition that divorces objective structures from subjective interests.

V

A very common objection presents itself at this point. If the subject who is to judge the legitimation of the existing social order on the basis of free thought is so defined in advance as to correspond with the demands of universality, then the judgement that is actually passed is hardly any cause for surprise. If the subject is already primarily oriented in its very subjectivity towards the domain of the state, it surely cannot do anything else but unconditionally accept the latter. This objection presupposes that the subject intrinsically possesses other, and more crucial, faculties that would be relevant to such judgement in the political context, but that are here effectively suppressed. However, that is precisely what would have to be shown. It is certainly true that the subject possesses various kinds of capacities and is therefore able to consider things from the most diverse of perspectives. Thus the subject relates to the world through knowledge and enquiry, it develops specific feelings concerning itself and other people, it pursues adventure for the sake of new discoveries, and it seeks out the realm of aesthetic experience.

But these manifold expressions of richly variegated subjectivity have nothing immediately to do with the realm of politics or right. As far as the legitimation of given forms of life is concerned, the only relevant consideration is whether the latter serve to facilitate and promote or to deny and impede the praxis of the *acting* subject in relation to other social agents. The fulfilment of the other aforementioned dimensions of experience does not appear to belong to the domain of right at all, but rather to that of *culture* in the broader sense of the word. And the express redemption of its claims reveals a certain tendency to interpret all the substantive content of human life in terms of legal right. The cultural wealth of forms of life is also a desirable end in general, but it does not affect the core institutional question that is the only relevant consideration here.

As agents, human subjects are characterised by a certain constitutive universality. It is true that the specific circumstances, the concrete ends, and the particular course pursued in any given case of action are highly individual. But our practical orientation to an end in general, the connection between activity and purpose, the logic of the particular steps required to attain the end, the practical appropriation of the world that is involved – these are all features that any one agent shares with every other agent. It is not the variable content of action, but the *intrinsic structure of praxis* that provides the basis of universality in practical matters. Social institutions must provide the appropriate framework since their very existence is grounded in their capacity to facilitate all collective action where individual subjects accomplish their respective ends. As long as they fulfil this role, we may properly claim that subjects, in the true sense of the word, can recognise themselves in the existing social world. This is what creates and sustains the spiritual unity in which agents and their world can meet under the sign of ethical life.

I shall summarise the argument by way of conclusion. *The Hegelian theory of right can be defended as an account of forms of life that are accepted precisely insofar as they are clearly seen to promote the domain of praxis.* The rational character of the social world and its relevance for human action are intrinsically connected. The crucial concept is that of the subject itself as the fundamental principle of orientation in the modern world. On the other hand, the already widespread and, through the modernisation process, indefinitely expanding pluralism of cultivated subjectivity in its various modes of knowledge, feeling, experience and desire is not directly relevant in this connection. What is essential here is simply the basic structure of praxis, which binds all acting subjects together. The question concerning the 'aesthetic transformation of the life-world'[6] should be addressed independently of the core issue concerning political legitimation. Hegel's political anthropology, at any rate, considers human subjects, insofar as they are essentially dependent, as practical agents upon the support of institutions. For it is the latter that already predefine the historical context of real human action without which individual subjects would exist as purely noumenal beings in a realm of their own, or simply populate the aesthetic sphere as so many wavering and indeterminate phenomena.

The prior substantial character of institutions that do not merely lie at the disposal of our individual attitudes thus bestows an objective and external place of support for the subject. In this minimal condition of human life, we may still perceive a trace of that 'metaphysics' that Hegel wished to mediate harmoniously with history without thereby sacrificing it to sheer historical relativism. The important point to recognise is that institutions are neither simple products of chance, nor social-technical constructs to serve the limited purpose of the common preservation of life. They must be interpreted rather as sedimented forms of spirit that essentially sustain the rational character of human action.

To be sure, everything depends on whether the relationship between practical subjectivity and institutional objectivity can still be explained from the perspective of human action. It is obvious that such a theory was motivated primarily by the experience of alienation in the post-Enlightenment period. The theory was only prepared to accept forms of non-alienated social life that permitted the subject to actualise its own ends in its own world, albeit in a way that was not always entirely transparent to the subject itself. If happiness is defined by the ability to live a fulfilled life, and a fulfilled life is attained through the deliberate and unhindered pursuit of practical ends, then Hegel's new

---

[6] Cf. my essay under this title in R. Bubner, *Ästhetische Erfahrung* (Frankfurt am Main 1989).

conception of ethical life provides the appropriate historical site for such a life. The institutional structures that lie beyond our immediate disposal correspond therefore to our aspirations to freedom. It is in this way that Hegel attempts to revive, for the modern age, the ancient Aristotelian demand for an ultimate identity between private and political *eudaimonia*.

HISTORY

5

TRANSCENDENTAL PHILOSOPHY AND THE PROBLEM OF HISTORY

Given its essentially narrative form of exposition, the discipline of history is not amongst the components of Kant's revolutionary philosophical attempt to reground knowledge from a transcendental perspective. Yet there is a sense in that history does now come within the purview of philosophy, although it had never been regarded as part of philosophy as long as it remained under the classical aegis of *rhetoric and the literary canon*. The role that history begins to play in the Kantian enterprise of philosophy is defined by the need to mediate the opposition between the two worlds to which we belong as rational beings and as empirical agents. 'Whatever conception of the *freedom of the will* one may form in terms of metaphysics, the will's manifestations in the world of *phenomena* – that is, human actions – are determined in accordance with natural laws, as is every other natural event. History is concerned with giving an account of these phenomena, no matter how deeply concealed their causes may be, and it allows us to hope that, if it examines the free exercise of the human will on a large scale, it will be able to discover a regular progression among freely willed actions. In the same way, we may hope that what strikes us in the actions of individuals as confused and fortuitous may be recognised, in the history of the entire species, as a steadily advancing but slow development of man's original capacities'.

These opening remarks of Kant's essay *Idea for a Universal History with a Cosmopolitan Purpose* (1794), designed for a general readership, express that exoteric core of transcendental critique that can effectively be communicated to the enlightened public of the age. The *dualism* of the two worlds of nature and freedom can never, in principle, be reconciled. But the public understandably expects some explanation of the actual play of freedom within history, and this expectation can be satisfied by an unsystematic or narrative account. *Narrative* was the principal traditional category for all historiography. And here it assumes a cosmopolitan colour insofar as what appears merely confused and irregular from the perspective of the individual subject can nonetheless be presented as a regular development of human capacities from the perspective of the species, which is slowly but continuously advancing towards a condition of right that will ultimately hold throughout the world. This 'discovery' of meaning in the course of world history itself derives from the intention of establishing *right* on earth in general. It is only in the light of this idea that the infinitely various individual and re-countable histories of human action can ever be integrated as some kind of whole.

This familiar perspective of transcendental philosophy in relation to history, in its broadly exoteric form, should be distinguished from *the inner structural problems* of transcendental philosophy that became the object of explicit philosophical attention along the path from Kant to idealist thought in general. Not yet in the work of Kant himself, but certainly in that of his immediate successors, we can see that history acquires a new significance for the practice of transcendental philosophy.

Kant's critical philosophy expresses fundamental doubts concerning the theoretical paradigm that had long been represented by the discipline of metaphysics. The dogmatic claims of this allegedly 'highest science' have largely evaporated in the interminable and irresolvable clash of dialectical contradictions. But the successful modern development of the exact sciences has now provided us with a new model for a future kind of metaphysics that could meet the required scientific criteria. We must simply focus our attention upon the *a priori* conditions, conceptual in kind, that already possess necessity as far as the constitution of rigorous science within the domain of possible experience is concerned. We can clearly recognise this necessity without making any metaphysical claims or groundless assumptions precisely because the human mind has only to look within itself to find it. The human mind is already organised in a quite specific fashion that makes it possible for us to acquire properly scientific knowledge in the *a posteriori* encounter with the experienced world.

In elucidating these conditions of possibility, transcendental philosophy employs a kind of *reflection* that does not, as reflection, enjoy the same status of *a priori* necessity as the conditions it uncovers. Necessity belongs to the conditions of knowledge in comparison with the material content for which they provide the conditions. And objective validity belongs to the actual cases of knowledge that have been rendered possible by those *a priori* conditions. But the very reflection that reveals the logically necessary relationship between *a priori* conditions and *a posteriori* knowledge plays no role in either. Considered more closely, therefore, transcendental philosophy, which exercises its critical task by means of this specific kind of reflection, only represents a preliminary level of a truly definitive system of philosophical knowledge that has yet to be erected on this basis.

Kant himself had intended to supplement and complete the critical philosophical foundation for which he has become so famous with a further systematic and doctrinal contribution, but only succeeded in supplying the latter in part. The early idealist attempts to continue the transcendental approach were motivated entirely by the hope of bringing Kant's own unfinished work to its full and final completion. That is why transcendental philosophy soon assumes the systematic features it does in the work of Fichte and Schelling. The old metaphysics, which Kant had rightly revolutionised because of its inability to justify its own scientific claims, was now finally to accomplish its original intentions. A definitive 'science' or body of knowledge was to emerge from the fire of 'critique'. But this process of reconstruction had left the task of defining and locating the site of transcendental reflection an open question. For the resolute system-builders, this no longer represented a crucial problem once they had taken the emphatic step from negative 'critique' to constructive 'science'. But a new conception of history nonetheless arose precisely in connection with this residual problem of accommodating transcendental reflection within the totality of systematic philosophy.

In the first instance, history is certainly not yet treated in the manner of Hegel's later comprehensive and self-contained *Encyclopaedia of the Philosophical Sciences* – that is, as an authentic part of philosophy expressly concerned with the objective reality of spirit. At this point, history is still understood entirely in very traditional terms as an 'a-theoretical' domain that intrinsically eludes comprehension through relevant laws or principles. But precisely as a field that cannot be brought under any *a priori* laws, history nonetheless comes to assume a specifically articulated relationship of its own to the sphere of knowledge that is governed by *a priori* principles. Fichte was the first thinker who undertook to bring history into a direct relationship with the systematic structure of transcendental philosophy in this way. Fichte presented his own philosophical programme in his essay of 1794 *On the*

Concept of the Doctrine of Science, a work that also effectively provided the stimulus for Schelling's early philosophical development.[1] Fichte here elaborates the contemporary task facing any philosophy that would truly think the implications of Kant's thought through to a satisfactory conclusion, and thereby effectively advance from the merely 'critical' standpoint to the articulation of genuine philosophical knowledge, as already promised by traditional metaphysics. Fichte therefore outlines a 'Doctrine of Science' that can answer the fundamental transcendental question as to how genuine knowledge is possible, and does so in properly 'scientific' form precisely by seamless derivation from an absolutely ultimate or first principle. Philosophy as the doctrine of knowledge is thus the science of science as such, or the knowledge of knowledge in general.

Fichte's *Doctrine of Science* essentially reconstructs the system of knowledge that is already internal to and contained within the human mind itself.[2] It thus brings a pre-theoretical content, which reveals the presence of reason even without the intervention of the philosopher, into a new and expressly scientific form. The already implicit necessary and *a priori* dimension of experience is here systematically expounded in its very necessity. It is transcendental reflection that mediates between the content and the form, between the human mind and the explicitly philosophical doctrine of knowledge. This reflection can only operate if it presupposes the inner correspondence of both sides that allows the *Doctrine of Science* to claim truth in the first place. But this presupposition cannot itself be derived precisely because it necessarily precedes all legitimate derivation. We cannot even properly or systematically show that philosophical reflection, in attempting to reconstruct our *a priori* system of knowledge, does indeed relate to actual universal structures of the human mind. And this is because reflection presents itself as a free act of knowing that is not yet accounted for or contained within the reconstructed system of knowledge itself. Insofar as knowing expressly relates itself solely to itself in this philosophical act, it serves to indicate the proper direction of further enquiry, but not yet its actual result. We may certainly assume that such free direction of the mind upon itself must imply a relevant spiritual principle. The only question concerns whether this philosophical act of reflection also involves everything that is necessary to the rigorous explanation of knowledge in general.

---

[1] Cf. Schelling, *Über die Möglichkeit der Form einer Philosophie überhaupt* (1794).

[2] For the following, cf. Fichte, *Über den Begriff der Wissenschaftslehre*, §7.

The persisting uncertainty here is immediately confirmed, in Fichte's eyes, by the history of philosophy, which essentially represents nothing but a series of attempts undertaken by the human spirit, with greater or lesser degrees of success, to grasp and comprehend its own character. Implicitly everything is already there to be seen within the mind itself, and the human spirit therefore needs only to concentrate attention upon itself, but this is a slow and gradual process. 'The human spirit, blindly groping this way and that, at first emerges into the twilight and only from there can it then advance towards the full light of day'.[3] Immediately inspired by the transcendental rebirth of philosophy, Fichte does not hesitate to point out the full significance of the destination of the path in question. But the entire length of human history, which only now possesses a fully mature philosophy in the shape of the *Doctrine of Science*, reveals the long series of repeated efforts that have been required to bring the human spirit to genuine self-awareness. Even for the system that now claims finality for itself, the story of all previous philosophical efforts only serves to mirror uncertainty as to whether the newly intended reconstruction itself will effectively establish its own validity. That inner correspondence between the human spirit and the system of reason, in the light of which alone transcendental reflection can properly be pursued, must therefore remain an indemonstrable assumption that can only be legitimated by the success of the rest of the philosophical programme as a whole.

At this point of the argument, a rather delicate one as far as his systematic conception is concerned, Fichte goes beyond the specific reference to its own history that is already internal to the discipline of philosophy and appeals to the concept of the progressive history of the human species in general, an idea in which the eighteenth century had expressly formulated its aspiration for some ultimate condition of moral and cultural perfection. It is Kant's philosophy of history 'from a pragmatic point of view' – namely, one that focussed attention upon the regular unfolding of man's rational capacities in the developmental process of the species as a whole – that served here as the inspiration for Fichte.[3a] The governing idea is that of an unfolding process,

---

[3] Fichte, *Gesamtausgabe* I, 2, p. 143.

[3a] Additional inspiration stems from Ernst Platner, *Philosophische Aphorismen nebst einigen Anleitungen zur philosophischen Geschichte. Erster Theil. Neue, durchaus umgeschriebene Ausgabe*, Leipzig 1784, §13.

in a greater or lesser degree that cannot precisely be determined, in which real human beings come to identify themselves with their ultimate vocation as rational moral beings. But if Kant had hesitated to ground such an approach in explicitly transcendental-philosophical terms and had therefore quite consciously pursued his thoughts on the philosophy of history solely within the broader domain of enlightened literary activity in general, Fichte broke decisively with this distinction of genre based upon the different perspectives of strict theoretical grounding and popular pedagogics respectively. The idea of the moral perfection of the human species is thereby introduced directly into the internal systematic structure of transcendental philosophy itself. And this naturally involves further important modifications in the concept of history. History is no longer simply universal history as interpreted from the perspective of reason, but is the philosophical *history of the human spirit coming to full awareness of itself in and as the system of philosophy.*

History opens up the space for a species of reflection that is certainly oriented to ends insofar as it strives to mediate between the implicit reality of spirit and the explicit philosophical reconstruction of the latter, but is not subject to any rules or principles derivable by conceptual necessity. Fichte interprets this tension between end and justification in metaphors appropriate to the philosophy of history. 'If our doctrine of knowledge is an accurate exposition of the system (of the human spirit), then it is as utterly certain and infallible as the latter; but the question is precisely whether or to what extent our exposition is really accurate; and we can never provide a strictly grounded argument for that, but only one that provides probability in this respect. The exposition claims truth only to the extent and only on condition that it is indeed accurate. We are not legislators but historians of the human spirit, not journalistic authors but pragmatic and historical ones.'[4] Since the transcendental philosopher does not prescribe but merely reconstructs what the universal structures of the human spirit must be like, the necessity in question lies entirely with the structures themselves, and not with the reflective activity through which the philosopher retraces that necessity. The only thing that can rigorously be derived here is what can already claim *a priori* validity for itself. The free act of the philosopher brings no new certainties into play, but simply follows the logic of

---

[4] Ibid., p. 146 f.; also see Fichte, *Grundlage der gesamten Wissenschaftslehre* (1794), GA 1, 2, p. 282.

something that is intrinsically certain. And history performs a key role with regard to this remarkable combination of the freedom that belongs to the reflective act and the necessity that belongs to the relevant task of reconstruction.[5]

It sounds like another variation on the same theme when the early Schelling, in a first tentative contribution to the question 'Is a philosophy of history possible?' (1797/98), ultimately defines the possession of history in terms of the lack of a genuinely *a priori* theory.[6] He thereby dissolves all earlier conceptions both of natural history and the history of the human species. The new and systematic 'universal science' envisaged by early idealist thought had overcome the fundamental opposition between philosophy and experience that found exemplary expression in the very term meta-physics. Philosophy is now no longer concerned with what essentially lies 'beyond' the physical world. 'The object of philosophy is the actual world'. The philosophy of nature, as Schelling conceived it around this time, undertook to conceptualise theoretical experience in a unified and consistent fashion. But was it possible for the philosophy of history to accomplish something analogous for the domain of practical experience? Obviously not, if one understands experience here to imply the absence of any knowledge framed in terms of genuine principles. But that remains unavoidable if the possession of history itself effectively signifies that the human being must always continue to have unforeseen and unforeseeable experiences in the future.[7]

We can only be said to have *experience* in the realm of praxis to the very degree in which laws and principles still fail to hold sway there. But there can be no laws for a history that is determined precisely in the Kantian sense as the intrinsically free approach towards the ideal of the human species as a whole. 'If man therefore possesses history (*a posteriori*), he only does so because he has no history (*a priori*); in short, because he does not so much bring his history with him, as first bring

---

[5] It is astonishing that Emil Lask does not pursue this point in his book, *Fichtes Idealismus und die Geschichte* (1902). This work emerged within the context of the neo-Kantian interest in the philosophical problem of 'value', where the logical enigma of history became a central issue, especially for Rickert. 'We shall merely consider how the problem of the irrational permeates the entire development of German Idealism, and thereby look more closely at the path this process takes throughout the work of Fichte' (E. Lask, *Gesammelte Schriften*, vol. 1, p. 79).

[6] Schelling, 'Ist eine Philosophie der Geschichte möglich?', in *Sämtliche Werke* 1, p. 464 ff.

[7] Cf. the parallel formulation in Schelling's slighter later *System des transzendentalen Idealismus* (1800), SW III, p. 588 ff.

it forth through himself. [...] Everything that we cannot ourselves determine *a priori* [...] becomes history for us.' Since the relevant realm of experience here is not that of nature but of man himself, the 'fact that we have history' appears to be 'an effect of our own limitedness'. Renunciation of the limitedness that still binds us in favour of complete self-determination is what creates the *a priori* of theory out of the *a posteriori* of experience. And systematic philosophy would thereby attain its final culmination there where knowledge and actuality would correspond with one another entirely. 'The more the limits of our knowledge are extended therefore, the narrower the limits of history become'.

It is obvious that our capacity for knowledge and our dependence upon history are connected with one another. For as long as we have still to attain the culminating point of perfect knowledge, we will remain dependent upon new and unforeseen experience for acquiring real knowledge of ourselves, and history as such will continue to exist. If history only exists because our knowledge of ourselves remains defective, then the eventual perfection of knowledge in the systematic sense would equally bring history to a standstill. But if history ultimately vanishes in the completed system of philosophy, the philosophy of history itself is a futile enterprise insofar as its object only exists for as long as the relevant knowledge is lacking. Schelling concludes that philosophy of history is impossible for this reason. We can see here how history is reduced to nothing but a lack of knowledge that itself returns to haunt the idealist programme of systematic philosophy at a crucial point. For this lack of knowledge affects the very certainty with which the system would grasp the object in question. This lack allows the object to exist, while eliminating the lack would merely eliminate the object. This disconcerting remnant of uncertainty, in spite of all the grand gestures of philosophical 'construction', only shows that systematic philosophy cannot fully evade that original remoteness that always belonged to the historical domain over against the realm of theory.

This fact is only obscured rather than revealed in its full significance when Schelling further extends Fichte's ideas by effectively incorporating reflection upon history into his *System of Transcendental Idealism* (1800). The 'Preface' announces that this system, with which Schelling first presents himself before the public as an independent thinker, while essentially reaffirming the fundamental principles of Fichte's *Doctrine of Science*, nonetheless also undertakes to extend the latter by presenting 'all the parts of philosophy in a continuous form'.[8] The original impulse to complete the system of transcendental philosophy, which Fichte had formerly initiated over against Kant, now begins to turn against Fichte himself. Schelling believes he has found the appropriate means of securing such internal continuity by now expounding the whole of philosophy as 'the progressive history of self-consciousness'.[9] For those interpreters who read idealist philosophy essentially in terms of its effective influence upon the modern historical world-view, such an idea certainly sounds straightforward enough, but it involves considerable difficulties as soon as we look more closely at the systematic structure that Schelling envisaged here.

The human spirit, according to Schelling, posits all the structures it requires in the original act of the ego that generates self-consciousness. As the original form of all positing and unifying, this act does not itself appear as such to consciousness. That it should do so requires the re-constructive activity of philosophy as a 'free imitation' of that act in transcendental reflection.[10] This second act is temporal for it follows upon the first original act, which is not itself temporal because it first posits time along with itself. The problem that confronts our 'philosophical ingenuity' consists in the precise imitation or repetition of what was originally posited. A *free repetition* after the event does not itself possess the necessity that accompanies the original positing of all structures. This is where history enters as a form of exposition that can 'recount the actions which have been decisive as it were for the history of self-consciousness and present them in their interconnected character'.[11]

No necessity belongs to history, which is a narrative, at a temporal distance, of past actions. It is the historical narration that first creates the interconnection between these actions. The methodical adaptation of a *historical mode of exposition* imitates the necessary interconnection between the primary acts of self-consciousness that are freely repeated in the philosophical act of reflection. The re-constructive interconnection, which here takes the place of *a priori* necessity, appears convincing through its articulation in terms of 'epochs', which can only ever be determined *ex post*. It is by appeals to *epochs* that we generally attempt

---

[8] Ibid., p. 331.

[9] Compare the very similar remark in Schelling's *Abhandlungen zur Erläuterung des Idealismus der Wissenschaftslehre* (1796/97), SW I, p. 382.

[10] SW III, p. 395 ff. [11] Ibid., p. 398.

to grasp in concentrated segments a range of historical material that could never be surveyed in merely summary compilation. The introduction of epochal segments into the history of self-consciousness is a means of articulating order in place of mere succession. The historical metaphorics involved are by no means to be identified with the subject matter as such, which we are thematising here from the ultimate perspective of philosophy itself.

In itself, self-consciousness 'has' no history. It is simply perceived through a historical optics by the philosopher whose free reflection upon self-consciousness always comes too late. Since he must strive to identify, after the event, something that does not itself transpire in a temporal dimension at all, the *a priori* appears to him as if it were historical. The philosopher makes a virtue out of this predicament by introducing epochal segments into the exposition and unfolding a subsequent narrative that posits a re-constructive interconnection in place of a purely transcendental logical necessity. The historical dimension thus represents a methodical transformation of lack on the part of a transcendental philosophy that strives for systematic completeness, but is constrained to operate with a form of reflection that finds no appropriate place within the system itself. The unmasterable character of the reflection with which alone the philosopher is able to approach the *a priori* structures that are the object of enquiry represents an element that ineluctably falls outside the structure of the philosophical system.

One should acknowledge that the recourse to history that is required for the methodical elaboration of a system of philosophy is as much a symptom of the *finitude of philosophising* as it is a victorious solution of ancient questions through the miraculous achievements of idealist thought. Most readers regard the idealist philosophy of history as a bold projection of certain direct intuitions concerning the human spirit onto the historical material available. This interpretation gives rise to the familiar image of history as a wholly transparent process of development in which the spirit comes to full awareness of itself, a process that may well satisfy the interests of reason but has always been accused of excessive 'idealisation'. Apologists and critics of philosophical idealism alike would regard their interpretations as confirmed by just such an image. But the latter really only reveals one aspect of the idealist approach to history, the one that emerges, for example, in Fichte's lectures on the *Fundamental Characteristics of the Present Age* (1806). Of course, the most astonishing and controversial model of this approach always was and still remains the philosophy of history elaborated by Hegel in his later years at Berlin. Hegel's famous first book, the *Phenomenology of Spirit* (1806), actually points in a rather different direction, although this work can also be superficially conflated with his philosophy of history and thus subsumed within the single unified trajectory that is supposedly characteristic of 'the idealist conception of history'. Before we address this issue specifically, we must first clarify, at least briefly, the place and significance of the *Phenomenology of Spirit* in Hegel's thought.

On careful consideration, we can see that the *Phenomenology* belongs to a whole series of works that attempted to elucidate the idealist programme of systematic philosophy in an essentially *methodical* manner. Hegel's *Phenomenology* begins from the point at which the early Fichte and his disciple Schelling attempted to define the peculiar status of transcendental reflection, wavering as it did between a systematic constitutive role and an inadequate integration within the system of philosophy. The comparison with historiography thus recommended itself more on procedural grounds than on any substantive grounds. In principle, the *Phenomenology* undertakes to develop the same approach, although the work grew far beyond the task of providing incidental elucidations for appropriate philosophical procedure, and effectively constitutes the substantial 'first part' of the system itself.[12]

Hegel's theory concerning the various 'forms of appearance' of spirit is not a philosophy of history obscurely conflated with some kind of psychology. Critics have often assumed this, ever since Rudolf Haym rejected Hegel in the vein of nineteenth-century liberalism.[13] Nor indeed is it an ideologically distorted and schematic account of the social development of mankind, as one might be tempted to believe since Karl Marx first compared it with 'the standpoint of modern political economy'.[14] For if we simply consider the actual sequence of phenomenological 'shapes', constantly moving back and forth as they do in purely chronological terms, it is quite clear that the work is not primarily interested in the interpretation of real history at all. It is essentially designed as a

---

[12] On the genetic and conceptual issues involved here, cf. my essay, 'Hegel's Concept of Phenomenology', included in this book as Chapter 6. The following discussion builds upon the conclusions of this earlier investigation.

[13] R. Haym, *Hegel und seine Zeit* (1857), Leipzig 1927, p. 243.

[14] K. Marx, *Ökonomisch-philosophische Manuskripte* (1844), in K. Marx, *Frühe Schriften*, vol. 1, edited by H. J. Lieber and P. Furth (Darmstadt 1962), pp. 641 ff., and particularly p. 646.

kind of 'preparation'[15] for an authentic philosophical system, and proceeds by engaging with and clarifying the structure of reflection. Reflection is not merely the means through which the conceptual labour of philosophy itself is accomplished, but also represents a characteristic challenge for philosophy in general insofar as reflection, structurally speaking, already lies within all forms and shapes of pre-philosophical consciousness. This circumstance can hardly be a matter of indifference to the philosopher since the latter is also dependent upon the activity of reflection and cannot claim any exclusive power or authority over its various expressions.

Once Hegel has pronounced his verdict upon the inspired pretensions of 'higher wisdom', exposed the vacuous claims of immediate and intuitive knowledge, and prescribed a clear methical approach for any philosophy aspiring to properly 'scientific' status, he must proceed to determine the precise relation between philosophical reflection and the reflection that is implicit in all forms of pre-philosophical consciousness. He does so by analysing the different shapes of consciousness and deciphering the structural moment of reflection that the shapes in question, as so many given views of the world, do not as such bring to conscious awareness. The philosopher reveals the true reflective character of the various shapes of consciousness themselves and thereby elevates them step by step beyond their initial level. In doing so, the philosopher helps to prepare, in the interest of systematic philosophising, the standpoint from which the system itself can begin.

Hegel calls this standpoint 'absolute knowing', and characterises it explicitly as one that can no longer be described as one shape of consciousness amongst many others. For here, *reflection* no longer plays an uncharted role in the continuing process, but has now become fully conscious of itself. But this standpoint of absolute knowing can only be attained if reflection in general can be surpassed and sublated precisely through the methical procedures of reflection itself. The phenomenological 'exposition of appearing knowledge' undertakes to fulfil this task. 'Now since the present exposition only has appearing knowledge as its object, it does not appear itself to be that free science that moves expressly in its own distinctive shape; but from the perspective of this standpoint it can be regarded as the path which natural consciousness takes in pushing forward to true knowing'. Along this path

---

[15] Hegel, *Phänomenologie des Geistes*, edited by J. Hoffmeister (Hamburg 1952), p. 31; *Hegel's Phenomenology of Spirit*, trans. A.V. Miller (Oxford 1977), p. 20.

we 'wander through the series of shapes .... as so many appointed stations'[16] until the re-constructive process of appearing knowledge comes to rest in true knowing at the only level that is appropriate for the system of philosophy.

The *Phenomenology* locates this process in the dimension of history – that is, of 'spirit externalised in time'.[17] The historical perspective on spirit corresponds to its purely 'appearing' existence before it achieves its own total self-possession as spirit. The truth of spirit would therefore be the pure 'aether' of the logical dimension where all temporal factors disappear. The quasi-historical procedure adopted by the *Phenomenology* must be explained, on the other hand, from its relationship to the system.[18] The indispensability of the reflective approach for any philosopher who aspires to the system and the inappropriateness of the means for the task in question here come together to present the first hurdle to systematic philosophising *before* effective construction of the system can properly begin. In this situation, the exposition of the history of consciousness serves to clarify the sense and significance of the required system before we have the categories of the same at our full conceptual disposal. *What appears as historical is precisely what can not yet be brought into fully adequate theoretical form.* The appearing forms of spirit are the inadequate forms in which the truth of the matter can only inadequately be grasped by the powers of the pure concept.

At the level where the concept finally finds itself in full possession of its objects, 'historicity' no longer represents a potential limitation of its sovereignty that must be methodically dispelled. In its essential structures, historicity now opens itself to the concept from the general perspective of objective spirit, that is to say, from the perspective of 'right'. At the close of the *Philosophy of Right*, history emerges as the scene where reason realises itself within the domain of political actuality. And this domain is one that still has to be determined and decided in the context of world history itself. 'Right' is not considered here simply from the perspective of establishing a perspicuous organisation of the institutions. On the contrary, it finds itself ineluctably drawn into the

---

[16] Ibid., p. 66 f.; *Phenomenology of Spirit*, pp. 49 ff.

[17] Ibid., p. 563; also p. 557 ff.; *Phenomenology of Spirit*, pp. 491 ff.

[18] For a completely different reading, see Terry Pinkard's interesting book, *Hegel's Phenomenology. The Sociality of Reason* (Cambridge 1994). Pinkard is influenced by Robert Pippin's interpretation of Hegel as a theorist of modernity. 'The *Phenomenology* offers a dialectical-historical narrative of how the European community has come to take what it does as authoritative and definitive for itself' (p. 13.)

domain of those competing collective 'spirits' in terms of which Hegel describes the plurality of legally and constitutionally organised nation states.[19]

The essentially concrete character of existing 'right' necessarily exposes the totality of ethical life, which allows agents who claim freedom in the name of reason to lead a 'universal life'[20] securely embodied in institutions, to the play of contingency within the broader framework of world history. With a cautious quotation from a Schiller poem that is symptomatically entitled 'Resignation', Hegel leaves the resulting process to 'world history as the world's court of judgement' without thereby illegitimately indulging in eschatological prognoses, optimistic utopias, or internationalist activism.[21]

---

[19] Hegel, *Elements of the Philosophy of Right*, §340. The expression 'spirits of the peoples' must be properly interpreted here given the inevitable ideological suspicion that it merely expresses the irrationality of the 'special German path' supposedly prescribed by a Romanticism remote from genuine political reality. It has been very convincingly shown that the expression actually derives from the French Enlightenment as expressed in the work of Voltaire and Montesquieu. The early Hegel is already familiar with it from his reading of the latter.

[20] Ibid., §258. See the preceding chapter.

[21] Cf. the proceedings of the Stuttgart Hegel Congress, *Die Weltgeschichte–das Weltgericht?*, ed. R. Bubner/W. Mesch (Stuttgart 2001).

6

HEGEL'S CONCEPT OF PHENOMENOLOGY

I. Preliminary Remarks

In order to shed light on the origins of Hegel's concept of phenomenology, I will begin by considering some of his first essays.

The irretrievable loss of the ancient Greek's sense of freedom and political unity must have had the most profound meaning for Hegel and his Tübingen friends Schelling and Hölderlin. The fragmented age in which they lived seemed far removed from that all-encompassing spirit which had animated the "genius of nations" "from the days of the past." The "power of unification" they demanded from life had "disappeared from the lives of men" altogether, as Hegel was to lament in one of his early notes. This insight into the modern world's inherent lack of unity is the axis around which much of his early thinking turns.

The leitmotif of Hegel's juvenile writings is religion, and his first, main concern is to rethink religion against the backdrop of Kant's moral philosophy. For the young Hegel, religion revealed a state of "positivity," of unquestioning submission to authority and blind adherence to doctrine. According to this understanding, positive religion stands diametrically opposed to religion rooted in practical reason's concept of morality. The limits of an ideal of religion based on morality become blatant, however, when theology, in its turn, appropriates Kant's concept of practical reason, together with his doctrine of postulates, to reinforce its authority and produces a particularly *intractable form of orthodoxy*. At the turn of the eighteenth century, Tübingen's divinity students could point to actual instances of how religion becomes

This chapter was originally published in G.K. Browning (ed.), *Hegel's Phenomenology of Spirit: A Reappraisal*, pp. 31–51. © 1997 Kluwer Academic Publishers. Reprinted with kind permission of Kluwer Academic Publishers.

distorted at the hands of a "priesthood" which "poses as reason," as the unknown author of the *Earliest System Programme of German Idealism* (1796 or 1797), polemically puts it.[1] It is important to understand the terms of this reversal.

The Enlightenment's critique of religion, aimed at purging superstition's historical content from the rational core of "natural" religion, loses its cutting edge when confronted with a theology which also claims to be grounded in reason and is, therefore, equipped to defend itself against the possibility of critique. As a weapon of critique, the concept of positivity is only effective to the extent it confronts such problems of appropriation head-on. In the revisions to the introductory sections of the manuscript, known to us as the *Positivity of the Christian Religion*, Hegel develops a more acute methodological awareness to deal with these problems.[2] Hegel's insight, in the second *Preface*, that religion takes on different forms according to the spirit of the times it serves, is intended to prohibit defining the positivity of religion by means of the abstract universality of the Enlightenment's concepts of human nature. These "simple" concepts, which exclude all particularity and difference, have become "important only in recent times" and are the culmination of a "long series of stages in cultural development, extending over centuries."[3] But because they "fix" the results of this same

---

[1] English translation in H.S. Harris, *Hegel's Development Towards the Sunlight*, 1770–1807 (Oxford 1972), p. 511. *Das älteste Systemprogramm des deutschen Idealismus, G.W.F. Hegels Werke*, 20 vols. (Frankfurt am Main: Suhrkamp, 1986), vol. I, 234–36. Above all, G.C. Storr, professor of theology at the University of Tübingen during Hegel's time there, is intended as the main target of the author's polemics. See Schelling's letter to Hegel from the beginning of January 1795, and Hegel's reply at the end of January, as well as Schelling's letter of February 4, 1795; *Briefe von und an Hegel*, ed. J. Hoffmeister (Hamburg: Meiner, 1969) vol. I, 13f, 16f, 21. (For the English translation of a selection of Hegel's letters see *Hegel: The Letters*, trans. C. Butler and C. Seiler (Bloomington: University of Indiana, 1984).) For further insight see also the first *Zusatz* (supplement), written in the winter of 1795–96, to the *Positivität der christlichen Religion, Werke* I, 192f. The identity of the author of the *Oldest Systematic Program* is still disputed. Franz Rosenzweig, the discoverer of the fragmented manuscript, maintained that Schelling was the author, but that the text was written in Hegel's hand. For our purposes, the question as to whether it was Schelling or Hegel can remain open; in the light of the letters, it is obvious that both shared the same contempt for theological sophistry. For further discussion see *Das älteste Systemprogramm. Studien zur Frühgeschichte des Idealismus*, ed. R. Bubner, *Hegel-Studien* (Bonn 1973) Beiheft 9.

[2] *Early Theological Writings*, trans. T.M. Knox, (Chicago: University of Chicago Press, 1948), 167–181; *Werke* I, 217–229. The revisions to the *Preface* of the *Positivity* essay were written September 24, 1800.

[3] *Ibid.*, 168; *Werke* I, 217–18.

cultural development and, thereby, transform all "variations in national or individual manners, customs and opinions" into "accidents, prejudices and errors," universal concepts themselves foster positivity. Over the years, however, enlightened critique has become so "empty" and "wearisome" that a "need" has arisen to recover the *relative naturalness and necessity* of religion's historical forms constituting the objects of enlightened critique.[4] According to Hegel, a positive religion can be appropriate to a given time and, in this way, completely natural for the people who believe in it. Only when "another mood awakens," only when the spirit of the age "begins to have a sense of itself and to demand freedom in and for itself," does the true positivity of a religion manifest itself to those who now have an "ideal of humanity hovering" before their minds which corresponds to their newly won sense of freedom.[5]

The revised *Preface* to the *Positivity* essay, briefly discussed, was written a few months before Hegel moved to Jena to embark on the first stage of his academic career. Although its central concern is still the problem of religion, this short text comes close to an understanding of philosophy which will inform subsequent essays. The *Fragment of a System*, written during the same period, maintains, however, "Philosophy has to give way to religion."[6] For only religion can raise us above reflection and its biased standpoints of thinking to the level of spirit; that is, only religion can dissolve the obdurate antithesis of finite and infinite, produced by reflection, in infinite life. Later on in the essay, however, Hegel concedes that religion *per se* is not absolutely necessary, and characterizes it as "*any* elevation of the finite to the infinite."[7] The advantage of religion over other forms of unity, for example, the "most perfect integration" of the "happy people" of ancient Greece, consists in the correspondence religion has with the given historical situation. Where "integration with the age" is impossible or would result in a false peace based on accommodation, the intervention of that philosophy, capable of elevating the pure ego completely above the totality of everything finite, is certainly not inferior to religion. Hegel had in mind Fichte's principle of *Tathandlung*, the first positing act of the absolute ego, which, as far as the distortions produced by

[4] *Ibid.*, 170, 172; *Werke* I, 221, 222.   [5] *Ibid.*, 170; *Werke* I, 220.
[6] *Systemfragment von 1800, Werke* I, 419–427, 422; *Fragment of a System* (1800), *Early Theological Writings*, 309–319, 313 (my translation, [Cara Gendel Ryan])
[7] *Ibid.*, 317; *Werke* I 425.

reflection are concerned, compares favorably to religion's power of reconciliation.[8]

The exact point can be located, however, where Hegel's insights into religion overtly display their true philosophical force. As sketched out, Hegel's historical understanding of positivity grew out of his critique of the enlightened critique of religion and the parallel ways, alluded to but not worked out in the *System Fragment*, in which religion and philosophy correspond to the needs of the time and can be viewed from the perspective of historical contingency. At the very beginning of the essay *Faith and Knowledge* (1802),[9] both sides of the parallel merge together in a philosophical explanation of transformations which Hegel now sees as taking place within philosophy itself. "Culture has raised this latest era so far above the ancient antithesis of reason and faith, of philosophy and positive religion that this opposition of faith and knowledge has acquired quite a different meaning and has now been transposed into the sphere of philosophy itself."[10] Hegel briefly evokes the hypocrisy of theological orthodoxy and the ever-more vacuous, ever-more abstract critique of positive religion, in order to account for the levelling of all differences, the increasing indistinguishability among traditional fronts, as a manifestation of the age and the work of culture. What is decisive here is that Hegel has now come to see philosophy as entering into these transformations and as understanding itself historically. In this way, he sets the stage for a more complex and nuanced interpretation of philosophy, an interpretation which he conceives as being carried out by philosophy within the framework of its own historicity.

This new understanding of philosophy seems to have inspired the early work of the Jena years. It will be shown how Hegel's first critical essays take shape around a philosophical task from which, in the course of the system's formation, the conception for a "phenomenology of spirit" will eventually arise. The following inquiry, however, does not promise either a seamless historical or philological reconstruction of the path this development took.[11] Given the incompleteness of what has

[8] *Ibid.*, 318–19; *Werke* I, 425–27.

[9] *Glauben und Wissen oder Reflexionsphilosophie der Subjektivität in der Vollständigkeit ihrer Formen als Kantische, Jacobische und Fichtesche Philosophie, Werke II, 287–432; Faith and Knowledge,* trans. W. Cerf and H.S. Harris, (Albany: SUNY, 1977).

[10] *Ibid.*, 57, (translation modified); *Werke* II, 287.

[11] We have O. Pöggeler's on-going research to thank for uncovering the circumstances surrounding the writing of the *Phenomenology of Spirit* and presenting all available philological

come down to us from Hegel's early writings, such detective work would be in vain, anyway.[12] Rather, the focus of this chapter is the question of the systematic meaning of Hegel's concept of phenomenology, as far as it can be explained by his early development leading up to the work of 1807, and evolving from the problem as formulated in the Jena essays.

In what follows, the main interest is the *genesis of Hegel's concept of phenomenology*. In the light of the general question, *What is phenomenology*, I will begin by first considering philosophy's preparatory function as critique, and then, by way of contrast, highlight the logical character of philosophy's self-realization in speculation. Against the backdrop of this difference between philosophy as critique and philosophy as speculation, it will be possible to determine more precisely the systematic meaning of the *Phenomenology*, its function and methodological structure.[13]

II. Philosophy as Critique

What is striking about even a cursory reading of Hegel's first published essay, *The Difference Between Fichte's and Schelling's System of Philosophy* (1801), is that the concept of *cultural formation* [*Bildung*] is given a peculiarly negative cast[14] and is closely linked to the phenomenon of

---

evidence as the key to its structural articulation. See among others of Pöggeler's works, *Hegels Idee einer Phänomenologie des Geistes*, (Freiburg: Alber, 1993).

[12] In this connection, however, it is worth pointing out that Reinhold's "*Phänomenologie*" is largely ignored and, if one is allowed to speculate, most likely prompted Hegel's choice of title: K.L. Reinhold, *Elemente der Phänomenologie oder Erläuterung des rationalen Realismus durch seine Anwendung auf die Erscheinungen*, in *Beyträge zur leichtern Übersicht des Zustands der Philosophie beym Anfang d. 19. Jh.*, Heft 4, (1802). [*Elements of Phenomenology or the Explanation of Rational Realism by means of Its Application to Phenomena*, in *Contributions toward a More Facile Overview of the State of Philosophy at the Beginning of the Nineteenth Century.*]

[13] For a good standard work on the *Phenomenology* see W. Marx, *Hegel's Phenomenology of Spirit: Its Point and Purpose*, (New York: Harper and Row, 1975). In my opinion, the most important new work on the *Phenomenology* to appear in English is T. Pinkard's *Hegel's Phenomenology: The Sociality of Reason* (Cambridge: Cambridge University Press, 1994).

[14] The *Difference Between Fichte's and Schelling's System of Philosophy*, trans. H.S. Harris and W. Cerf, (Albany: SUNY, 1977) 89ff., 101, 177, 192–93; *Differenz des Fichteschen und Schellingschen Systems der Philosophie*, *Werke* II, 20ff., 33f., 119, 136. In the light of Herder's concept of *Bildung*, understood as the education of mankind up to its own humanity through the realization of reason and freedom, Hegel's use of the word is indeed curious. To my knowledge, only Fichte in his *Wissenschaftslehre* of 1794, gives the word *Bildung* a similar, negative emphasis: *Fichtes Werke*, (Berlin, 1971), vol. 1, 284–85; *Science of*

disseverance [*Entzweiung*].[15] At first glance, this association is anything but obvious; for why should philosophy feel compelled to object to and to polemicize against the culture of its time instead of simply accepting it as a preparatory stage played out on a non-philosophical level. The relation between general, intellectual culture and philosophy, however, is by no means arbitrary or unproblematic. In the culture at large, philosophy finds the "building blocks" of its future system as well as the obstacles to its self-realization as system. To capture the two sides of this ambivalent relation, Hegel coined the expression "the need for philosophy." The given historical conditions are such that they elicit philosophy, but not in the sense of a teleology directed toward bringing forth one more specific form of philosophy. Rather, the age expresses its need for philosophy negatively, as an emerging rupture between what already seems to exist and what, in fact, does not yet exist.

When the profusion of philosophic systems no longer provides any real satisfaction, and the longing for the one true philosophy has become all the more intense, the cultural realm lays the groundwork for philosophy by offering surrogates which only *seem* to respond to the need for philosophy. The age has, indeed, produced an abundance of systems during the short period from Kant to Reinhold and from Fichte to Schelling. This pell-mell pursuit, however, to create new systems, can never actually gratify the need for philosophy. In fact, the philosophic activity of the age is the real obstacle to the fulfillment of this need. Hegel's paradoxical diagnosis is twofold: it distinguishes between the given historical conditions underlying the spirit of the age, and *the one* philosophy which he provisionally characterizes by the necessity that it form a system and be based on the principle of speculation. Thus, for Hegel, in "an age which has so many philosophic systems lying behind it," the first response to the admitted need for philosophy finds its expression precisely in this disjunction in which the heightened

---

Knowledge, trans. P. Heath and J. Lachs, (Cambridge: Cambridge University Press, 1982) 251.

[15] Translator's note: The German noun *Entzweiung* comes from the verb *entzweien*, which literally means divide or split in two halves, sunder, separate, bifurcate, disunite, and in the extended sense of to turn people against each other or to sow dissension. Hegel's use of *Entzweiung* has been rendered in English by various translators as "bifurcation" (Benhabib), "diremption" (Surber), "dichotomy" (Harris). According to S. Benhabib, "*Entzweiung* is particularly important in the context of Hegel's early diagnosis of modernity and civil society as conditions of division, separation and alienation" (H. Marcuse, *Hegel's Ontology and the Theory of Historicity*, trans. S. Benhabib, [Cambridge: Cambridge University Press, 1987] 336).

intellectual and spiritual culture of the age, with its affinity for philosophy, is not identified either with any one of these received systems and
entrenched schools of thought, or with the unified idea of philosophy.
The one true philosophy is still to come!

What more precisely does Hegel find so problematic about *Bildung*?
Bildung is the crystallization of a way of thinking about the world in
which reflection and understanding have become dominant. Reflection tends to create uniformity by reducing the infinite multiplicity
of being to fixed, one-dimensional determinations of understanding
and, thus, renders every finite being as valid for understanding as the
next. The interconnections reflection establishes in this way consist in
the purely formal process of bringing one thought determination into
relation with another. The network of ensuing relations, generated by
reflection, rests on nothing more substantial than that the determinations stand in relation to one another. In this way, they are deprived of
their independent existence, and their genuine content is transformed
into the terms of the relations created by reflection. The thoroughgoing
differences, engendered by reflection, paradoxically also empower
reflection to promote unity in the realm of understanding. Reflection's
integration of thought determinations only camouflages the real differences, and its semblance of unity fixes the underlying disseverance all
the more as it progresses. Disseverance is perpetuated precisely because
it has disappeared from direct view behind the fake unity created by
what was, in fact, only reflection's simulated sublation of disseverance.

When *Bildung*, under the sway of understanding and reflection, determines the conditions of an entire age, life becomes alienated from
itself[16]; for the natural separations, inherent in all living processes, are
not counterbalanced by any true unifying principle. The relation of disseverance and unification is itself distorted. Disseverance first appears
within *Bildung* veiled in the semblance of unity created by reflection,
and beneath this veil the individual separations, caused by disseverance,
coalesce into a rupture within the spirit of the age. In this situation, the
need for philosophy makes itself felt in that the false unity created by
Bildung must be replaced by genuine unification. Reason, in its striving
toward the unconditioned, is called upon to free the oppositions from

---

[16] In his *Lectures on the History of Philosophy*, Hegel formulates the concept of *Bildung* in
much the same way and creates an historical parallel between the Enlightenment and the
ancient sophist movement with which, according to Hegel, the "principle of modernity"
begins; *Werke* XVIII, 404, 409ff., see also 435. For a similar analogy see the *Vorrede zu
Hinrichs Religionsphilosophie* (1821), *Werke* XI, 6of.

the understanding's fixed totality of limitations. This can only mean that reflection's domination has to be undermined, and that polemical fronts have been established in opposition to the cultural world.

It is not, however, simply a question of substituting existing thought structures with new systems proclaimed by the age to be more rational and more genuinely philosophical. To be able to see through the structures erected by contemporary philosophy, it is imperative to refrain from making systematic statements about philosophy which might alter the scene. In fact, Hegel intentionally begins his career as philosophical writer with *critical* essays, whereas his contemporaries try to outdo one another with more powerful, more totalizing new systems. The crucial insight, which secured Hegel's theoretical superiority and, down to the present, still lends fascination to his genealogical reconstruction of the history of philosophy, does not consist in a loftier, more all-encompassing philosophical principle, but rather in making apparent the relationships of dependency prevailing between philosophy and the spirit of the age.

III. Philosophy's Confrontation with the Age of Reflection

Kant, Fichte and Jacobi are the most emblematic representatives of what Hegel called *Reflexionsphilosophie*. Reinhold, however, who was the first to point out the synergistic relationship between philosophy and its historical moment, should be counted as no less symptomatic.[17] For Hegel,

---

[17] As is well known, the outward "occasion" for the *Difference* essay was the first installment of Reinhold's *Contributions to a More Facile Overview of the State of Philosophy at the Beginning of the Nineteenth Century* (1801). For the most part, later acquaintance with the *Beyträge* has been limited to Hegel's commentary. As a result, the tendency is to accept sight unseen Hegel's critical assessment. The later installments of the *Beyträge* (*Hefte* 1–6, 1801–3) remain by and large unknown. The tenor of Hegel's own essay is comparable to Reinhold's consideration of the historical situation in that Reinhold surveys the various philosophical systems of the age, their rise and fall, as well as describes the advent of the need for true philosophy. (In this connection, *Some Thoughts about Philosophical Systems in general and the Science of Knowledge in particular* is especially pertinent. The *Preface* for this installment of the *Beyträge* is dated March 30, 1801, and as the note in the *Difference* essay attests, was known to Hegel [*Difference essay*, 178–79; *Werke* II, 120].) In the face of Reinhold's lumping together of Schelling's and Fichte's systems in the name of Bardili's logic and his condemnation of both as "speculative philodoxy," Hegel, who was at this time a dyed-in-the-wool Schelling supporter and an equally adamant Fichte critic, felt directly called upon to account for the "difference" between the two systems (*Ibid.*, 79–80, 82, 174–75; *Werke* II, 9, 12, 116). Hegel also knew of Reinhold's article, *The Spirit of the Age*

Reinhold's *Beyträge* only "swim in the needs of the age." What was really required was a well-grounded theory which would account for philosophy's relationship to the prevailing historical conditions. Only such a theory would be able to prepare the way for a philosophy truly up to the task of meeting the needs of the age. In order to understand the loss of importance Reinhold suffered, in stark contrast to the prominence he enjoyed among his contemporaries, and why, in particular, his writings after 1800 sank into oblivion, it is necessary to look at the devastating effect Hegel's critique in the *Difference* essay had on Reinhold's future standing in the history of philosophy.

Reinhold's intention in the *Beyträge* was to survey the current philosophical landscape at the beginning of the nineteenth century by working through and amplifying doxographic knowledge from a historical perspective. It is hard to see how any real progress in philosophy could have been achieved in this way. For, on the one hand, the project of bringing together and preserving various viewpoints falls squarely within the purview of culture where any new viewpoint will be regarded indifferently as just one among others. On the other hand, the principle Reinhold took over from Bardili's logic, thinking *qua* thinking abstracted from its application to real knowledge, is only another manifestation of a culture already in the grip of understanding and reflection.[18] Reinhold's entire undertaking of bringing the current, historical

---

as the Spirit of Philosophy, published in Wieland's (Reinhold's father-in-law) journal *Neuer Teutscher Merkur* (March 1801, n. 3, pp. 167–93), (*Ibid.*, 178–79, *Werke* II, 120). As H.S. Harris has observed, this essay had a preliminary note which announced that it consisted of "fragments from a treatise" included in the *second volume* of the *Beyträge*. The "treatise" (*Beyträge* II, 104–40) was entitled: "On Autonomy as the Principle of the *Practical* Philosophy of the Kantian School – and of the *Whole* Philosophy of the School of Fichte and Schelling," (see Harris' note *Difference* essay, 178). Hegel alludes to both works. In the *Spirit* essay, Reinhold explains speculation in terms of the age's general tendency toward "egotism" and "impiety." Concealed behind the concept of transcendental philosophy and the mere semblance of speculation of Fichte's and Schelling's systems is only the interest of "philosophers going by the name Peter and Paul" in the free despotism of their individual egos. Reinhold voices similar objections in the *Beyträge* (for example, Heft I, 153f; Heft 2, 58). Hegel repudiates the moralizing calumny, but concedes Reinhold's point that the various forms philosophy takes on are determined by historical circumstances. From the perspective of the history of philosophy, there is, at any rate, a good deal more in common between Reinhold and Hegel of 1801, than the widely accepted view that Hegel's inspiration for the *Difference* essay was completely original. Hegel's polemics have contributed to an unfair picture of Reinhold's accomplishments.

[18] *Difference* essay, 187, 192; *Werke* II, 130f., 136. Compare also *Wesen der Kritik*, *Werke* II, 179f.

situation to the attention of philosophical consciousness, together with
the "discovery" of yet another viewpoint of philosophical abstraction,
becomes reintegrated into the current, historical moment and, through
this self-historicizing, contributes to reaffirming and reconstituting the
dominant culture.

Given the eclipse of an authentic speculative principle by reflection,
it is not surprising that the various careers made in *Reflexionsphilosophie*
were sustained not so much by reason as by "luck" and an "instinctive
inclination" of the age, which did not find satisfaction in the creation
of a definitive system, but in continuing to feel drawn to certain token
appearances of philosophy. What was sought after in these appearances
was more a matter of hoping to find something rather than actually
finding it.[19] The outward signs mirror philosophy's failure to intervene
in the actuality of the historical moment. Such an intervention would
have allowed philosophy to overcome its "unfree" side given through
the culture of the age.

Reflection having long since established its primacy in the cultural
realm, thus encroached on the philosophical realm. In a number of passages in the *Difference* essay, Hegel depicts the skewed relation between
reflection and speculation as one of "tyranny" and "alienation."[20] This
means that the finite side of the relation maintains its domination at
the cost of the infinite side and prevents the unity of both sides. The
subjection of speculation to reflection results in systems which are inconsistent and incomplete, as epitomized for Hegel in the philosophies
of Kant, Jacobi and Fichte.[21] The principle of culture, gaining entry
into the realm of philosophy, becomes absolute in these systems, and
disseverance is driven to its utmost extremes.[22] Hegel summarizes this

---

[19] *Ibid.*, 82, 114; *Werke* II, 12f., 47; see also *Wesen der Kritik, Werke* II, 181f.

[20] *Ibid.*, 115, 121f., 125; *Werke* II, 48, 53f., 59f; *Faith and Knowledge*, 6off., 143, 183; *Werke* II, 293f., 383, 425.

[21] Reinhold proclaimed that transcendental philosophy had come to an end by declaring himself to be for "rational realism" (i.e., Bardili's *Outline for the First Logic, Purged from the Errors of Previous Logics, Kant's in particular; not a Critique, rather a Medicina Mentis Primarily Useful for Germany's Critical Philosophy* [Stuttgart: Fromann, 1800]). Reinhold in following Bardili also criticizes Kant and Fichte and points to failings in both which Hegel takes over as his own. See in particular Reinhold's *Ideas for a Heautogony or Natural History of the Pure Absolute Ego [Ichheit], Called Pure Reason* in *Heft* I of the *Beyträge*.

[22] *Difference* essay, 101–2; *Werke* II, 34; *Faith and Knowledge*, 56–57, 61–62, 189; *Werke* II, 289, 295f., 430. Compare *Phenomenology of Spirit*, trans. A.V. Miller (Oxford: Oxford University Press, 1977), 15–16; *Phänomenologie des Geistes, Werke* III. 31–32. See also Reinhold's *Key to Philodoxy in general and to the So-called Speculative in particular* in *Heft* IV of the *Beyträge*, 186, (*Foreword* from March 21, 1802).

development in the conclusion of his essay, *Faith and Knowledge*, when he writes "the external possibility directly arises for the true philosophy to emerge out of this [completed] culture, to destroy the absoluteness of its finite elements and, at the same time, present itself as perfected appearance."[23]

In order to arrive at a more concrete understanding of Hegel's concept of philosophy, which has thus far only emerged thetically, it is necessary to turn to the concept of *philosophical critique*, as he develops it in his first published contribution to the *Critical Journal of Philosophy*. The essay, *Concerning the Essence of Philosophical Critique in general and its Relation to the Present State of Philosophy in particular*, begins as follows: "Critique, in whatever division of art or science it is carried out, calls for a criterion which is just as independent of the one who judges as of what is judged: not derived from individual phenomena, nor from the subject's particularity, rather from the eternal and immutable archetype of the subject matter itself."[24] If philosophical critique does not want "for all of eternity to set subjectivity against subjectivity," then "the idea of philosophy itself [must be] the condition and presupposition." The idea, therefore, is not contingent; it is defined in this context as the Absolute, and there can only be *one* unified idea because there are not many philosophies. Solely in reference to this idea, is it possible to evaluate modern philosophy's degenerate forms and its various, inadequate systems which have arisen in the course of reflection's cultural formation. Critique consists in measuring these results of reflection against the idea of true philosophy.

Criticism of philosophy's finite, historical forms is not identical with philosophy, however far removed it is from the level of what is being criticized. The idea of philosophy is always presupposed by the very activity of criticism and never realized by the philosophical standpoints constituting the objects of criticism. For this reason, it is just as important for philosophy "to recognize the multiplicity of spirit's reflexes, each of which must have its own sphere, as what is deficient and inferior about them."[25] By the same token, it is necessary to study disseverance's most acute forms in the sequence that the philosophy of reflection makes them absolute.[26] Conversely, it is also necessary to prepare specifically for *philosophy's emergence in its own age*.

---

[23] *Faith and Knowledge*, 189 (translation modified); *Werke* II, 431.
[24] *Werke* II, 171ff.   [25] *Ibid.*, 175.
[26] *Ibid.*, 181f.

What is imperative is that philosophy as critique actively confronts its own historical reality. For this reason, philosophy refrains, at first, from claiming to be just another system. Instead, it serves as a standard by which to judge the claims and pretensions of already existing systems. At this *preliminary* stage, philosophy attempts to lay hold of and sort out the multiplicity of its own limitations. It must comprehend its finite, contingent forms and "refute the limitation of the form [arising] out of its own genuine inclination."[27] Philosophy develops a *consciousness of the age* by becoming the direct object of its own critical inquiries; this means, philosophy strives to recognize itself in the already existing structures and thought formations and, with the idea of true philosophy always in view, to plot out, by means of critique, the entire field of its limitations.

Critique is the form of reflection in which true philosophy first steps into its time in order to sublate the prevailing historical conditions for itself. The relation of history and system becomes a legitimate concern for philosophy so long as critique has already worked through the historical, raw material of spirit.[28] This is why *critique is not yet speculation*. As Hegel writes in the *Essence of Critique*: "It must be necessarily believed that such knowledge is possible, if we are to expect critique to have a genuine effect, not merely the negative [effect] of destroying all limitations, but of paving the way for the emergence of true philosophy."[29]

---

[27] *Ibid.*, 175.

[28] O. Pöggeler's approach to understanding the philosophical task of the *Phenomenology of Spirit* is obviously influenced by Heidegger. This orientation manifests itself when Pöggeler maintains that Hegel places experience and the problem of history "at the center of metaphysics" so that "truth itself can be seen as historical and thus, in a certain way, also as 'a goal to be aspired to' [Streben] and as 'problematical,'" (*Hegels Jenaer Systemkonzeption*, in *Philosophisches Jahrbuch* (1963/64) 316f., 311, 308). This interpretation, however, fails to realize that Hegel, in according the problem of history a place in his system, is by no means interested in making truth dependent on history and, therefore, contingent. Rather, for Hegel, it is a question of endeavoring to comprehend such dependency in all its forms in order to rescue the truth of the one, atemporal philosophy from the influence of history and those inadequacies that undermined the viability of *Reflexionsphilosophie*, which was itself shaped by the spirit of the times. (See, for example, the *Phenomenology* 486–87; *Werke* III, 584–85.) In his reading of the *Introduction* to the *Phenomenology*, Heidegger, because he failed to distinguish sufficiently between phenomenology and logic and, thus, excluded from consideration the function phenomenology has in Hegel's system (*Hegels Begriff der Erfahrung* in *Holzwege* [Frankfurt am Main: Klostermann, 1980] 111–204), treats phenomenal spirit as if it were a manifestation of the Absolute. For an English translation of Heidegger's essay, see *Hegel's Concept of Experience*, trans. J.G. Gray (New York: Harper and Raw, 1970).

[29] *Werke* II, 185.

What Hegel here describes as the negative and positive function of critique foreshadows the passage in the *Introduction* to the *Phenomenology of Spirit*, where he defines the task of preparation as freeing science (and that means philosophy in its "unfolded and developed truth") from the character of being "merely an empty appearance of knowing." In order to combat the appearance of being untrue knowledge, it is not sufficient that science simply gives an assertion of its superiority over other modes of knowledge. It must turn against its own appearance and bring to bear a scientific "exposition of phenomenological knowledge."[30] The method appropriate to this exposition Hegel characterizes as a critically examining "way of *relating science* to *phenomenal* knowledge."[31] The logical structure of this mode of examination will be dealt with later on in this essay. I have here only suggested how Hegel understands the task of phenomenology.

For Hegel, philosophy as critique is *preparation* for genuine philosophical knowledge. The rather vague concept of preparation, however, must be defined in an adequately systematic way. Preparation is never carried out from a standpoint external to philosophy, but always works from within philosophy. It consists in a critical attitude by which philosophy establishes itself alongside other modes of knowledge. If, according to this explanation, critique does not exactly extend to the inner sanctum of philosophy, then at least it can be said that in some sense critique is itself already philosophy. For without the ideal of true philosophizing, presupposed from the beginning, critique will not be able to fulfill its function. The question arises, however, what more of substance can be achieved, if philosophy, in its capacity as critique, has already developed a speculative point of view. In short, what is the relation between philosophy and its preparatory function as critique, and how do we account for this relation? The answer to this question will now help to specify the systematic meaning of phenomenology. The analysis of its structure will be discussed at the end of this chapter.

IV. Logic or Phenomenology

The letter Hegel wrote Schelling on November 2, 1800, is generally cited as evidence for the turn in Hegel's thinking in which he begins to translate the themes of his early writings into the form of a system.

30 *Phenomenology*, 48–49, see also 15–16; *Werke* III, 72, 30–31.
31 *Ibid.*, 52; *Werke* III, 75.

"In the course of my scientific education, which began with the more subordinate needs of man, I was driven toward science, and the ideal of my youth had to be transformed into the form of reflection and, at the same time, into a system."[32] During the following years, in addition to the critical essays, Hegel drafted the initial version of his system comprising logic and metaphysics. In 1807, however, he came out with the first part of a system of sciences called the *Phenomenology of Spirit*. Needless to say, this raises problems which go far beyond the scope of historical, genetic concerns. The conundrum presented us by the *Phenomenology* of 1807, is to understand, on the one hand, how systematic philosophy realizes itself in speculation by beginning its career as phenomenology, and then, on the other, how to distinguish between philosophy's speculative and critical functions. This is closely connected to the question: does philosophy first come into itself as critique or as speculation?

In philosophy, reason is directed toward itself, deals only with itself and comes to know itself. In this unity of subject and object, arising from reason's self-reflection, philosophy is speculation and has reconciled the rigid oppositions produced by external reflection. In the *Difference* essay, Hegel understands reason's mediation of the oppositions created by reflection to be philosophy's appropriate activity, and he goes so far as to define *logic* as reason's apprehension of itself.[33] Hegel, however, is here reacting to contemporary debates and does not directly identify logic with philosophy. Only in conjunction with Reinhold's reworking of the "rational realism" of Bardili's logic does he refer to logic as being the testing ground for philosophy's speculative principle. Bardili's implied identification of logic with metaphysics was meant to cure the subjectivist reductionism of transcendental philosophy, and Reinhold, armed with weapons supplied by Bardili, waged his own battle against what he saw as the culmination of the principle of subjective idealism in a mere semblance of the Absolute – Fichte's and Schelling's "speculative philodoxy."

Hegel recognized, however, that Reinhold, in having based his whole approach to logic on the abstraction of thinking from its application, started out from unseen premises and was blind to the formal oppositions created by this abstraction. Only when logic is rightly understood can the truth of speculation first be proven; for logic must from the outset already have determined whether the antitheses created by

---

[32] Briefe von und an Hegel, Bd. I, 59.
[33] *Difference essay*, 87, 88, 96–97; *Werke* II, 17, 19, 28.

understanding have actually been overcome or are only assumed to
be so. The critique of Bardili and Reinhold offers a first glimpse of
the project Hegel will tackle ten years later in the *Science of Logic*. In the
Difference essay, however, he obviously still models what is essentially positive knowledge of the Absolute on Schelling's *System of Transcendental
Idealism* and his postulate of transcendental intuition. In the later texts
of the Jena period, Hegel takes the first, decisive steps toward realizing
his own conception of the Absolute.

Speculation comes into its own by *comprehending* by means of logic
what the *truth of reflection* is. Since this truth does not yet directly correspond to reflection's thinking as understanding, since reflection as
understanding does not recognize itself as reflection, or reflect upon
itself when it reflects, speculation destroys the false forms of unities
reflection as understanding creates. When reflection gives up the semblance of creating unity, upon which its fundamental antitheses tacitly
rest, it establishes true unity capable of including antitheses and becomes reason. The apprehending of reflection's truth thus constitutes
reflection's own self-understanding in that the insight into the origin
of its derivative, finite forms results from its own activities. Reflection's
turning back on itself to illuminate its inner nature constitutes logic's
real concern.

To be sure, this description of the role Hegel assigns logic in the
dialectical transition from reflection to speculation is anything but self-
explanatory. Karl Rosenkranz in his biography, *Hegels Leben*, however,
preserved an important excerpt from Hegel's Jena lectures (winter
semester 1802), which makes this transition less opaque. The argument
is as follows: philosophy, as the science of truth, recognizes that "infinite knowing or speculation," in which philosophy must move, stands
opposed to "finite knowing or reflection." In the latter, philosophy recognizes only the abstraction of the former and, in opposition to both,
sees nothing final, something untrue. "Thus, the objective concern of
true logic is this: to display the *forms of finitude* and not simply gathered together empirically, rather as they arise from reason, but being
robbed of reason by the understanding, they appear only in their finitude. – Hence, understanding's efforts to *imitate* reason in the creation
of identity must be set forth, showing how understanding's copying can
give rise only to *formal identity*. And in order to recognize the imitative
character of understanding, we must always keep the original [*Urbild*]
that it copies, the expression of reason itself, before our eyes. – *Finally*,
we must sublate the forms of understanding themselves by *reason*, we

must show what meaning and content these finite forms of knowing have for reason. Reason's way of knowing, so far as it appertains to logic, will therefore be reason's *negative* knowing. – I think that, inasmuch as it fixes the finite forms as such, logic can serve as an introduction to philosophy only from this speculative side, where it knows reflection completely and clears it from the path, so that it does not put any obstacles in the way of speculation and, at the same time, keeps the *image of the Absolute* as a mirror reflection so that we become familiar with it."[34]

In order for reason to comprehend understanding's finite character it must undermine the certainty understanding has in its reflective powers and, at the same time, clear the way for speculation. Reason accomplishes this task by bringing understanding's finite forms of thought into close proximity to their archetype. By making a complete survey of all forms reduced by reflection to mere finite appearances of the Absolute, reason simultaneously throws back, in a mirror image, an imitation of the infinite, the Absolute. Reflection's forms are understood as self-subsisting semblances of unity[35] which only, in fact, mimic the unity created by reason and are confined within a formal antithesis overlooked by reflection. It, thus, becomes possible to raise understanding to its truth in reason by translating the antithesis, persisting in the semblance of unity established by reflection, into the antithesis prevailing in the relation between the real unity and its copy. Because the former is no longer a genuine antithesis, it ceases to be an obstacle for speculation.

In other words, reflection, as the source of false forms of unity, and understanding, as the source of finite forms of thought, are brought into relation with reason. Reason shows that the totality of the connections it creates among understanding's finite forms is not one point of reference among others; rather, it constitutes understanding's highest level of unity, and conversely, reason in this way also exposes understanding's self-subsisting forms to be mere abstractions. The two sides of Hegel's proof, the creation of genuine unity and the negation of understanding's finite forms of thought, represent the process by which

---

[34] See *Introduction* to Harris and Cerf's translation of *Faith and Knowledge*, 9–10, where the entire excerpt is quoted (translation modified); Rosenkranz, *Hegels Leben*, (Berlin 1844; reprint, Darmstadt: Wiss. Buchges, 1969) 190f. Omitted here is the reference to the three-tiered structure of logic.

[35] Compare *Faith and Knowledge*, 170–171; *Werke* II, 413–14; and also *Difference* essay, 90; Werke II, 23f.

reflection is carried over into speculation. The "thinking of thinking,"[36] however, is the self-movement of logic's thought determinations. The characterization of logic as the speculative introduction to philosophy refers to the elevation of finite thought to infinite thought as the first moment of the scientific system and the first of philosophy's accomplishments. It is important to note that Hegel obviously at this stage still uses the concept of introduction in a non-technical sense, and it should not, therfore, be invested with the meaning of the more developed concept of introduction which will take shape in connection with the later, formalized system.

The *Science of Logic* similarly accounts for the advance made by speculation's elevation of thinking to the "loftier" sphere of reason by the seemingly "retrograde step" of aggravating the antinomies generated among reflective understanding's determinations. The *Logic* also maintains that so long as understanding has "taken possession" of philosophy, it directly recoils from becoming enmeshed in contradiction and attempts to gain ground against reason by imposing common-sense viewpoints and the "opinions" of every-day consciousness.[37] "But when these prejudices are carried over into the sphere of reason, . . . then they are errors the refutation of which throughout every part of the spiritual and natural universe is *philosophy*, or rather as they bar the entrance to philosophy, must be discarded at its portals."[38]

v. The Importance of Prescientific Consciousness

The ambivalence expressed in the passage just quoted is important for our question as to whether speculative philosophy, in the entirety of its system, consists in nothing more than the refutation of errors arising from reflection's entrenched standpoint, or whether reflection's views, prejudices and opinions *obstruct philosophy* and, therefore, must be eradicated beforehand. The further question thus arises, when does philosophy really begin as itself? The formulation of the problem in the *Logic* alludes to the *Phenomenology* and occurs in the same context where Hegel attributes opinions and prejudices to the special character of "phenomenological consciousness." The alternatives, however,

---

[36] *Encyclopaedia of Philosophical Sciences, Logic*, trans. W. Wallace (Oxford: Oxford University Press, 1975) §19.
[37] *Science of Logic*, trans. A.V. Miller (Atlantic Highlands: 1990) 45–46; *Werke* V, 38.
[38] Ibid.

to refute errors by means of philosophy or to discard prejudices at the "portals" of philosophy, both contain a residue of an unresolved problem which must be dealt with in the context of the reciprocal differentiation between phenomenology and logic. I will return, therefore, to the question posed earlier and attempt to bring it together with the original problem, philosophy as critique.

As we have seen, *Reflexionsphilosophie* took shape within a general process of cultural formation and governed the thought of the age. In contrast, philosophy as critique had the task of preparing the way for the emergence of an authentic, speculative system. This advance work of critique was essential because reflection had not only permeated common-sense attitudes of everyday consciousness, but also the very principles upon which contemporary philosophy had built its systems. In these historical circumstances, the spiritual need for philosophy calls for speculation to provide genuine insight into the structure of reflection. This need for true philosophy can only be satisfied by logic, the thinking of thinking, with which philosophical science as system begins.

Logic, however, does not concern itself with every-day understanding, its prejudices and opinions behind which reflection conceals itself.[39] For logic, which thinks speculatively, only those prejudices are pertinent which have worked their way into the sphere of reason, where it is then logic's function to expose and refute them as errors resulting from reflection's ubiquitous influence. The superior science demonstrates to understanding reason's importance and, in the process, simply destroys the pretensions to science understanding so arrogantly flaunts. In this way, logic knocks down what ordinary thinking, in total independence from science and its role in science, believes itself to be.[40] For speculation, consciousness' dubious claims to autonomy constitute an obstruction and, accordingly, speculation maintains only a negative attitude toward consciousness.

For unscientific consciousness this imbalance is obviously less precarious than it is for science, since the former can get along without the latter but not the other way around. Only at the risk of remaining abstract and undermining its own scientific principles, can philosophy conceal the asymmetry of this relation. It is, therefore, in the interest

[39] *Difference* essay, 98ff; *Werke* II, 30ff. See also Hegel's Krug review first published in the *Critical Journal of Philosophy*, January 1802, under the title *Wie der gemeine Menschenverstand die Philosophie nehme, dargestellt an den Werken des Herrn Krug, Werke* II, 188ff.
[40] *Phenomenology*, 14–15, 49 *Werke* III, 29–30, 72.

of its own self-realization that philosophy educates prescientific consciousness to the point where it can gain entry to the level of science. Should consciousness in its autonomy continue to be problematic for science, then only because it demands to be initiated into the mysteries of science itself.[41]

The *Phenomenology of Spirit* seems to encourage such an understanding. It is usually read either as the path science maps out for consciousness in science or as an introduction to science which is meant to persuade consciousness of the necessity of attaining a philosophical standpoint.[42] To read the *Phenomenology* in this way, however, gives rise to certain difficulties, if it assumes an indifferent coexistence between science, which is not concerned with consciousness' lack of scientific knowledge, and consciousness, which is predisposed toward science and requires only to be shown the way. This description does not take into account the decisive role a phenomenological explanation of consciousness plays not only in consciousness' own coming into science and its taking possession of an already independently established philosophical standpoint, but in obtaining this standpoint at all and, thus, in the coming-to-be of science.

It is important to see that Hegel describes the relation between unscientific consciousness and science as an antithesis in which each side appears to the other as "the inversion of truth,"[43] so that without further consideration a decision about the truth or untruth of either side would be, at this stage, almost impossible or reached only by chance. Ordinary thinking, in its absolute independence from science, must be taken seriously as a rival power which is left unconvinced when science, for its own purposes, sublates the untruth of the other side of the antithesis. In the face of the competing power of consciousness' independent positions and claims to knowledge, any attempt to steer consciousness to the level of absolute knowlege would be inappropriate or at best arbitrary. For this would assume, on the one hand, a philosophical standpoint which has not yet been established in its truth, and, on the other, a willing,

[41] *Ibid.*, 7–8, 14–15; *Werke* III, 19–20, 29–30.
[42] In his *Das Problem einer Einleitung in Hegels Wissenschaft der Logik*, (Frankfurt: Klostermann, *second edition* 1975), H.F. Fulda extensively argues this thesis in its systematic implications while, at the same time, maintaining an understanding of the *Phenomenology*, based on the later *Logic* and *Encyclopaedia*, as proof for the necessity of a standpoint biased toward philosophical science. See *Science of Logic*, 48–49; *Werke* V, 42–43; and also *Encyclopaedia*, remark §25.
[43] *Phenomenology*, 15, 49–50; *Werke* III, 30, 72–73.

"malleable" consciousness which is already predisposed to science. Instead, the actual *antithetical relation* between science and consciousness' prescientific positions must be dismantled, for the antithesis is
artificial.[44] So long as science and consciousness can only see the inversion of the truth in each other, an illusion prevails which completely
misdirects all of scientific philosophy's efforts. Philosophy must defend
itself against this illusion and divest consciousness' opposing positions
of their autonomous power by making them manifestations of itself;
that is, philosophy must *confront* the illusion and force consciousness to
relinquish its positions, not, however, in order to raise consciousness to
the level of philosophy, but to insure the possibility of philosophy *tout
court.*

   The way opens up for philosophy as soon as the opposition between
consciousness and science, first confronting philosophy, begins to abate
on its own accord. That the pretensions and claims with which consciousness reproaches science gradually subside is not because science,
for the sake of pacifying consciousness, has paid tribute to them by
acknowledging that they are justified. On the contrary, it is the proof
of philosophy's superiority as a science that it knows how to impute
to prescientific consciousness the *doubt* it raises with regard to the legitimacy of its claims against science. The "thoroughgoing doubt," the
"despair,"[45] experienced by ordinary understanding and consciousness
thus becomes the same process described, in regard to philosophical
science, as the phenomenological "preparation" which first establishes
spirit's true standpoint.[46]

   Up to now, philosophy has manifested itself as critique, that is, as
a critical confrontation with an illusory antithesis in which philosophy
stands over against consciousness as an opponent. At this stage in the
development of science's relation to consciousness, the need for an
adequate method becomes urgent.[47]

---

[44] Compare *Jenenser Realphilosophie* I. ed. J. Hoffmeister (Leipzig, 1931–32) 266, Anmerkung
   II to the fragment "*Die Wissenschaft.*"
[45] *Phenomenology* 49–50; *Werke* III, 72. – The idea is already contained in Hegel's *Habilitation's*
   theses of 1801: "VI. Idea est synthesis infiniti et finiti et philosophia omnis est in ideis. VII.
   Philosophia critica caret ideis et *imperfecta est Scepticismi forma*" (Rosenkranz, *Hegels Leben*,
   158f.). In the *Difference* essay, Hegel similarly calls one variety of philosophy, "genuine
   scepticism," which does not actually fulfill the need for philosophy (*Difference* essay, 193–
   94; *Werke* II, 136–37). See also the essay, *Verhältnis des Skeptizismus zur Philosophie*, *Werke* II,
   especially 239f., 249, 224, 228, as well as the *Encyclopaedia*, §78, and remark §81.
[46] *Phenomenology*, 20; *Werke* III, 38.   [47] *Ibid.*, 56; *Werke* III, 80.

VI. The Structure of Phenomenology

By emphasizing how phenomenology confronts unscientific consciousness at each stage of its development and, thus, simultaneously helps philosophy come into its own right, I have raised more questions concerning concrete analyses of the *Phenomenology* than can be adequately answered. For the purposes of this chapter, however, it is important to discuss in more detail what has been generally referred to as the positions of ordinary understanding and prephilosophical, unscientific consciousness. For Hegel, the medium of philosophy is spirit. The forms of consciousness which compete with philosophy must be defined, therefore, by corresponding categories. In the realm of spirit, whatever stands in opposition to philosophy must be a manifestation of spirit, and one in which spirit appears in a specific mode of untruth. If, from an ontological perspective, the forms consciousness assumes in opposition to philosophy are regarded as manifestations of spirit's unmediated or incomplete existence, then they can also be regarded as becoming preliminarily integrated into spirit's realized, concrete existence of total self-mediation in which philosophy first moves freely.

Spirit, however, in the totality of its abstract forms of appearance, is also *consciousness*. It, therefore, subsumes all the different, individual shapes taken on by ordinary understanding, common sense and culture, as well as the entire spectrum of corresponding philosophical viewpoints arising from inadequately realized systems and their symbiotic relation to the prevailing intellectual level of cultural formation.[48] In the *Philosophy of Spirit*, as carried out in the context of the *Encyclopaedia of Philosophical Sciences*, Hegel offers a structural analysis which construes consciousness as being always knowledge of something, that is, consciousness of an object and consciousness of itself. This analysis is clearly at odds with the function the concept of consciousness has in phenomenology.[49] In a phenomenology of spirit, what the truth of consciousness is, should not be positively stated, as is the case in the *Encyclopaedia*; for this assumes that all differences between consciousness and spirit have been worked through and are already thoroughly

---

[48] Compare, for example, the *Encyclopaedia*, remark §415.

[49] This can already be observed in the chapter "*Phänomenologie des Geistes oder Wissenschaft des Bewußtseins*" from Hegel's Nürnberg *Philosophische Propädeutik* (1809), *Werke* IV, 111; *The Philosophical Propaedeutic*, trans. A.V. Miller (Oxford: Oxford University Press, 1986) 55. (The English translation does not retain the chapter heading, "Phenomenology of Spirit or Science of Consciousness.")

integrated into spirit's absolute standpoint. For the purposes of phenomenological inquiry, concrete proof must be given for all the successive, individual shapes consciousness assumes, even the false knowledge
of itself derived from its uncritical and uncriticized self-understanding.
In order to attain the level in which a science of spirit can be realized,
consciousness must, therefore, shed its abstract appearances of being
something other than spirit and abandon the putative autonomy of its
phenomenal existence in favor of finding its real existence in spirit.[50]

If the contrast just drawn between the concept of consciousness and
its phenomenological function turns out to be valid, important methodological problems emerge in conjuction with phenomenology. It is easy,
however, to overlook these problems, especially if the main focus is the
wealth of material supplied in the *Phenomenology,* and the concern is
to think through this material immanently. This has been the starting
point for traditional interpretations, and the source of fascination the
Phenomenology exerts on its readers. As critique, however, the method
appropriate to phenomenology can not, at first, be put on a par with
speculative method which finds its model expression in logic. Then
again, how can such a distinction be adequately drawn, when scientific philosophy is itself engaged in speculation?[51] The solution to this
problem is usually sought for in correspondences between logical and
phenomenological structures. If the aim is to refashion the *Phenomenology's* general framework after the *Logic,* what comes first to mind is the
"Doctrine of Essence," which starts out with the transitional category of
Being constituting the Other of reflection.[52] This is plausible given that

---

[50] Compare *Phenomenology,* 56–57; *Werke* III, 80–81.
[51] H.F. Fulda's closely reasoned argumentation attempts to address this paradox. For the
most part, he bases his argument on the famous statement at the end of the *Phenomenology* that for every one of science's abstract moments there is a corresponding, individual
shape of manifest spirit (*Phenomenology,* 491; *Werke* III, 589). In a comparison with speculative logic, Fulda tries to get to the root of the logic specific to the *Phenomenology* through
a more concrete understanding of the *Phenomenology's* techniques and methodological
form. All told, this results in a subtle interpretation of the concept of correspondence
(Fulda, *Zur Logik der Phänomenologie von 1807, in Hegel-Studien,* Beiheft 3, 1966). – Fulda's
line of reasoning concerning the *Phenomenology's* formal structure seems to me to be on
the right track. The question is, however, whether it is legitimate to base such an interpretation on a formulaic and synoptic statement as encapsulated in the sentence drawn
from the last chapter of the *Phenomenology.* – It is not by chance that what is still by far the
best grounded attempt to track down behind every individual shape of the *Phenomenology*
a corresponding moment in the *Logic* comes up against its limits after the *Phenomenology's*
third chapter. See W. Purpus, *Zur Dialektik des Bewuß tseins nach Hegel* (Berlin: de Gruyter,
1908).
[52] *Logic,* Bk. II, 390; *Werke* VI, 13. See also *Encyclopaedia* §414.

phenomenology does seem to move within the sphere where "being-in-itself" and "being-for-self" are united. It becomes obvious, however, to formulate the problem in this way can not account for the difficulties which arise in the concrete application of such determinations within the *Phenomenology*. Although Hegel indeed brings the realm of consciousness' individual shapes, in the sense of their abstract appearances, in relation to spirit's realm of truth, this contributes little to pinpointing what is specifically characteristic about the method intrinsic to phenomenology.

A more successful approach would be to focus on the idea of a phenomenological *preparation* for science. From this perspective, the importance of what we expect phenomenology to achieve will lie in an on-going critique of consciousness' seemingly autonomous standpoints and in exposing the bogus nature of the opposition between science and consciousness. This goal can only be realized when consciousness' various opinions and levels of self-understanding are taken seriously and given a hearing,[53] whereas it is up to speculation to destroy both aspects by leaving them to perish as reason strives toward systematic knowledge.

In order for critique to fulfill its function, it must first be conceded that each of consciousness' individual, phenomenal shapes actually understands itself as a totality and as constituting the truth. As the *Phenomenology* progresses, the focal point undergoes a radical shift in perspective. The philosopher becomes directly engaged in a dialogue with the various phenomenological standpoints consciousness assumes. It is now *our* reflection as observer which inquires into consciousness' self-understanding, that is, the for-it of consciousness is examined, as to what it is in-itself and what its truth is for us.

From the perspective of real knowledge, the "for-it" means *certainty*, and the "in-itself," *truth*, while the incongruence of certainty and truth is crystallized in the concept of *opinion*. Insight into this incongruence constitutes consciousness' *experience* of itself. Experience means knowledge is brought to bear upon consciousness from the outside and indicates that consciousness must accordingly modify its present understanding of itself. Consciousness has to realize that what it took to be the truth and independent being of things is, in fact, nothing other than the objects of its own reflection; this is, however, very different

---

53 For further insight see R. Wiehl, *Der Sinn der sinnlichen Gewißheit*, in *Hegel-Studien*, Beiheft 3 (Bonn 1966).

from what consciousness originally believed about the nature of objects and its relation to them. In experiencing the loss of the object's being-in-itself, consciousness corrects its former opinions and achieves an integration of truth and certainty and, in terms of the *Phenomenology's* overall development, this means consciousness has advanced in its own self-knowledge. What first was the "for-it" of consciousness has now to be understood as "for us or in-itself," and the further insight resulting from this methodological maneuver must be reintegrated into the for-it of consciousness.

The insights consciousness gains in this way, however, are always immediately *forgotten*,[54] and consciousness must, once again, move between certainty and truth. In improving and correcting its previous knowledge, consciousness suffers a loss at the next stage of its development. In the language of consciousness this is to be described as nothing more than reestablishing its standpoint in all its immediacy, and the phenomenological method must once again deal with a similar problem translated into the terms of a higher level of awareness. From the side of phenomenology, self-certain opinions about the truth must give way to reflection. This move helps clarify for us the relation between consciousness and science by showing that it is consciousness' experiences which rectify the discrepancies between what the truth in itself is and what consciousness believes it to be. This process is resumed so long as consciousness is able to adopt new standpoints as a consequence of having forgotten its previous experiences. The process, however, is not open-ended. It comes to a halt the moment certainty and truth coincide, and consciousness has no other objects to fall back upon other than itself.[55] At this last stage in the development of the *Phenomenology*, the refutation of consciousness' standpoint is carried out by consciousness itself, and it ushers in the moment of absolute knowledge. Since there is no longer a consciousness to be distinguished from philosophy, philosophical science can now begin as itself unhindered.

The function of method in the *Phenomenology* is to impute to consciousness, whose authority was initially granted on the basis of certainty and the bare assertion of truth,[56] the form of reflection originally practiced by the phenomenological observer. Consciousness, thus, carries out the process of reflection originally introduced by phenomenology and, in its turn, reflection is integrated step-by-step into the opposing

---

[54] *Phenomenology*, 64–5, 71, 102–3, 141; *Werke* III, 90, 98, 134–5, 180.
[55] Compare *Jenenser Realphilosophie* I, 267.   [56] *Phenomenology*, 141; *Werke* III, 180.

standpoint. Reflection sheds the role of being something external to consciousness, as the two seemingly conflicting standpoints of phenomenological observer and consciousness gradually merge together to form an identity of perspective. The observer's standpoint, however, exists only in its opposition to the successive standpoints assumed by consciousness and, conversely, the internal standpoints of consciousness come into view only in opposition to the observer's external standpoint. In this way, philosophical science emerges on the scene thoroughly implicated in what first appears to be an antithetical relation between consciousness and observer.

The truth of phenomenology, however, is that it is not really a standpoint at all; rather, it is the disguised mode by which philosophy prepares the way for its emergence as a true science of spirit. Phenomenology finally rids itself of the appearance of being a standpoint the closer consciousness and observer come to actually forming an identity. Once the standpoints have entirely disappeared into each other, there is only one standpoint left over, that of absolute knowledge. Absolute knowledge, however, is no longer a standpoint. It is the first moment in which philosophy begins to realize itself as genuine system.[57]

If the phenomenological standpoint does not have any independent truth of its own and acquires meaning only in opposition to consciousness, then consciousness' standpoint is no less dependent on phenomenology for the truth of its existence and, taken in isolation, is merely the expression of inflated opinions and self-aggrandizing claims. That consciousness has not yet carried out reflection for itself indicates the for-it of consciousness has not yet been mediated. It is only a form which can be indiscriminately adopted by any content whatsoever, whereas consciousness' given form can be held to be certain regardless of its content. Consciousness' certainty of all things is paid for by the empty, indeterminate *otherness* of all its knowledge. This indeterminate knowledge, coupled with the form of mere certainty, results in consciousness' standpoints becoming dogmatic. When consciousness, however, takes over the function of reflection previously performed by the phenomenological observer, and reflects for itself over the truth of its own experiences, it realizes that they were always laid out in the form

---

[57] It is important to guard against the standard sceptical objection to "absolute knowledge" as being an endpoint which Hegel dogmatically presupposes from the beginning of the *Phenomenology*. For a detailed discussion of this problem see my essay *What is Critical Theory?*, in R. Bubner, *Essays in Hermeneutics and Critical Theory*, trans. E. Matthews (New York: Columbia Press, 1988).

of reflection. With this insight, consciousness prevails against the obdu-
rateness of its standpoints, undermines its fixed, abstract appearances,
and becomes what it is – reflection.

By means of reflection, the mode of thinking peculiar to consciousness, philosophy confronts consciousness on its own terrain of cultural
formation and reveals that reflection is the hidden motor force behind
the entire progression of shapes consciousness assumes. Confronted
with the truth of its own reflective nature, consciousness can no longer
sustain its standpoints. The phenomenological critique of consciousness' individual shapes is the course philosophy pursues in helping
consciousness, incapable of self-knowledge, to be what it is, namely, reflection. For only reflection can open up the possibility for philosophy
to be what it is, namely, speculation. Under the rubric of phenomenology, speculation manifests itself as reflection; for only as reflection can
it have an effect on current thought and reduce the illusion, as it prevails in consciousness' thinking and its standpoints, to a manifestation
of itself. Freedom from illusion is for this reason tantamount to saying that *without the explicit connection to prevailing thought or the spirit of
the times, philosophy is incapable of defining itself.*[58] It is this insight which
Hegel realizes in the *Phenomenology of Spirit.*

[58] For further consideration of Hegel's insight, see my essay *Philosophy Is Its Time Compre-
hended in Thought*, which first appeared as a contribution to the Gadamer-Festschrift
(*Hermeneutik und Dialektik* I [Tübingen: Mohr, 1970]), and is translated in *Essays in
Hermeneutics and Critical Theory*, 37–61. Translated by Cara Gendel Ryan.

7

ROUSSEAU, HEGEL, AND THE DIALECTIC OF ENLIGHTENMENT

I

Rousseau was the first Enlightenment thinker who fully grasped the dialectical character of the movement that effectively sought to clarify and shape all forms of life in terms of reason. Enlightenment for Rousseau represents not only an advance but also, and inevitably, a loss. For the universal dissemination of the light of reason nonetheless leaves morality itself in darkness. 'Telles sont les moeurs d'un siècle instruit: le savoir, l'esprit, le courage ont seul notre admiration; et toi, douce et modeste vertu, tu restes toujours sans honneurs! Aveugles que nous sommes au milieu de tant de lumières!'[1]

Blindness in the midst of illumination – this paradoxical diagnosis was anything but self-evident at the time. The earlier front in the modern struggle for emancipation from prejudice and tradition was oriented without a shadow of doubt towards the idea of progress. The customs and practices that had been handed down from generation to generation, the inherited forms of knowledge, the belief in and deference towards authorities in general – in short, the entire world that was yet to be illumined by the pure and undefiled light of reason – seemed only to survive on the basis of ignorance or force, or a certain fear of using one's own rational powers. The pre-Enlightenment world had no authentic right to exist, but only persisted because of the essentially backward character of current historical conditions. The active overcoming of such conditions amounted therefore to liberation from the forces of superstition and timidity. Human beings can only enter into undiminished self-possession if they are prepared to cast off the

[1] J.J. Rousseau, *Lettre à d'Alembert* (1758), Paris 1967, p. 85.

restrictions the effects of which they have for so long failed clearly to perceive.

In reflecting upon this necessary path of progress, which he both supports and welcomes, Rousseau also acutely observes the inevitable distance from original human existence, which it brings in train. Rousseau grasps something that had escaped the first protagonists of Enlightenment in their moment of almost religious enthusiasm for change: that the progressive rationalisation of forms of life dissolves that immediate and dependable sense of self-evidence that first vouchsafes an ethically unproblematic domain of praxis for human beings. Enlightenment signifies the self-reflective renunciation of unreflective forms of life, and it provides no substitute for the latter. This gives rise to a realm of ambiguity and hypocrisy, of hot-headedness and cold-heartedness, where human beings attempting at last to realise their own identity reap nothing but the experience of failure. And it is here that we first begin to sense a fundamental alienation from ourselves, from one another, and from nature.

It should be noted, of course, that Rousseau is not simply sounding the same theme as the conservative critics of Enlightenment. For they followed the English example of Edmund Burke in reversing the question of political legitimation, directly challenging the fundamental assumption that ascribed all rights to the protagonists of the new and assigned none to tradition itself. Given the aforementioned premises of Enlightenment thought, the idea of progress presented itself as the kind of emancipation from irrationality that had been implicitly inscribed in historical development from the beginning. The conservative critics, on the other hand, argued that the successful survival and continuing existence of the tradition enjoyed a fundamental right of its own simply by virtue of its superiority over all prospective changes and innovations. It was therefore the prophets of the new who should really be challenged to account for their supposed legitimacy.

That was not Rousseau's question. His diagnosis of the dialectic of Enlightenment is concerned to show that the socio-cultural process of development that leads from man's original condition unwittingly destroys the capacity to lead an undiminished life as a gift of nature. A kind of universal historical fate therefore afflicts this ambivalent development. To step forth from the garden of paradise was implicit in man himself, but the experience of universal decadence also dates from that same moment. We increasingly develop and come closer to ourselves through the arts and sciences, through technical innovations, through ever more refined forms of behaviour, but we also ceaselessly lose touch with ourselves in the very process. Since it is impossible for us to explain exactly how this has come about, we can at best describe it. The verdict on the eventual result, as it appears at the height of the modern Enlightenment, cannot therefore be grounded theoretically, but can only be articulated in moral terms.

The exemplary theme of Rousseau's thought, constantly presented in various ways from the revolutionary first *Discourse on the Arts and Sciences* through to the educational novel *Émile*, is a sense of astonishment at the historical fact that virtue and knowledge have proved to be mutually incompatible. Rousseau here renews an ancient question that can be traced right back to Plato's critique of the Sophists: does self-conscious reflection essentially belong to the nature of human existence or does it not rather undermine it? In an age of Enlightenment that is characterised by recognition of cultural relativity, our awareness of historical development is intensified accordingly, not least through the actual encounter with peoples whose forms of life must appear as wild and primordial in our eyes. The alien Other provides the highly cultivated European with a mirror in which he recognises what he can no longer be if he is to be what he actually is. The historical fate of the species 'man' seems therefore to be characterised by the bifurcation of culture and morality. Derrida has rightly shown in his substantial essay on Rousseau that the lamented distantiation from nature springs directly from the character of man himself, that it was always already there and can never be healed by any naive 'return to nature'.[2]

The cardinal concept, as introduced especially in the second *Discourse upon the Origin and Basis of Inequality amongst Mankind*, is that of 'perfectibilité'.[3] It is the capacity to perfect oneself that essentially distinguishes the human being from the animal. This thought effectively suggests an open-ended anthropology allowing for developments that cannot in principle be controlled in advance.[4] It is thus difficult to foresee the degree and level to which mankind can collectively perfect

---

[2] Cf. J. Derrida, *De la Grammatologie* (Paris 1967), II 3, 1; *Of Grammatology* (tr. G.C. Spivak, John Hopkins University Press, 1974), pp. 165ff.

[3] J.J. Rousseau, 'A Discourse on the Origin of Inequality', pp. 54 and 74, in: J.J. Rousseau, *The Social Contract and Discourses*, tr. G.D.H. Cole (London 1973).

[4] Cf. the survey of the issues in E. Behler's essay, 'Die Idee der unendlichen Perfektibilität des Menschen in der französischen und deutschen Romantik', although Behler omits any discussion of Rousseau in this connection. The essay appears in *Gallo-Germania. Festschrift für R. Bauer*, ed. E. Heftrich and J.M. Valentin (Nancy 1986).

itself, and the specific direction this development will take. But we must at least assume the human capacity for unlimited further development if we are properly to grasp the present state of things. Rousseau takes pains to emphasise that this trend to perfectibility only ensues thanks to certain conditions and circumstances that might well have been different. And he ascribes the path that the human race as a whole has actually taken to a 'baleful chance' (*funeste hazard*) that should never have transpired from the perspective of the highest human good.

In this way, Rousseau's approach effectively refuses the framework of a historical teleology oriented to the idea of providence or a teleology established through the wisdom of nature itself, the notions that would subsequently define the philosophy of history in Herder and Kant. In their work, the play of chance and the unexpected turn of events, the inequalities and antagonisms of history, function essentially as a spur to the fuller and richer unfolding of 'humanity'. The obstacles that hinder our own petty plans and subjective intentions that motivate our actions actually form part of a greater plan that we actors cannot immediately survey, but that nonetheless guides and governs the overall development of the historical process. That is why we can trust that those aspects of the course of the world that we cannot control or understand still ultimately serve the attempts of the human race to realise itself as such.

Rousseau does not share this trust. He finds no intelligible meaning in the thought that human beings attain their cultural perfection at the cost of their natural mode of life. He never tires of repeating that human beings have essentially procured their own unhappiness. None but human beings themselves can be held responsible for this, least of all that 'nature' that originally predisposed all things in the most excellent fashion. Rousseau's argument thus effectively culminates in a kind of theodicy of nature.[5] Even the ultimate act through which the human race would shape its own destiny, through which it would finally put an end to the false trails and violent compulsions of history, must itself be seen as a resurrection of our original natural state. And Rousseau is thinking here of the social contract that in the economy of his thought systematically corresponds to the aforementioned critique of culture.

Through this fundamental 'contract', human beings who are essentially free by nature mutually confirm their freedom in lasting form

---

[5] Rousseau, *Second Discourse*, note IX.

precisely by sacrificing their dangerous and purely individual freedom to the constitution of society as a 'corps moral et collectif'. This contract provides the only possible cultural response to that loss of nature that is occasioned by culture itself. For we effectively establish ourselves once again in the act through which the people properly *is* a people ('l'acte par lequel un peuple est un peuple').[6] This astonishing formulation shows that we can only escape the dilemma identified here through the fundamental decision to make ourselves into what we properly are. The salvation of our 'nature' essentially depends upon a moral-political kind of 'decision'.

II

Whereas Rousseau persists in a posture of denunciation, Hegel effectively neutralises the relevant problem within the context of his overall perspective upon history. The immediate reaction to the growing doubts concerning the blessings of the Enlightenment is now succeeded by an analysis that dissolves the original moral protest. If, for Rousseau, we have procured our own unhappiness precisely by distancing ourselves from nature through culture, then we alone are responsible for the lack of integrated life that permeates modernity. Rousseau proclaims his discovery in reproachful tone in order to open the eyes of his contemporaries to the crucial loss that is facilitated, if not indeed encouraged, beneath the glittering surface of civilising 'progress'. But anyone who wishes to go beyond the denunciation of the historically necessary betrayal of nature must take a further step, one capable of providing a coherent explanation for such a scandalous phenomenon.

This is the step that Hegel takes, after his own early writings, by interpreting the intellectualised world of the Enlightenment as an incomplete product of the human struggle for self-understanding and self-determination, one that therefore still requires its appropriate completion and fulfilment. The path that humanity has broached must be followed through to its end, but pursued in such a way that the undesirable results of the same process are not perpetuated in an ossified manner. The decisive issue, therefore, is to overcome the initially diremptive effects of the Enlightenment with respect to social life and to re-establish the fractured relationship between thought and

[6] Rousseau, *Contrat social*, I, 5; *The Social Contract*, loc. cit., pp. 172ff.

actuality. In Hegel's view, it is only a powerful systematic philosophy that proceeds in a dialectical manner that can effectively address this problem.

The external factor that led certain thinkers, in contrast with the prevailing view, to regard the Enlightenment as one stage along a further path of development rather than as the ultimate destination, were the events associated with the French Revolution, which soon displayed the ugly face of terror to the European public that had initially welcomed it so enthusiastically. Schiller sought an escape from the dilemma in the idea of an essentially non-coercive or aesthetic education of man that would help to produce a genuinely human being in the first place. Hegel, adopting a general historical perspective, interpreted the Enlightenment as the result of a process of reflection that now must itself be subjected to further reflection if the unsatisfactory consequences that had revealed themselves were to be overcome.

Hegel's argument can be summarised as follows: Man essentially owes his independence to the tireless labour of reflection. But at the same time, this labour of reflection has effectively produced a second actuality alongside the original one, and the opposition between the two is simply reinforced with every further exercise of reflection. This situation is experienced as a kind of alienation. For the effective world of enlightened culture now confronts the original world of given norms and practices without being able to reconcile itself with the former, but also without being strong enough to absorb or put an end to it. As long as such opposition persists, there is a felt need for unification, even though the purely reflective understanding is powerless to accomplish this.

The problem must therefore be addressed at a deeper level if the power of the prevailing alienation is truly to be broken. In order to identify the 'opposition' in question precisely as an opposition, and thereby to characterise the standard current assumptions as false ones, Hegel appeals to an elementary living sense of the whole that binds all such forces and impulses together and forbids us to treat any single moment involved as unilaterally independent of the others. Since the reflective labour of the 'understanding' tends to produce an independent world of its own in just such a one-sided fashion, it lacks that kind of free perspective upon the 'whole' that would show how the relevant moments have come into sharpened opposition with one another. Over and beyond the standpoint of reflection, therefore, we must articulate the need for unification and internal connection, one that is capable of relativising the acts of reflection without simultaneously basing its own existence upon them.

In his first published work, Hegel writes in this regard: 'The more stable and splendid the edifice constructed by the understanding [*des Verstandes*] is, the more restless becomes the striving of the life that is entangled there as a part to escape from it, and to raise itself to freedom. Insofar as life as reason steps into the distance, the totality of limitations is at the same time nullified, and connected with the Absolute in this nullification, and thereby grasped and posited as mere appearance. The diremption [*Entzweiung*] between the Absolute and the totality of limitations has disappeared.'[7]

In the light of this elementary feeling for life as a whole, the rationalistic edifice is experienced as a constricting force that cannot satisfy the need for unity. For the socially and culturally produced unity of the present has merely been bought at the cost of diremption. And on closer inspection, the brilliant facade of contemporary life actually reveals all the breaks and lacerations under which enlightened humanity still suffers without properly grasping why it does so. This interpretation of the current state of culture also indicates the general direction in which a solution is to be sought and the restless disquiet of a vaguely sensed dissatisfaction can be properly articulated and directed. The task is to establish a new kind of unity that is not oriented, in marked contrast with the idea of progress, to some mythical origin of uncontaminated nature. Rousseau's model, on this view, is trapped in an essentially immediate opposition between a unity that was once enjoyed and a modernity that has since forfeited it. The new unity, on the other hand, must be able to recognise and include its own opposite if it would end the suffering imposed by diremption.

Vainly priding ourselves upon the achievements of the culture of the understanding, we have forgotten that the perfecting of reflection leads to the perpetuation of that opposition that is posited with every instance of reflection. We must establish a critical distance with respect to the interpretation that enlightenment offers of itself. Instead of simply abandoning ourselves to the process of enlightenment as one of ineluctable historical necessity, the initially confident achievements of reflection must be interpreted as moments within a larger context,

---

[7] G.W.F. Hegel, *Differenz des Fichteschen und Schellingschen Systems der Philosophie*, 1801 (Hamburg 1962, p. 13); *Difference between Fichte's and Schelling's System of Philosophy* (tr. H.S. Harris and W. Cerf, State University of New York Press, Albany 1977, p. 90).

albeit one that cannot be established as long as enlightenment simply triumphs. Such a context, in which the world of the understanding would no longer function as a substitute for concrete life, can only be descried once we have succeeded in articulating an appropriate relationship to the Enlightenment itself and relativising its one-sidedly dogmatic character. And Hegel describes this, in contrast with the 'understanding' [*Verstand*], as the work of 'reason' [*Vernunft*] insofar as it is the expression of the Absolute.

The wounds of reflection as something that can only be healed through reflection itself is a constant theme throughout Hegel's work, although it progressively appears there in an ever more differentiated form. The early political and theological writings project this new unity that is to be produced in Hegel's own time in the wake of the French Revolution as a reconciled shape of life, as a community of love conceived in essentially pneumatological terms. Later on, a practical and a theoretical aspect begin to emerge specifically in their own right. The theoretical dimension eventually assumes the form of a self-contained encyclopaedic system, whereas the practical dimension is treated in terms of the 'ethical world' that is expressly thematised as a philosophy of right. In a famous letter to his young friend Schelling, written when Hegel was still in search of his own philosophical identity, he made the following comments about these two aspects of his developing project: 'In the course of my intellectual education, which began from the subordinate needs of mankind, I inevitably found myself driven forth to Science, and the ideal of my youth also inevitably transformed itself at the same time into the reflective form of a system; and now I ask myself, while I am still occupied with this, how I can find my way back towards intervention in the lives of men'.[8]

The coherent system, one still in the process of genesis when Hegel wrote his letter, is developed precisely to enrich the philosophical 'Idea' with all the required essential content and thus to heal the cleft between concept and reality. The greatness, or the failure, of the Hegelian system depends essentially upon the degree to which this concept of total mediation can itself be sustained. The ethical world, on the other hand, represents a historically developed reality that is supposed to facilitate a political form of life that lies beyond legal positivism and the abstract interiority of pure morality. The modern constitutional state, as conceived by Hegel, has relinquished that opposition between

---

[8] Hegel, letter to Schelling of 2 November 1800.

subjectivity and substantiality, between reflection and actuality, that initially defined the terms in question. The plausibility of a practical philosophy that attempts to overcome the one-sided character of the Enlightenment critique of social institutions depends upon the degree to which it also permits reason to offer a well-grounded affirmation of the *status quo*, and not merely a stereotypical repudiation of the latter. I do not wish to discuss here these still vigorously contested claims that Hegel's fully elaborated conception effectively implies.[9] But it is certainly easier to endorse Hegel's original vision of a new unity along such lines than it is to accept the actual execution of this project in all particulars and details. But I now return to the principal theme under discussion.

III

Hegel's critique of the Enlightenment also appears at an important juncture in his *Phenomenology of Spirit*. In the course of the *Phenomenology*, which displays all the shapes of historically determined consciousness as stages along the path of spirit's self-actualisation, the task is precisely to clarify the apparent right with which a specific social product of culture [*Bildung*] is presented as actuality itself. 'Culture' is here described in a pejorative fashion, and discussed under the rubric of 'self-alienated spirit'. We see how the artificially produced world of culture posits, over against the original one, a second actuality in which the cultured individual disappears amongst his fellow cultured individuals. The world of culture is created above all through language, which is where the mediated character of spirit acquires explicit existence for itself. Insofar as the individual expresses himself, he is thereby effectively present for others, and social existence itself immediately assumes the shape of language.

In contrast to current perspectives strongly oriented to the theory of communicative interaction, Hegel does not regard the linguistically constituted community as the final word of reason, but rather as its mere *semblance*. For the more actuality is replaced by language, the more it forfeits its own substance. The domain of culture thus presents us with an 'absolute and universal perversion and alienation', and the

---

9 As far as the actual development of Hegel's system is concerned, I refer the reader to my earlier study, *Zur Sache der Dialektik* (Stuttgart 1980); and with regard to the *Philosophy of Right*, to my forthcoming book, *Polis und Staat* (Frankfurt am Main, 2000).

language that expresses this process perfectly encapsulates the content of such a world. 'The language of disintegration is the perfect language and is the true existing spirit of this entire world of culture'.[10] The 'speech fully aware of its own confusion', which Hegel finds exemplified in Diderot's portrayal of 'Rameau's Nephew', represents the cynicism embodied in the linguistic articulation of this fundamental alienation. Hegel's inspired exploitation of Diderot's glittering satire rightly belongs amongst the most celebrated and brilliant passages of the *Phenomenology of Spirit*, as well as providing an outstanding example of fertile interaction between philosophy and literature.[11]

At that time, Hegel was familiar with Diderot's unpublished text only through the translation by Goethe. But he immediately perceived the embodiment of refined insanity in the nephew of the famous composer Rameau as an extreme expression of the internal paradoxes of the Enlightenment. Diderot describes this figure as a mixture of 'bon sens et de déraison', as a witty but wretched existence that belongs to the chattering intellectual environment of the coffee-house, but is wholly inappropriate, and expressly recognises it is inappropriate, as far as the reasonable conduct of human life is concerned. 'Rien ne dissemble plus de lui que lui-même', as Diderot puts it.[12] It is from this that Hegel derives the 'speech fully aware of its own confusion' that so typifies the realm of culture.

In contrast to this, Hegel presents the 'language of the simple consciousness', whose honourable character soon falls victim to the arts of rhetoric. There is an obvious self-deception involved here, for the world of culture cannot itself be undone by the means of culture itself. In a passage that is clearly aimed at Rousseau, Hegel writes: 'If the simple consciousness finally demands the dissolution of this whole world of perversion, [. . . .] then this demand cannot mean that reason should relinquish once again the spiritually cultivated consciousness which it has acquired, should simply submerge the fully developed wealth of its moments once again in the simplicity of the natural heart, in the immediate wildness of the animal consciousness, which is also described as nature or innocence. On the contrary, the demand for this dissolution

---

[10] Hegel, *Phänomenologie des Geistes*, ed. J. Hoffmeister (Hamburg 1952), p. 370 f.; *Phenomenology of Spirit*, tr. A.V. Miller (Oxford University Press 1977), p. 316f.

[11] Cf. H.R. Jauss, *Ästhetische Erfahrung und literarische Hermeneutik* (Frankfurt am Main 1982), p. 490 ff., and the dissertation by R. Groh, *Ironie und Moral im Werk Diderots* (Munich 1984), which also refers to Jauss in this connection.

[12] Diderot, *Oeuvres choisies* (Paris 1884), p. 392.

can only be directed to the *spirit* of culture itself, in order that it might return out of its confusion to itself as *spirit*, and win for itself a still higher consciousness'.[13]

Instead of the moralistic repudiation of the ambiguous consciousness that dissipates all content in its brilliant chatter, the task is rather to lift, to 'sublate', the world of culture into a higher and more comprehensive shape of spirit. This shape has been implicitly prepared in the background insofar as 'the disintegration of consciousness that expresses itself and is conscious of itself as such' is indeed appropriate to an actual world in which everything appears as vain and futile. This consciousness, as Hegel says, 'knows how to give correct expression to each moment in relation to the other, in general, how to express accurately the perversion of everything; it knows better than each what each moment is, no matter what its specific character may be. Since it knows what is substantial from the side of the disunion and conflict that is united within the latter, but not from the side of this union, it understands very well how to pass judgement upon it, but has forfeited the ability to grasp it'.[14] The proximity between loss of actual substance and the insubstantial chatter surrounding it is much closer than one imagines. The dialectical strategy consists precisely in transforming the prevailing alienation into the sudden insight that consciousness and actuality correspond with one another and constitute an identity. The mediation has therefore already transpired; the only task is to recognise this mediation for what it is, and thus awake from the confusion that surrounds us.

The original opposition through which the 'cultured' consciousness has become divorced from historical actuality can effectively be resolved insofar as we grasp precisely the manner in which consciousness and actuality do relate and correspond to one another. The further development of spirit depends upon a contradiction that spirit has itself engendered and that spirit is therefore equally capable of resolving – an example of the ancient theme of the power that heals the wound it first created. The true relationship between spirit and world will ultimately be identified as religion, which for its part represents the last phenomenological shape of consciousness before the final standpoint of absolute knowledge that concludes and re-traverses the entire preceding development.

---

[13] Hegel, *Phänomenologie*, p. 374; *Phenomenology*, p. 319.
[14] Ibid., p. 375; *Phenomenology*, p. 320.

But we have not yet arrived at such a position. The world of culture itself gives rise to the shape of believing consciousness that the Enlightenment in the proper sense now feels called upon to oppose. And here Hegel offers an approach that is well worth taking seriously. His interpretation suggests that the official Enlightenment campaign against 'superstition' is itself a product of the world of culture. In contrast to the perspective that is generally presented in textbook accounts of the period, the progressive critique mounted by the Enlightenment is directed not against the obscurantist remnants of an ancient but persisting tradition, but against a partner that has the same origin as the Enlightenment itself. The struggle between the respective forces of light and darkness is thereby demoted to the status of an immanent engagement between two aspects of a single shape. Following this line of thought, Hegel essentially relativises the Enlightenment by presenting it as the result of, rather than the motive power behind, the world of culture. The authentic claim to independence originally raised on behalf of free reflection is thereby inserted within a much broader historical context.

The relevant shapes of consciousness fail in each case fully to understand their own essential character. Over against their own self-interpretation, therefore, they must be reminded that they themselves represent phases of a broader overall development. The Enlightenment is also subjected to such a transformative interpretation. Its self-proclaimed 'struggle with superstition' now appears as an invention of the protagonists of enlightenment that serves to legitimate their own ambiguous existence, and thereby belongs to the domain of deliberate deception that is characteristic of the 'cultured consciousness'. But in truth, the spirit has already advanced beyond this. The arguments and conflicts of the Enlightenment culminate in the 'absolute freedom and terror' of the French Revolution. This destructive experience reveals that the time now calls for a new shape of spirit that is no longer characterised by the delusory confusions of the world of culture. For it is manifestly clear that the Revolution is unable to discover any non-violent resolution to the problem of uniting knowledge with virtue, of uniting free reflection with a properly human life.

The new unity of ethical life, of which the early idealists had originally dreamed, is here assigned its appropriate place in the perspective of world history. Hegel, who harboured a certain philosophical patriotism and hoped to do his part in teaching speculative philosophy 'to speak German', watches in the *Phenomenology* as self-conscious spirit 'passes over into a new country', moves, that is, from France over into Germany.[15] From the nineteenth century up until today, critics of Hegel have recommended that we cross this border in the opposite direction. Comparison with the French situation is supposed to help and correct Teutonic traditionalism, as if this chapter of the Enlightenment had not already revealed its consequences. This is an issue that has remained acutely topical throughout the second half of the twentieth century.

IV

I should now like to draw some general conclusions from the two principal reactions to the 'dialectic of enlightenment' that we have previously discussed. To this end, I present a series of theses that, at least in part, run counter to a number of convictions that are widely and fondly entertained at the present time.

The principal result of our discussion indicates that the general process of continuous rationalisation cannot be consolidated as a new form of life that offers new certainties to human beings who have lost the old ones. Thus my first thesis asserts: *the Enlightenment can provide no answer to the question concerning a new form of life in the modern world.* This question itself is naturally a product of the Enlightenment, since the older traditional forms of social life were never troubled by this question. For then one lived as one had always lived, as earlier generations and ages had already shown one how to live, and as human beings would continue to live in future in accordance with their very nature. The sense of solidarity and harmony with the cosmos or with an essentially divine order of the world created the required confidence and trust in the continuities of the accustomed form of life.

Once this unquestioned stability becomes problematic, the deliberate challenging of tradition spontaneously generates a felt need for new criteria that can orient our practical and social life. The existing world is required to demonstrate its legitimacy, is abandoned to potentially critical exposure by all and sundry, is subjected to a radical critique that cannot itself be ultimately grounded. This generates a historical dynamic without any *telos* in which it might eventually be fulfilled and thereby come to rest. For the task of critical examination and justification can never, in principle, be concluded. Critique is always capable of finding new objects to criticise, including the actual consequences of

---

[15] Ibid., p. 422; also cf. 350; *Phenomenology*, p. 363.

its own interventions at earlier stages of the process. The fact that this activity of critical reflection is capable of being extended indefinitely results in the unlimited consumption of finite resources. The historian Koselleck has spoken in this connection of the essentially 'accelerating tendencies' of the modern age. Thus my second thesis: *rationalisation is a continually self-generating process without end.*

The activity of critique was originally pursued on the assumption that the world was more irrational than it was rational, and that the dissemination of enlightenment required a tireless struggle to dispel the remaining darkness. The longer the struggle persisted, the greater the resulting illumination of the world would become. Persisting irrationality would be gradually eliminated thanks to the activity of reason. But the fact that, despite undeniable progress in certain respects, the battle front remained much the same, the fact that enlightenment impulse still continued to find itself in the position it had reached in the seventeenth and eighteenth centuries, strongly suggested that something had gone fundamentally wrong. The resulting disillusionment over the unfulfilled programme of enlightenment was subsequently analysed and addressed in different ways. I suggest that we can distinguish three specific forms of response to this situation.

One response is to transform the formerly imminent goal of real historical change into an ever-more distant and receding goal, so that the anticipated revolution on earth finally disappears in the end of time itself. This postponement to the point of an unachievable utopia results from the eventual recognition that the process of change itself has now assumed essential pride of place. It is in this way that the 'eschatological' faction attempts to explain the continuing failure to realise the original programme of transformation. And here in part we can witness the re-emergence of those theological premises of the classical notion of progress that secularising thought had formerly rejected (Walter Benjamin provides a good example).

An alternative attempt to come to terms with the continuing dynamic of rationalisation as a permanent predicament can be identified, surprisingly enough, in the response of aesthetics. One may well ask what the one phenomenon has to do with the other. Modern aesthetics arises when the pressure of modern scientific knowledge dissolves the older idea of teleology, which once endowed the actually existing world with a comprehensive and sustaining sense of meaning. Once this metaphysically grounded meaning is placed in question, man himself must recover this loss of meaning through the powers of his own reason, as manifested in the theoretical knowledge of science and the practical attempt to transform the world in accordance with human wishes. But as long as science still remains incomplete – for there is always so much more to know – and as long as the practical transformation of the world also appears unfinished, the aesthetic perspective would seem to offer a possible route of escape. For the latter permits us, at a stroke, to act as if the world did possess meaning, as if we were indeed at home there, without our having to redeem this imaginary reconciliation of subject and object by providing a proper theoretical justification and a corresponding practical effort to bring it about. There are certainly signs that now, at the close of the modern age, a creeping aestheticisation of the life-world represents the required escape from the dilemma of an essentially unfulfilled and unrealisable process of rationalisation.[16] Adorno has contributed some essential insights in this connection.

Finally, there is a third possible way of compensating for the dialectic of enlightenment. Here I am thinking of the philosophical theory of communicative action, which has recently come to assume the role of an ethics. This approach undertakes to institutionalise the process of critical reflection itself. The free-floating activity of reflection is no longer simply restricted to a negative critique of the existing state of affairs, because this activity lacks any authentic orientation as such. The procedural forms of rational communication in general are now consolidated as a form of life in its own right. The methodical pursuit of unforced argumentation provides the linguistic model for a feasible, rather than imaginary, form of social interaction that can assume a 'substantial' character without arousing the charge of irrationalism. In my opinion, this idea suffers from a problematic idealisation of our linguistic resources, which are never simply the untarnished mirror of reason, but are always also an expression of the historical conditions of understanding and misunderstanding. The sophistical aspect that Hegel identified in the language of culture can only be denied at the cost of incurring self-deception or imposing a kind of philosophical edict. Language is not liberated from distortion simply by defining it independently of real linguistic praxis. There may well be good reasons for subscribing to the postulate that language must not betray the

---

[16] For more on this, cf. the essay 'Mutmaßliche Umstellungen im Verhältnis von Kunst und Leben', in my collection *Ästhetische Erfahrung* (Frankfurt am Main 1989). It is obvious that Habermas wishes to provide a systematic response to the melancholic neo-Marxism developed by Max Horkheimer and Theodor Adorno during their period of emigration in California and presented in the *Dialectic of Enlightenment* (1947).

universal for the merely particular. But this demand does not prevent this happening even and precisely in the name of reason where certain interested parties are concerned. Although he has defended the communicative model of reason with considerable verve, Habermas has not yet succeeded in resolving the problem of the resulting degeneration of language, unintended and unanticipated as it is.

My third thesis asserts: we can identify three ways of addressing the paradox of enlightenment that the promised unification of theory and praxis has not been achieved despite all efforts directed to this end: (a) an eschatological explanation, which effectively repeats earlier theological elements, (b) an aestheticising solution, which leaves the desired reconciliation hovering in the hypothetical mode of an 'as if', and (c) a linguistic substitute, which imagines social life in the light of the idealised rules of language. *But none of these possible approaches is capable of compensating the felt deficit within the life-world that has been produced by the process of rationalisation in general.*

The danger that threatens the genuine success of enlightenment is grounded in the dogmatism of the latter itself. If this is indeed the case, it is possible to understand why the continuous struggle to maximise rationality can never reach an end where a new life, one that is more than a thematisation of the old one, could properly begin. But as long as the historical process continues to live off circumstances and conditions that it cannot renew, it cannot avoid interpreting and elevating itself as the desired end in question. This predicament generates an ambiguous state of constantly rekindled hopes and permanent disillusionment, where the supposed progress more nearly resembles a vicious circle and the associated mood wavers between the extremes of enthusiasm and bitterness. In my opinion, Hegel had already grasped the curious predicament of modernity with incomparable clarity, and had also analysed its core elements. It is quite true that Rousseau's moralising protest against the accomplishments of civilisation is more appealing to the ears of the present age. In this respect, there are many contemporary disciples of Rousseau who do not realise that this is what they are. But Hegel's diagnosis of the situation is nonetheless a superior one.

Hegel rightly felt that his contemporaries had failed to grasp the process in question as a characteristic condition, that they had misunderstood the versatile activity of critical reflection as if it were itself a substantial comprehension of the actual world. He was also right in encouraging enlightened reflection to relativise its own claims, to take its proper place within a broader context of rational structures where it would represent a part rather than the whole itself. Hegel's own proposal was designed to re-articulate the modern constitutional state as a similarly differentiated whole that would no longer be torn apart by the abstract opposition between the existing world and the exercise of critical reflection precisely because the substantial character of social institutions was capable of meeting the claims of free subjectivity. In this way, the autonomous individual would finally be able to feel at home in the actual surrounding world. Hegel's proposal, in the historically concrete form of the Prussian reform state of the time, has remained an object of continuing controversy. In substantive terms, the socialist tradition effectively inherited Hegel's project, but projected it into the future realisation of a truly free society. That has certainly brought us no closer to the desired end, as all historical experience during the last century has clearly demonstrated.

Hence my concluding thesis: *the dialectic of enlightenment will not be consolidated unless and until the process of rationalisation can be 'sublated' within a broadly accepted form of life in which reason is visibly articulated as such for everyone.* To this extent we can say that Hegel's proposal – in one concrete form or another – is still a historical task that confronts us.[17]

---

[17] Cf. the concluding chapters on the European project in my book, *Polis und Staat* (note 9).

8

CLOSURE AND THE UNDERSTANDING
OF HISTORY

This chapter undertakes to elucidate three basic issues. Starting from a discussion of Hegel's philosophy of history as the exemplary expression of a historically oriented form of thinking, I examine the judgements that Hegel's nineteenth century successors passed upon his project. For there were basically two ways in which they typically reacted to the appearance of definitive closure that marked the Hegelian standpoint (Section I). Then I analyse the specific claim that is actually mounted by Hegel's system with respect to historical time (Section II). And, finally, I attempt to clarify the task of historical reflection regarding the formal structures that underlie the controversial claim to historical closure on the part of philosophical thought (Section III).

I

The controversy concerning the definitive and conclusive character of Hegel's philosophy effectively broke out almost immediately after his death. The 'Young Hegelians' argued for the necessity of developing Hegel's philosophy beyond the systematic shape it had assumed in the hands of its original creator, and finally completing it as a 'philosophy of action' oriented to the future. This approach, now adopted from the perspective of political *praxis*, effectively repeated an argument that had already been broached with regard to *systematic* philosophical issues in the wake of Kant's thought. For at the very close of the eighteenth century, the early idealists, starting from the 'premises' that Kant himself had supplied, undertook the task of enthusiastic speculative reconstruction in philosophy in the name of a renewal of metaphysics. The transcendental philosophy of Kant had intended to ground the possibilities and limits of metaphysics as a science of pure reason. But Kant himself, according to their objections, had halted at a halfway point, and a further, and final and decisive, step was still required. This is what Fichte had expressly demanded, and he had been followed here by the anonymous author of the so-called *Earliest System Programme of German Idealism.* And Hegel's *Encyclopaedia of the Philosophical Sciences* would ultimately represent the final fruition of the movement that had wanted to move out beyond Kant precisely by appeal to Kant.

In attempting to develop Hegel's philosophy further, the Young Hegelians initially took issue with the *Encyclopaedia* and its claim to provide a definitive synthesis of all relevant knowledge. For they had rightly observed that Hegel alone, in contrast to his idealist predecessors, had been bold enough to bring *metaphysics and history* into the most direct relationship. The intellectual development that led from Reinhold through Fichte to Schelling had essentially been concerned with providing better foundations for a projected system, conceived in the light of Kant's discovery of the *a priori* dimension of knowledge. But Hegel himself was initially concerned with a rather different problem. Hegel's intention, from the critical writings of his Jena period through to his first major work that appeared under the enigmatic title of the *Phenomenology of Spirit,* lay in systematically elaborating the necessity of a specific historical emergence of the desired system.[1]

Hegel's observation of his philosophical contemporaries had shown him how the various proposals for such a system had simply overtaken one another in turn and all fallen victim to their own time without being able to recognise and understand this process itself. The task that now forcibly imposed itself upon Hegel's mind was that of anchoring the idea of systematic philosophy firmly and explicitly in the demands of the time itself and thus mediating between the external conditions for the actual appearance of such a philosophy. It was a question of carefully identifying the influence of those irrational factors at work in the immediate appearance of philosophical thought upon the historical scene. Hegel solved this problem by reflexively expounding the entire history of spirit up to the point where he could make his own philosophical voice clearly heard. That is how the *Phenomenology* comes to represent a 'preparation' for his own system of philosophy.

The Polish aristocrat August von Cieszkowski was the first thinker who attempted to overcome Hegel's thought precisely by developing

---

[1] I have pursued this issue in further detail in Chapter 6 of this book, 'Hegel's Concept of Phenomenology'.

it even further. The outsider Cieszkowski applied this typically post-Kantian strategy for the purpose of opening up Hegel's philosophy of history to the dimension of the new. He criticised the Hegelian position for concerning itself solely with the past when the real task of philosophy was to try and shape the future. Moses Hess, Arnold Ruge and the early Marx would soon come to share the same perspective and join with others in forming the 'Young Hegelian' faction. In his *Prolegomena to Historiosophy* of 1838, Cieszkowski adopted Hegel's own speculative approach in order to oppose the self-limitation of philosophy to the retrospective understanding of reality. Philosophy and history must rather be fused together to become what Cieszkowski called 'historiosophy' as a means of addressing the needs of the future. For otherwise, the required 'realisation of the vocation of mankind' would necessarily remain unfulfilled. The question concerning the future thus intrinsically belongs to the philosophical comprehension of history, and cannot artificially be excluded from the purview of the latter.

'The totality of world history, therefore, must absolutely and thoroughly be understood within the speculative trichotomy; but given the freedom that belongs to further development, it is not itself a part of history – namely, that which has already transpired, but precisely the totality of history that must thereby be grasped in an organic and speculative manner. But the totality of history is itself determined from the perspective of the past and the future, of the path that has already been traversed and of the path that remains to be traversed, and this gives rise to the primary demand: to vindicate the knowledge of the essence of the future in the eyes of speculation'.[2] For the epochs of the ancient and the modern world will necessarily be succeeded by the third 'synthetic' epoch that represents the task of the future. Spirit cannot simply dwell in the self-comprehension of the present but must rather acknowledge its essentially 'self-activating character'. In accordance with the laws of previous development, a 'philosophy of action' must now undertake to shape the coming, and final, age of human history.

'In Hegel, the practical dimension is still absorbed in the theoretical, has yet to distinguish itself properly from the latter, is still regarded, so to speak, as a tributary of the theoretical. But the true and authentic vocation of the practical is to be a particular and specific, and indeed

---

[2] *Prolegomena zur Historiosophie* (reprint Hamburg 1981), p. 7f.

even the highest, level of spirit'.[3] Cieskowski adopts the chiliastic perspective of the imminent end of days, and effectively continues the programme of Enlightenment philosophy of history as it had been formulated, for example, by Condorcet. In his *Esquisse d'un tableau historique des progrès de l'esprit humain* of 1795, Condorcet, an aristocratic sympathiser with the French Revolution who also became one of its victims, already attempted to prophesy the future on the basis of the laws that had supposedly characterised the previous development of mankind. As the final link in a continuous historical chain, the coming epoch will inevitably bring the attainment of human perfection, where happiness, fame and virtue await us. And the understanding of history we have already acquired permits us to anticipate a logical end to all previous development. This orientation towards a final end, the theological roots of which have been clearly explored by Karl Löwith[4], also enters directly into the dialectic of theory and practice elaborated by the Young Hegelians in immediate relation to their contemporary world.

The tradition of historicism, on the other hand, provided an alternative way of appropriating and inheriting the insights of the Hegelian system. With his idea of 'culture' [*Bildung*], Herder had already suggested the unpredictable and complex variety of developments in and through which historical mankind is capable of discovering and actualising its essential character as 'Humanity'. This approach certainly salvages something of the teleological perspective of a 'Providence' that effectively underlies the philosophy of history, but it refuses to adopt a precise position with regard to the end and completion of the historical process. Herder himself thinks about this process in entirely immanent terms, and historicism takes up and further accentuates this perspective. In the midst of actual historical development, it is never possible for us to determine when and where that development might attain its appointed end and thus arrive inevitable at a final position of stasis. For the processes of cultural development are capable of being continued indefinitely. Although this ongoing process – that is, the constant creation of continuity – no longer rests upon some anticipation of a final end, it does not thereby sink back into a flow of arbitrary change. For the production of new connections and relationships can, in principle, proceed for ever.

---

[3] Ibid., p. 120.
[4] Karl Löwith, *Meaning in History* (Chicago 1949).

The historian Johann Gustav Droysen, himself a student of Hegel's, expressed this particular approach in his lectures on method that present his systematic doctrine of history: 'However deeply rooted in the needs of the human spirit the desire to clarify both the origins and the ultimate ends of humanity may be, however persistently theological and philosophical speculation alike, arguing from the self-certainty of the finite human spirit, have attempted to pursue this general aim, the very nature of the empirical sciences, focussed as they are solely upon the here and now, reveals the impossibility of ever penetrating to the first origin or to the end of days'. And Droysen continues: 'if all our investigations recognise or comprehend the ethical and social world as a ceaseless and continuous process in which ends and purposes are connected with one another through the links of an infinite chain, then the ultimate end or purpose that moves, embraces and drives all the others, the highest unconditional and conditioning purpose, the end of ends [*der Zweck der Zwecke*] can never be grasped and known along the path of empirical knowledge'.[5]

The difference between philosophy and the positive sciences lies in the empirical principle that characterises the latter in contrast to any quasi-theological conception of some 'absolute mover'. Human aims and purposes can only validly be understood in the context of the here and now of experience, and it is therefore meaningless to try and transcend this limitation and connect them to an ultimate end that would itself no longer be succeeded by new aims and purposes and further processes of continuity. Although this appeal to empirical experience certainly reflects the self-understanding of the emerging discipline of autonomous history, we must nevertheless operate with some caution here. For in spite of these efforts to establish history as a rigorous discipline of its own, there remains a crucial difference in approach over against the method of the natural sciences, which proceed by observation and the production of hypotheses on the basis of empirical data. For although one can approach nature through the process of scientific experiment, the historian must rely rather on the process of interpretation. No historical 'fact' is ever immediately accessible to us because it belongs by its very character to the past, even if the historian, such as Thucydides, for example, sets to work immediately after the events he is to describe. Generally speaking, historiography proceeds by way of interpretation based upon the investigation of the relevant sources.

[5] J.G. Droysen, *Historik* (1868), ed. R. Hübner, Munich 1971, p. 269 f.

But historical sources do not spring forth spontaneously on their own account, and must therefore be brought to speak, as it were, in a methodical fashion.

In rejecting the idea of some transcendent mover standing behind the historical process, Droysen can naturally refer to the pervasive theological metaphorics of Hegel's philosophy of history, which of course does speak of theodicy and our knowledge of God. The new scientific ideal of autonomous history must be defended against such metaphysical notions. In a very similar way, Dilthey would later claim that Hegel's philosophical recourse to history was itself productive, even though the metaphysically grounded system as such could only distort the picture. 'Insofar as life in its totality, insofar as experiences, processes of understanding, historical connections, the power of the irrational, now take the place that Hegel ascribed to universal reason, we are faced with the problem of how the science of history itself is possible. This problem did not exist for Hegel. His metaphysics had already disposed of it as a problem. But today our task is the reverse one – namely, to recognise the given phenomenon of historical expressions of life as the genuine foundation of historical knowledge'.[6]

The historicist successors of Hegel did not attempt, therefore, to extend the dialectic into the field of real history, as the politically motivated Young Hegelians had done. On the contrary, they rejected the pretensions of dialectic precisely in the name of real history. It was not the *future* but the *past* that functioned for them as the criterion of historical criticism. But in both cases, the relationship between spirit and reality is explicated in a one-sided and reductive manner. The central and crucial point of Hegel's systematic philosophy, which had consisted in a knowledge of the *present* on the basis of an actually accomplished 'absolute knowing', fell victim to the demands of one or other of the dimensions of time regarded as dominant in each case.

Now the orientation to the present, the essentially *contemporary character* of the Hegelian system, depends upon the idea that 'the labour of the concept', although it always was, is and will be active in the world, has expressly realised its end and purpose, after many turns and attempts in the history of philosophy, only in Hegel's own epoch, if not in Hegel's own thought itself. For otherwise, systematic philosophy would once again have remained yet another project, haunted in turn by the shadow of being historically conditioned. Instead of philosophy's being in a

[6] W. Dilthey, *Gesammelte Schriften*, VII, Göttingen 1958, p. 151 f.

position to fulfil its concrete task of 'grasping its time in thought', it would then merely give uncontrolled expression to the changeable spirit of the time. Hegel's famous formula from the 'Preface' to the *Philosophy of Right* articulates the essentially dialectical relationship of spirit and history: it is not the time that determines philosophical thought, but rather the latter, which is to sublate the former.

We have now outlined the two basic reactions to the Hegelian philosophy that have continued to exercise an influence from the nineteenth century onwards. The original Young Hegelian appeal to shape the future actively reappears in all those forms of social philosophy that understand themselves in progressive political terms. It is above all the various types of Marxism, in pursuing a winding path between orthodoxy and revisionism, that consciously sustained this hope and aspiration for the future. This kind of enterprise would now seem to have come to a final end. The historicist reinterpretation of Hegel, on the other hand, has effectively toned down the stronger claims associated with a systematic philosophy of spirit, and continued to develop in a broadly hermeneutical direction. The active process of 'understanding' can never in fact reach a final goal because every new historical present must in turn animate the past that lies behind it and strive to reconnect that past with itself.

II

First, it is necessary to clarify precisely how what we have called the essentially contemporary orientation of Hegel's thought assumes a central place in the self-understanding of this philosophy. It was Hegel's critical engagement with his own contemporaries, as we saw, that marked the beginning of his attempt to articulate philosophy in a systematic fashion. Hegel's most important early essay, composed during the period of his collaboration with Schelling in Jena, formulated a certain 'need of philosophy' grounded in the prevailing diremption of the epoch marked by the 'philosophy of reflection' that was characteristic of Kant and his immediate successors.[7] And this bifurcated condition of the modern age, which penetrates the social forms of life themselves, must now be reconciled through the unifying power of philosophical thought. This is the historical aspect that occasioned the Hegelian

---

7 G.W.F. Hegel, *Differenz des Fichteschen und Schellingschen Systems der Philosophie* (1801).

attempt to produce a comprehensive and self-contained system of philosophy.

The lectures that Hegel later offered on *The History of Philosophy* continued to develop this idea: 'The deeds of thought would seem initially, insofar as they are historical, to be a matter pertaining to the past and therefore to lie somewhere beyond *our actuality*. In fact, however, what *we* are, we also are historically, or more precisely: just as in this region, that of the history of thought, what is past is merely *one* dimension, so in what we are the universally imperishable is indissolubly connected with what we are historically'.[8] 'It is the universal spirit that is grasped thinkingly by philosophy; it is that through which philosophy thinks itself and thus forms the determinate and substantial content of philosophy. Every philosophy is philosophy of its time, is a link in the entire chain of spiritual development; philosophy therefore can only procure satisfaction for the interests that are appropriate to its own time'.[9]

These remarks clearly formulate the principal problem of all philosophy – namely, its double subjection to historical and systematic demands. The problem is by no means a new one, and has existed ever since Plato engaged with the pre-Socratic thinkers concerning the truth of being. Aristotle introduced his *Metaphysics*, which continued this question productively and thereby established certain lasting criteria for Western culture, with a brief historical outline of previous philosophical speculation. The whole problematic therefore cannot simply be interpreted as a symptom of intellectual decadence typically marking a later age overburdened by too much historical awareness. It is nonetheless true, after the Kantian revolution, which emphatically broke with the power of traditional metaphysics, that the tension between the historical site of thought and its supra-temporal aspirations has only been accentuated further. This predicament is not something that can simply be avoided – either by appeal to the ideal of a *philosophia perennis* timelessly prevailing over and beyond the realm of historical transformation, or by abandoning oneself to the waves of time that dictate the pulse of fashion to the exponents of philosophical opportunism.

Hegel's strategic response to these difficulties is to conceptualise the thinker's relationship to the contemporary age as something that is not *external* to philosophy at all. He thus prepares a way of integrating

---

[8] Hegel, *Geschichte der Philosophie, Werkausgabe* (Suhrkamp), vol. 18, p. 21.
[9] Ibid., p. 65.

that relationship as a specific manifestation of philosophy itself. This approach dissolves that opposition between the unity of philosophy as such and the plurality of its historically appearing forms, which has always provided the protagonists of 'healthy common sense' with cheap and ready arguments for their scepticism concerning the very possibility of ultimate philosophical truth. For Hegel, 'spirit' is not itself some transcendent entity whose status could simply be challenged by invoking examples of historical relativity. It is conceived rather as living movement of self-actualisation on the model of the Aristotelian *energeia*, which seeks expression in its own appropriate form. The life of spirit for Hegel thus consists precisely in the ongoing process of externalisation and re-appropriation. The various historical forms it assumes do not represent a loss of its essential substance, but rather demonstrate its intrinsic power to express its own character. For these forms are the forms of spirit itself as manifested through time. They are its forms, but spirit is not simply identical with them.

Since the spirit is not simply dispersed in some arbitrary multiplicity, but rather governs the relationship between its authentic universality and the plurality of external perspectives adopted with regard to it, it is capable of preserving its own *identity* precisely *in and through* these perspectives. The single enduring spirit, which the labour of the philosophical concept perpetually serves, expresses itself in historical terms, and does so necessarily. In this way, Hegel dialectically undermines the independence of an age that allegedly preserves its stubbornly particular character throughout the unfolding processes of historical time. For Hegel, there is no such thing as the existence of 'time', and in addition the existence of 'spirit', in such a way that the two could essentially come into conflict with one another. The time at issue here is not the chronometric time of the clock, but rather the horizon in the context of which new connections and relationships are constantly forged and shaped. Time is not the domain of mere chance and arbitrary change, but the very site of mediation and the inauguration of sense and significance.

That is why *world history* and the *temporal reference of thought* are so intimately connected in Hegel's eyes. As Hegel puts it in *his Lectures on the History of Philosophy*: 'What is to be shown is how the spirit of an age shapes the entire actuality and destiny of the latter in accordance with its own principle – and to present this entire structure in a properly comprehending fashion ... would constitute the object of philosophical world history in general. ... One consequence that follows from this is that philosophy is entirely identical with its time. Hence philosophy does not stand above its time, and is the knowledge of the substantial content of its time. Just as little does the individual, as a child of his time, stand above the latter. He simply manifests in his own form the substantial content of the time, which is the individual's own essential being. No one can truly get beyond his time, any more than he can get out of his own skin. On the other hand, however, philosophy does in accordance with its inner form stand above its time insofar as it thinks what the substantial spirit of the time is and thus makes that spirit into its object. Insofar as philosophy transpires within the spirit of its time, that spirit forms the determinate worldly content of philosophy.

'At the same time, however, philosophy, as the process of knowing, is also beyond that specific content it places over against itself in thinking. But it does so only in a purely formal fashion since it truly has no other content. But this knowing is precisely the actuality of spirit, the self-knowing of spirit, and the formal distinction is thus also a real and actual distinction. It is this knowing that then produces a new form of development, and such new forms are simply modes of knowing. Through the act of knowing, spirit posits a distinction between knowing and that which is. This in turn contains a new distinction, and thus it is that a new philosophy also arises. Philosophy constitutes, therefore, already a further character of spirit; it is the inner birthplace of that spirit which will later emerge in the shape of actuality'.[10]

What is crucial here is the necessary process through which spirit, in accordance with its very essence, both roots itself within a specific time and overcomes the specific shape it has given itself there. Spirit requires the first moment in order to manifest itself at all rather than simply dissolving as an empty fiction; but it also requires the second moment because no time-conditioned expression is ever sufficient to grasp philosophy completely without remainder. The actual *historical emergence* of philosophy has here been made the principled object of thought for the first time. In Hegel's view, philosophy must explicitly acknowledge its own mediation in and through history, while recognising that this admission neither impairs the authentic rational claims of philosophy nor results in an irrationalist position. For the unavoidable fact that philosophy has emerged historically in a specific manner can itself be productively and consistently transformed into an essentially philosophical insight. The labour of philosophical thought is the complementary moment that belongs to the historicity of spirit itself: the

[10] Ibid., p. 74 f.

unitary and substantial character of spirit as such must be deciphered within the specific historical forms of its appearance – that is, recognised and identified over and beyond the limited shapes of its epochal self-manifestation. Without the interpretive labour of philosophy, which discovers the permanent within the temporal, the historically self-articulating spirit would lack the echoing voice that effectively corresponds to it. The spirit is only properly grasped and understood as what it truly is when its given and specific actuality is transcended.

One could also express this dependence of a specific epochal content upon philosophical articulation in the following way: world history would never advance without the ceaseless activity of *probing interpretation* that rationally clarifies the concrete historical material presented to it and thus enables us to connect the latter with the broader context that ultimately embraces all periods and segments of time. If we only understand a single phase of this process, we cannot be said to have understood anything at all. To do philosophical justice to one specific phase is precisely to penetrate its surface to expose the substantial core, and thus to reveal its intrinsic connection with the whole. The difficult process of differentiating between the surface appearance, to which indeed the most striking and conspicuous features of an age may well cling, and the valid content that is concealed beneath that appearance involves establishing this connection with the totality of all times, even though the specific age in question only represents a single aspect of that totality. Philosophical interpretation is only really possible through this continual movement oriented as it is towards a totality that is itself never given at any particular time, and can indeed never be given in its entirety.

What I am principally concerned to challenge here is the frequently expressed view that Hegel's philosophy of history is actually based upon a metaphysics that is essentially enthroned beyond history itself and functions like some sovereign puppeteer pulling the strings of historical change.[11] It is quite true that metaphysics had always been conceived

---

[11] As, for example, in the otherwise highly instructive study by O.D. Brauer, *Dialektik der Zeit. Untersuchungen zu Hegels Metaphysik der Weltgeschichte* (Stuttgart 1982), when the author claims that 'what essentially transpires in the field of history, on Hegel's understanding of the historical domain, is nothing other than absolute spirit itself' (p. 166). This conclusion is all the more surprising since Brauer has already presented us with a detailed examination of Hegel's attitude to the 'Historical School of Law' (Savigny and Hugo) and Hegel's own theory of the institutional forms of the 'national spirits' in history – that is, the domain of 'objective spirit'.

as the absolute science of supra-temporal truth and thus as a science intrinsically incapable of entering into any direct relationship with time. But the idea of some omnipotent and omniscient director of events at work behind the scene of history belongs to those purely pictorial theological images of a transcendent God that Hegel is known to have explicitly repudiated ever since his earliest writings on religious and political themes. For it was the false 'positivity' of Christian dogma that had led to the loss of any concrete understanding of reality, and the task that presented itself to Hegel was precisely to situate and locate the full weight of reason *within* the historical and ethical life world itself.

It is obvious, of course, that reason does not effectively manifest itself in history in an essentially *uncontaminated* fashion. That is precisely why it requires to be deciphered by philosophical activity that simultaneously penetrates and transcends the status quo and thereby assists in expressing the overall significance of history as such. For it is never the case that the objective course of things simply unfolds independently while the reflecting observer stands by and watches. The subject, and its entire potential for reason, is entwined and involved in the very texture of the historical process itself. This is true both for the practical interests in which particular individuals are caught up and for the particular ways in which the reason of individuals is mediated with the universal. History develops by virtue of the unfolding and ongoing reflection that arises within specific historical situations and thereby as such also influences the historical process.

The *exemplary position* of philosophy in interpreting its own time in the light of broader historical perspectives can best be compared with the role of the 'world-historical individuals' who are also described in Hegel's *Philosophy of History* with the antiquated title of 'heroes' or with the rather modern expression, 'agents'.[12] 'They were practical and political individuals. But they were also thinking individuals who possessed insight into what was needful and what was *appropriate to the time* [*an der Zeit*]. That is precisely the truth of their time and their world, the next genus, as it were, that already lay within. Their task was to know this universal, the next and necessary level of their world, to make it their own end and to place all their effort therein. That is why these world historical individuals, the heroes of a specific time, must be acknowledged as the individuals of insight. What they say and what they do represent

---

[12] On this, cf. E. Angehrn, 'Vernunft in der Geschichte?', in *Zeitschrift für philosophische Forschung* 35, 1981, especially pp. 347 f.

what is best in the time. Great individuals willed as they did in order to satisfy not others, but themselves. What they might have received from others in terms of well-intentioned suggestions and advice would rather have been too narrow or inappropriate for them; for it is they themselves who showed the greatest understanding here, they from whom, on the contrary, all others have first learned to understand or appreciate the matter, or at least to accommodate themselves to it. For the more advanced spirit is the inner soul of all individuals, but it is the unconscious inwardness which the great men have first brought to consciousness for them. That is why the others now follow such leaders of souls, for they sense there the irresistible power of their own innermost spirit made manifest before them.'[13]

A great deal has been written about these 'world-historical individuals' who pursue their own interests and passions, but nonetheless succeed, despite the natural limitations of those interests, in unwittingly furthering and promoting the universal significance of the whole. And I do not intend to enter into this dispute here.[14] I am solely interested in the comparison that can be drawn with the interventions of the philosopher who is also rooted in a specific time. The important actor on the world political stage does not entertain the universal, the idea of progress or the happiness of humanity, as his end or purpose. Just like everyone else, he acts under conditions of contingency. But his concrete ends subsequently reveal themselves as ones that have furthered the process of historical development. Such an effect is impossible for outsiders or eccentrics who are so far out on the edges of things that their marginal activities are incapable of exerting any significant influence at all. Successful change cannot but reveal the great extent to which it is directly connected with the whole. It is in this way that others, whose own perspectives could never have disclosed so much, can nonetheless effectively recognise themselves in, or at least give their own consent to, the paradigmatic step that has been taken here.

[13] Hegel, *Vorlesungen über die Philosophie der Geschichte, Werkausgabe*, vol. 12, p. 46. Hegel, *Lectures on the Philosophy of History*, trans. J. Sibree (London 1861, reprint New York 1956), pp. 31–32.

[14] Observation of the events transpiring in Europe at the close of the twentieth century surely occasion some doubt about the well-established view that it is essentially anonymous structures, complexes of social groups, and purely functional changes that determine the course of history, and that the older traditional claim that it is individual human beings that make history is properly deserving of the contempt into which it has fallen. Who could genuinely explain the emergence of a figure like Gorbatchov on the basis of the 'nomenklatura' alone?

This view has been cruelly caricatured to imply acceptance of some fascistic 'leadership principle' in which the leader simply commands and the mass blindly follows accordingly. But what those with genuine *insight* here diagnose and practically apply in advance of broader public acknowledgement is simply the particular situation that is striving to emerge into the light of general social awareness. That is why the matter in question essentially concerns everyone, and is not something that some singular individual has imposed on all. A perceptive understanding of the actual situation requires extremely well-developed awareness of the fundamental structures and the potential tendencies within and beneath the surface appearance that is immediately evident to everyone. There is no doubt that great individuals such as Caesar and Napoleon, as agents, were men wholly dedicated to and absorbed in their own ends, but their acts also explicate the time in a way that was not otherwise accessible to their contemporaries.

No one else is as capable of determining his position at the time as convincingly as such world-historical individuals. For this requires the ability to anticipate the shape of the whole development from a single fixed point in the midst of unfolding events. As long as things are still in a state of flux, matters can take an unforeseen course. But the exemplary agent here resolutely grasps this potentiality and intervenes to shape the course of events, actively setting the actuality of the here and now in relation to the general direction of development. The only one who can be compared to the world-historical individual in this respect is the philosopher, whose conceptual understanding does not of course prophetically illuminate the time through practical intervention, but rather clarifies it explicitly through subsequent reflection.

It is thus an under-estimation of the complexity of Hegel's theory of spirit when it is interpreted in the closed and definitive fashion that turns it into some kind of secularised eschatology. There were in fact some in the Hegelian school who defended the view that world history effectively had concluded with the present age, that it had attained a definitive end without further possibilities of significant spiritual development.[15] But Hegel himself never spoke of an 'end' understood in this way.

---

[15] Cf. K.L. Michelet, *Geschichte der Menschheit in ihrem Entwicklungsgange seit dem Jahre 1775 bis auf die neuesten Zeiten* (Berlin 1859). In order to avoid the ominous date of 1789 as the decisive step into modernity, Michelet chooses the year of the Battle of Lexington [1775] during the American War of Independence. As far as the middle of the nineteenth century is concerned, Michelet regards Germany, the French Empire, and North America

III

This unorthodox comparison between philosophers and world-historical individuals is intended to challenge the usual claim that Hegel's philosophy of history essentially views the totality of events from a supposedly God's-eye perspective. But such an arrogant approach, remote as it is from the actual phenomena, is characteristic neither of the methodological procedure of the dialectic in general, nor indeed of Hegel's particular attitude to history, which, he tells us, 'we are to consider as it is'.[16] Hegel's realism, which must be strongly emphasised here, is animated by the intention of passing beyond the universality of thought as stubbornly maintained by the standpoint of reflection to penetrate the concrete actuality of historical events, but without forfeiting the trust that even this last particularised domain of experience can also disclose its rationality. This perspective ultimately relies upon a conception of the genuinely concrete character of reason, which is developed more precisely in the *Science of Logic*.

Hegel's logical model of 'speculation' implies a second-order reflection of reflection, or the self-application of the original act that already underlies all of our thinking. In the shape of this meta-reflection, Hegel intrinsically denies the universal status usually ascribed to thought by recalling the source of such thinking in the processes of abstraction. The initial exercise of reflection dissolves the given characteristics of something and reduces them to the universal features of a concept, while the second stage of reflection shows that the status of the concept in question is merely the result of an artificial intellectual operation.

as existing in a state of harmonious balance that gives good reason to hope for lasting peace and stability. In recent times, Francis Fukuyama has created some controversy with a comparable thesis concerning the 'end of history' in a work that also appeals to Hegel in this respect (*The End of History and the Last Man*, New York 1992). Fukuyama follows the originally Marxian claim, popularised by Alexandre Kojève, that Hegel's genuine philosophy of history is to be found in the *Phenomenology of Spirit*, and specifically in the chapter on the 'Master and Slave'. I have already pointed out the difficulties involved in this interpretation of Hegel's philosophy of history. Fukuyama's second error is the belief that historical facts are in a position to confirm his central hypothesis that, given the end of socialism, the liberal democracies of the Western type have succeeded in resolving relevant social contradictions and have definitively established themselves as the last word of political organisation. It has rapidly become clear that this too is one more 'interpretation' of events and, like all such interpretations, will in turn be relativised by subsequent historical developments. After 11 September 2001, we can see that the whole picture has changed dramatically in this respect. One should never, as long as history continues, attempt to sound 'The Final Trumpets of the Last Judgement'.

[16] Hegel, *Philosophie der Geschichte*, *Werkausgabe* vol. 12, p. 22; cf. also p. 20.

The concept cannot therefore be taken as the definitive resolution of the initially problematic question until it has been properly mediated in turn with its original starting-point. This methodically developed reversal and return does not imply the simple repudiation of the abstractive accomplishments of thought in order to restore, as it were, the *status quo ante*. But it does demand that we do not merely remain at the level of a universal that persists in independent isolation over against the given particular. For the universal as conceived and produced by reflection can only be obtained at the cost of relinquishing what makes the particular precisely this particular. The sublation of the artificially fixed opposition of moments here is directed towards the initial operation of reflection itself, but it is intended to restore the true richness of the matter at issue. By this indirect dialectical path, the full content of actuality, initially threatened by the negative power of reflection, is to be re-established by virtue of its own power.

The greatest challenge posed by the speculative dialectic is therefore not the one-sided emphasis upon thought as such. This is of course the burden of the usual objection that idealism conflates the real with mere thought. The greatest challenge lies rather in the claim that the self-relativisation of reflection produced by speculative reversal reconnects precisely with the genuinely *concrete character* of actuality itself. In other words: it is not reflection as thinking that is the scandalous moment here – for Hegel rightly observes that simply as human beings, and prior to all philosophising, we cannot possibly refrain from thinking. Consequently we always already stand in a certain opposition to actuality. But what is difficult for us to grasp is that the methodically exercised reflection of reflection does not have to lead us away from actuality into empty meta-levels of thought, but is quite capable of doing justice to actuality in its most original and concrete character. The general resistance to this line of thought is based upon the inherited schema of a fundamental *opposition* between subject and object, one so deeply rooted that it is difficult to evade. But once we properly recognise that subject and object are not intrinsically opposed by nature, but that they have become divorced from one another solely as a result of the separating act of reflection, we can overcome and relinquish the familiar conviction that actuality possesses a genuinely concrete wealth that a thought inevitably mired in abstraction can never hope to capture.

Now it is particularly in relation to history that this obsession with abstract *objectivity* is most misleading. The peculiar character of the historical domain cannot possibly derive from some independent reality radically detached from the activity of consciousness and spirit. We emphasised at the beginning of our discussion that the so-called historical facts are always the products of interpretation. They may well assume a fixed form over a long period of time as far as the general view of historians and the public is concerned. Thus they come to be regarded as certain and reliable. But this only remains the case until relevant revision suggests itself through further research and reinterpretation on the part of succeeding generations, which from their new level of retrospection rearrange and freshly re-articulate the former data. The debate concerning the beginning of the First World War is a familiar example here, but most of the established 'facts' of history can become similar matters of controversy. It is the living character of the ceaselessly interpreting spirit that creates, as it were, the concrete contours that a given historical event comes to assume in retrospect and within which it is subsequently transmitted. The human sciences appropriated and appealed to this indelible and original character of the spirit when they inherited the tradition of Hegelian speculation in the context of their own hermeneutic methods. From Dilthey through to Gadamer, the human sciences have fundamentally attempted to grasp historical reality as the authentic expression of something that is basically oriented to self-articulation in concrete forms.

If we return now to Hegel's *Science of Logic*, we can see that the last chapter of this work is particularly important as far as our central question is concerned. It is here that one of the most obscure texts in the history of philosophy attempts to clarify its own character and status. For at the end of the *Logic*, Hegel expressly thematises the definite and conclusive nature of the 'science' of philosophy as a whole. And, surprisingly enough, this turns out to be a question of *method*. The typically modern scientific reflection upon method, since Bacon and Descartes, posited clarification of the appropriate procedures as something prior to the actual acquisition of knowledge. And the critical enterprise of Kant's transcendental philosophy also followed the demands of this twofold approach insofar as it undertook to examine the limits and possibilities of knowledge before moving on to the substantively 'doctrinal' exposition and development of knowledge. In Hegel's dialectic, the situation is precisely the other way around. The concept must begin immediately with the matter itself, in order to move out from the initial mode of immediacy through the mediation of reflection, and realise, in gradual steps, through the procedures of reflection the full content of the 'matter at issue' [*die Sache selbst*].[17] That is why the explicit reflection upon method stands at the *end*, where there are no longer any new substantial moments to be considered, and essential clarity concerning the entirety of the previous development can be acquired.

The approach that is thus characteristic of a substantively oriented dialectic corresponds to Hegel's fundamental critique of the 'fixated' positions spontaneously generated by the 'philosophy of reflection', positions that remain caught up within the tensions of reflection and are incapable of establishing a properly transparent self-relation. The target of this critique is pre-eminently Kant, who is frequently charged, as in the 'Introduction' to the *Phenomenology of Spirit*, for example, with specifically obstructing access to the real issue by concentrating his entire attention upon refining the methodological instruments of philosophy. On the other hand, the dialectic does not simply set to work in a blind and immediate fashion, but proceeds rather from the indispensable insight that a beginning must always be made at a specific and determinate point, if indeed a beginning is to be made at all. The ineliminable immediacy of the beginning stringently indicates the further path to be taken insofar as that immediacy is itself to be sublated in turn. This basically represents the proper method for working into and working through the substantive materials that the concept is striving to explicate and articulate in their entirety. In the first place, the method consists simply in its application, and cannot be made into a separate object of investigation in its own right. Once the effort of appropriating the full wealth of substantive content has taken place, the dialectical method that was at work in the process can be brought specifically to transparent clarity.

'Accordingly, what is to be considered here as method is only the movement of the concept itself, the nature of which movement has already been recognised for what it is; but *first*, there is now the added *significance* that the *concept is everything*, and its movement is the *universal absolute activity*, the self-determining and self-realising movement. The method must therefore be recognised as the unrestrictedly universal, internal and external mode; and as the absolutely infinite force, to which no object, presenting itself as something external, remote from and independent of reason, could offer resistance or persist as a particular nature in opposition to it, or could not be penetrated by it. It is

---

[17] For further discussion on this, cf. my earlier study 'Die "Sache selbst" in Hegels System', in R. Bubner, *Zur Sache der Dialektik*, Stuttgart 1980.

therefore *soul and substance*, and anything whatever is comprehended and known in its truth only when it is *completely subjected to the method*; it is the method proper to every subject matter because its activity is the concept'.[18]

Closure here is defined in relation to a specific task, just as the 'beginning' was defined in relation to the same task. The mediated overcoming of the initial immediacy of the 'beginning' was accomplished through the speculatively refined and elaborated application of reflection, which, after successfully appropriating the relevant content, returns to the level of immediacy in order to inaugurate a new beginning.[19] This is what closes the circle of development in each case. But in truth we are confronted here, in Hegel's famous metaphor, with a 'circle of circles'.[20] Thus we cannot properly claim that the dialectic, under the logical control of constantly operative reflection, actually comes to an end at a specific point, that reflection is abruptly and arbitrarily terminated, and that a peaceful and henceforth unbreakable silence finally descends upon the whole process. Since Hegel has reinterpreted the ancient idea of the 'absolute' in essentially processual terms, there are always new cases of beginning and closure to be found. We are not presented with the eternally self-same stream of becoming, as in Heraclitus, or with the eternally self-same being, as in Parmenides. We are presented rather with tasks of thinking that call forth the exercise of reflection and the successful immersion in the matter at issue until it is recognised that 'the concept is everything'. And this is the point at which we look back methodologically over the previous course of development.

The tasks in question do not unexpectedly fall to us from heaven, any more than they present themselves as the selfsame tasks throughout every possible epoch. Hegel's provocative claim is that *the tasks of philosophy are always shaped by their own time*. This implies that we must properly identify the pressing tasks within the context of the specific epoch, and this is something that already requires the investment of explicit conceptual effort. Considered on this level, the immediacy of the beginning appears as the necessity of connecting directly with the time, which, although already characterised by a certain pre-philosophical aspect, nevertheless awaits penetrating definition and determination

---

[18] Hegel, *Wissenschaft der Logik*, ed. G. Lasson II, p. 486; *Hegel's Science of Logic*, trans. A.V. Miller (London: Allen and Unwin 1969), p. 826 (translation modified).

[19] Ibid., p. 499; *Science of Logic*, pp. 838ff.   [20] Ibid., p. 503 f.; *Science of Logic*, p. 842.

through the concept. Viewed from this perspective, we may say that every age and every time is latently philosophical, just as philosophy itself necessarily remains bound up with its time as its given point of departure. We can never externally determine or decisionistically decree a definitive end to the constantly required labour of mediation between existing actuality and active conceptual grasp. The dialectical engagement with the matter at issue can only be described as 'closed' when there is no disturbing remainder still to be mediated. This transpires when philosophy, from a position analogous to that occupied by the world-historical individuals as elucidated earlier, paradigmatically succeeds in establishing a relationship between concrete actuality and the universal. And that in turn simply signifies the process in which the previous course of history is articulated as a whole in relation to the present age.

The whole simply *is* rationally comprehended history as such, the history that continues to unfold and remains permanently oriented in turn to a potential totality. The full wealth of the totality of history changes with the respective standpoint from which it is presented, but this history always forms a certain whole as configured in relation to the present. We cannot avoid recognising, therefore, that from the perspective of the most advanced historical consciousness, history is neither a mere collection of facts, as in the ancient notion of 'historia', nor a completely open-ended and purposeless series of events. History is always the entirety of history considered in explicit relation to that site, within history itself, where we thematise and represent it to ourselves. This enterprise can certainly come to an end in the sense that it generates a seamless unification of the universal and concrete actuality. But that is also precisely the hour that calls for renewal of the same task. The owl of Minerva begins her flight only with the falling of the dusk. But every evening heralds a new day.

AESTHETICS

9

FROM FICHTE TO SCHLEGEL

I

The history of the human spirit is richly characterised by the presence of constructive misunderstandings. This can surely be explained by the fact that certain ideas crave direct expression even before they are capable of finding an adequate formulation for themselves. Such ideas naturally attach themselves to some already existing intellectual constellation that initially appears to provide confirmation or deeper justification for them although they have in fact already opened up quite new paths of thinking.

This state of affairs should be distinguished from the processes of 'affirmation' and 'critique'. In the former case, a given thought or developed theory is imitated or further varied by some successor. In the latter case, some explicit position of contrast and contestation is assumed instead. Productive misunderstanding, on the other hand, arises whenever we appeal to a certain theoretical position that appears to anticipate our own, and thereby fail precisely to recognise the difference that has in fact already been opened up between them.

One can of course claim that the hermeneutic appropriation of anything always involves a process of 'understanding differently' and that the boundary between correct reproduction and adoption of new horizons of interpretation can never therefore be drawn precisely or definitively. But this hermeneutical observation, justified as it is, does not necessarily commit us to that happy form of intellectual defeatism that apostrophises every reception of ideas already formulated by others as an inevitable transformation and effect of distance, as an oscillating play of reflections and counter-reflections. The deconstructive school inspired by Derrida has now advanced to the extreme of deliberately eliminating the difference between understanding and misunderstanding. In fact, we must acknowledge that increasing distance from the immediate situation of transmission facilitates a much broader perspective upon the original contexts of meaning and influence. And historical research has also often been able to expose sources and materials that were not recognised or were simply unavailable at an earlier stage. In this case, therefore, it is precisely the subsequent distance or estrangement with respect to the original situation of transmission that permits a more nuanced judgement concerning the process of understanding and misunderstanding. One should not capriciously squander this advantage by appealing to a claim that leads to total indeterminacy, the claim that because all understanding necessarily involves 'understanding differently', there is therefore no way that understanding can be reliably checked and examined as such.

The best examples for the aforementioned problem of productive misunderstanding are generally to be found in *situations of crisis* and *epochal transformation*. For it is here that we see the old and the new entwined in a process where there is insufficient clarity concerning the precise character of the issues and problems involved. The emergence of post-Kantian thought is a particularly instructive episode in this respect, and that is one reason why this development has been so comprehensively explored. For the more narrowly philosophical innovations of the period are also connected with the social transformations of the revolutionary epoch, and with all its related hopes and expectations for the future. And this combination of factors involves a certain aesthetic turn with regard to the problem of modernity, with an express concern for the unification of life and art that has also exercised its influence upon the avant-garde movements of the twentieth century. It is this complexity that renders analysis of the period so difficult.

In the following discussion, I shall concentrate my remarks on the path that leads 'from Fichte to Schlegel' on the assumption that the perceptive insights of the young Friedrich Schlegel are directly connected with Fichte's *Doctrine of Science* through precisely the kind of productive misunderstanding we have mentioned. This specific focus of the discussion should naturally not tempt us to lose sight of the broader context of epochal change within which alone the development in question can properly be delineated. The question therefore concerns the way in which Fichte's attempt to provide a systematic foundation for the tasks of post-Kantian philosophy is effectively transferred and applied to an explicit programme of aesthetic reflection. In Schlegel's admittedly fragmentary projects and sketches, this idea is combined with that of a potential reorganisation of social life in which the artistic creator, the critic and the relevant public will come together to realise and promote an emerging historical tendency of the time. The misunderstanding lies in the fact that Schlegel appropriated Fichte as if the latter had specifically provided the authentic terms for articulating Schlegel's own project, as if indeed the extended and expanded constellation of ideas that resulted from this appropriation was precisely what the time itself demanded.

II

It is well known that the philosophical speculation that arose after Kant in response to the critical enterprise expressly intended to 'go with Kant beyond Kant'. No one believed that a still surviving shape of spirit was simply to be rejected or replaced by some entirely novel approach. On the contrary, it was widely felt that the 'Copernican Turn' represented by Kant's transcendental philosophy, grounding our entire theoretical and practical relationship to the world upon the central role of subjectivity, only encouraged the attempt to cast off the critical restrictions to which Kant himself still appeared to be fettered. What the emerging generation of thinkers were envisaging here was not so much the end of the European tradition of metaphysics as the thought of now finally bringing it to completion.

Kant's own reflection upon the extended history of metaphysics had only led him to the paradoxical conclusion that the supposedly ultimate discipline of pure reason actually presented nothing but an 'arena of never-ending conflicts' that was still very far from assuming 'the sure path of a science'. The idea of subjecting reason to a radical self-critique with respect to its own intrinsic limits and possibilities was intended precisely to open up the way for 'any future metaphysics that shall be able to present itself as a science'. So runs the eloquent title of the *Prolegomena* that Kant offered for the further elucidation of the first critique, which had quickly acquired a reputation for profound obscurity. The 'unfortunate fate that had always afflicted metaphysics' was finally to be dispelled.[1]

Fichte pursued the project in the form of a '*Wissenschaftslehre*'. His programmatic essay *On the Concept of the Doctrine of Science or of What is*

---

[1] I. Kant, *Prolegomena* A10.

Called Philosophy of 1794, which aroused immediate interest and attention, proclaims in the 'Foreword': 'The present writer is still inwardly convinced that the human understanding cannot possibly push beyond the limit which Kant, especially in the *Critique of Judgement*, has occupied, without however fully defining it for us, and has declared to be the ultimate limit of all finite knowledge … He has left for future ages the task of grounding the genius of the man who, from the level upon which the philosophising power of judgement then found itself, so mightily drew the latter, often enough as if led by some higher inspiration, towards its ultimate destination.'

Fichte was hardly lacking in audacity when he contested the title that traditional philosophy 'so called' had initially assumed for itself, and undertook to transform the latter into the fundamental science underlying all other human scientific knowledge – namely, into a *Doctrine of Science*. And twelve years later, in the celebrated 'Preface' to the *Phenomenology of Spirit*, Hegel would similarly declare his hope that philosophy might finally lay aside its traditional designation as the 'love of wisdom' and actually succeed in becoming 'Science'. The revolutionary pathos of the post-Kantian thinkers is therefore quite impossible to overlook. The emphatic claim here derives precisely from Kant's original insistence upon establishing the properly scientific status of philosophy, something that would historically realise the ultimate and authentic aim and purpose of traditional metaphysics.

Nonetheless, Fichte clearly admits in the quoted passage that he is incapable of doing more than decisively thinking Kant through to the end. For with the third Critique, expressly conceived as the systematic completion of the entire critical enterprise, Kant stood at the threshold of an even greater task. The impulse that Fichte himself communicated directly to his immediate successors was precisely that of actively appropriating the promised land that had been glimpsed. Thus Hegel, who had just gone off to Bern to assume his duties as a house-tutor, could write at Christmas 1794 in his first letter to his friend Schelling, who had remained behind at the *Stift* in Tübingen: 'How are things looking otherwise in Tübingen? Nothing real will come of anything unless someone like Reinhold or Fichte gets a position there'.

Schelling answered promptly on 6 January 1795: 'Philosophy has not yet attained its end. Kant has given the results, but the premises are still lacking. And who can understand the results without the premises? – A Kant perhaps, but how will that help the multitude? Fichte, on the last occasion he was here, said that one would have to possess the genius of a Socrates to penetrate Kant's meaning. With every day that passes I find this truer ... Fichte will raise philosophy to such a height that shall daze most of our previous Kantians. ... At the moment I am receiving his first reflections from Fichte himself, the 'Foundation of the Entire Doctrine of Science'. (It is not being publicly printed and is intended simply as a manuscript for his listeners.) I read it and found that my own prophecies were not disappointed'. And Schelling naturally also adds that his own work, inspired as it is by Fichte, will begin with an 'exposition of the critique of judgement according to my principles'.[2]

One thing is quite clear: the future of philosophy, which will also be its last and conclusive chapter, has already begun to take shape in the later thought of Kant. Its further advance now lies in the hands of a conscious elite that will go on thinking in the same spirit and will effectively reconstruct *the principles or presuppositions* that Kant himself had failed to present. Everything depends upon the active intellectual elaboration and further discovery of the necessary principles that will fully illuminate, both for the philosopher and for humanity in general, what has already been achieved. The next stage will therefore involve a creative process arising out of what has already been accomplished and proceeding logically upon a path that will finally ground and complete the latter in turn.

There is a further subsidiary observation implied in Schelling's letter. Fichte had also broken with the old philosophical tradition of the Schools, according to which the teacher lectured directly from existing compendia, which presented the material content of a given subject in a canonic fashion, and merely provided further elucidations of the prescribed text. Kant himself had still taught in this way. He would use standard works by Baumgarten, for example, as the basis for his lectures, and we can often study the genesis of his own views by examining the marginal remarks and annotations he added to his copies of the relevant texts. Fichte, on the other hand, was well aware that no one could find even the bases of his own systematic project already laid out in any of the contemporary philosophical literature. That is why, immediately after the aforementioned programmatic essay outlining his own intentions, Fichte produced the *Foundation of the Entire Doctrine of Science* of 1794 precisely as 'a manuscript for the use of his listeners', as

---

[2] Schelling's letter to Niethammer of 22 January 1795 and Schelling's essay *On the Ego as the Principle of Philosophy* of 1795 (*SW* I, p. 242 and 152 f.)

specifically stated on the title page of the work.[3] This approach, which
first announces some thematic problem in the context of *lectures* and
presents it as a means of encouraging an essentially *participatory thinking*
on the part of the listeners, is something that has also been adopted
since by philosophers from Hegel and Schelling through to Husserl
and Heidegger. After all, the 'collected works' of these thinkers consist
largely of lecture courses or their subsequent elaboration. And the trea-
tises of Aristotle, the so-called 'pragmatia', are also themselves derived
from compilations of lecture notes.

In Fichte's work on the 'Foundations' of the *Doctrine of Science*, the
'Foreword' provides further insight into the author's *intention* of encouraging his actively participating listeners to exercise their own intellectual autonomy, rather than simply presenting a text for consumption
by an anonymous general public. The author has deliberately eschewed
the use of any 'fixed terminology – the surest means by which devotees
of the letter [*Buchstäbler*] deprives every system of its inner spirit and
transforms it into a dessicated corpse', and has thereby encouraged his
intellectual collaborators to 'project along with him the future shape'
of the new philosophy. 'I did not wish to say everything, but rather also
to leave something for my reader to think for himself ... The Doctrine
of Science must not forcibly impose itself on anyone, but must itself
become a need, just as it was for its author'. The 'preliminary remark'
that prefaced the second edition of the work on 1802 was still promising 'the future appearance of a properly scientific exposition'. Fichte
effectively spent the rest of his life trying to present the definitive theory allegedly underlying all genuine knowledge claims in ever new, in
ever more comprehensible and transparent versions, until the late work
finally fell into almost impenetrable obscurity.

In truth, therefore, these apparently external facts connected with
the precise manner of publication reflect Fichte's own contribution to
determining the proper *task of philosophy*. Plato was traditionally said
to have rewritten his *Republic* no less than seven times. And Hegel
responded to this by claiming that he would dearly have revised his
Logic seventy-seven times.[4] Every author must appeal to the *captatio
benevolentiae*, must admit the imperfections of his achievements to the
reader while nonetheless encouraging the latter to reflect and study the

---

[3] For further details concerning the gradual way in which the text was first issued, cf. the
introduction to the Munich edition of Fichte's works (GA I, 2, p. 180 ff.).

[4] Cf. the concluding passage of the 'Preface' to the second edition of the *Science of Logic*
(1831).

matter with care. But this takes on a quite different note with Fichte. For here the matter in question is such as to demand of every reading subject the free actualisation of autonomous intellectual insight, and not merely the comprehending reception of what is communicated. The very structure of philosophical 'grounding' through the positing of the ego, through the oppositing of the non-ego, through the consistent process of perpetual mediation that ensues, projects the sort of principles that can never properly be grasped if they are not simultaneously produced through the original activity of the subject itself.

The cited passage from the 'Foreword' makes much of an opposition, that between the 'letter' and the 'spirit', which has a very venerable history behind it, including Plato's philosophical critique of 'writing' and the Biblical exegesis of the Christian Gospel. In the post-Kantian context under discussion, this ancient motif is intensified beyond its traditional application to become an explicit appeal: everyone can produce within himself, with the same transparency and independence, the self-same need for independent thought to which the author responded when he sought to establish the principles of systematic philosophy through clarification of the structure of the ego. The author thus expressly calls upon the active co-operation on the part of all free spirits, and the manner of lecturing he adopts, abandoning as it does the scholastic procedures traditionally involved, provides a germinating model for an *emerging community of readers* that will be able to emancipate itself from all alien and external principles and establish a new form of unity on the basis of the creative power of the spirit itself.

Schlegel's argument for the spontaneous exercise of free critical reflection naturally found an immediate point of contact with this social and methodological dimension of Fichte's pedagogic innovations. As Schlegel would write in retrospect: '[Fichte] first discovered and explicitly set forth, entirely on his own, the proper method of philosophy and organised the free activity of thinking for oneself as an art ... That is also why he possesed no disciples in the usual sense of the word, but only friends'.[5]

III

At the same time, it must also be emphasised that the originally and typically 'appellative' character of this intellectual approach as such

---

[5] F. Schlegel, *Aufsaetze in der Europa* (1803), KA III, p. 6. See note 7.

decided nothing with regard to specific *content*. And in this respect, the paths that in one sense served to bring Fichte and Schlegel together nonetheless proceed in quite different directions. For Fichte, as a systematic philosopher, the entire emphasis of the demand for unconstrained reflection lay in fulfilling the task of completing 'Science', something that meant absolutely nothing to Schlegel the young firebrand of a literary critic. The decisive difference in their respective approaches is already clearly revealed by Schlegel's preference for the literary form of the 'fragment'. Whereas Fichte's *Doctrine of Science* takes great pains to elevate the old-fashioned form of philosophy to the contemporary level of systematic 'Science' through the application of a transparent, because supposedly irreducible, self-grounding procedure, Schlegel articulates his own insights, equally deliberately, in terms of the 'fragment'.

Schlegel and his friend Novalis were both entirely agreed that the appropriate contemporary form for the philosophy of modernity was the *fragment* that is somehow capable of concentrating the many-facetted richness of thought within itself. For the fragment manages to leave things open, things that can themselves be thought out further through the unconstrained freedom of subsequent recipients and later generations.[6] The fragment must be fashioned in such a way as to provoke a further intense and energetic effort at subsequent comprehension and interpretation. The romantics were not simply content to present their literary works publicly as fragments, they also used the fragment form to debate the peculiarities of this challenging genre itself.

Thus Schlegel writes in a famous passage from the *Athenäum Fragments*: 'The fragment must, like a small work of art, be entirely detached from the surrounding world, as complete in itself as a hedgehog'.[7] Here the status of completion is rather surprisingly ascribed to the fragment insofar as it appears sealed off from its general environment. Like a hedgehog, the fragment displays its sharp spines outwards in order to emphasise its polemical contrast with the everyday world. The whole point of the fragment lies in a radical and decisive concentration of the universal within the particular.

---

[6] Cf. my essay 'Gedanken über das Fragment. Anaximander, Schlegel und die Moderne' (*Merkur* 529, 1993).

[7] F. Schlegel, *Kritische Friedrich Schlegel Ausgabe*, ed. E. Behler et al. (Paderborn 1958–). vol. II, p. 197. Henceforth abbreviated as KA.

In another passage, Schlegel writes: 'A dialogue is a chain or a wreath of fragments. An exchange of letters is a dialogue on a larger scale, and *memorabilia* are a system of fragments. There is still nothing that is fragmentary in form and material, at once entirely subjective and individual, that is also entirely objective and forms a necessary part of a system of all the sciences'[8] There are a number of factors involved in the complex play of differences between Schlegel and Fichte here. Schlegel, and likewise his friend Schleiermacher later, expressly regarded the 'dialogue' as the paradigmatic form of expression for that Platonic philosophy to which they would dedicate their joint labours of translation in the modern and romantic spirit of 'collaborative philosophising'. The use of memorabilia and the letter form, on the other hand, would characterise Schlegel's own novel-fragment *Lucinde*, a work whose general libertine and erotic-aesthetic atmosphere so scandalised denizens of the contemporary salons that Schleiermacher felt compelled to defend it publicly in his own *Confidential Letters Concerning Lucinde*.

According to the fragment we have just cited, there is still, strictly speaking, no pure example of a fragment that, at the highest level of contemporary thought, could be formally subjective and simultaneously objective as part of an emerging philosophical system. The 'fragment' thus appears as a kind of *expository pendant* to Fichte's *Doctrine of Science*. 'It is equally fatal for the spirit to have a system and not to have one. We shall therefore have to decide for both'.[9] This call to dissolve the dilemma between fatal compulsion and unbearable anarchy, which itself represents a kind of meta-theoretical reflection on the desire of the epoch to construct the definitive philosophical system, naturally culminates in a plea for the 'fragment', a form that is capable of harbouring content even while requiring further intellectual and spiritual activity in order to realise its proper nature.

IV

While Schlegel privileges the fragment as the appropriate form for the presentation of ideas, the Fichtean Doctrine of Science, which originally inspired him, aims explicitly to provide the complete and compelling demonstration of the *ultimate scientific ground and justification* of all the sciences. The argumentation behind the programmatic essay *On the*

---

[8] Ibid., p. 176.　　　　　[9] Ibid., p. 173.

Concept of the Doctrine of Science of 1794 can be briefly summarised as follows. Fichte is convinced that the rational core of philosophy essentially constitutes a 'science'. He is thus continuing to build upon Kant's original critical effort to establish philosophy upon 'the sure path of a science'. But whereas Kant had employed transcendental reflection to accomplish this ambitious aim by revealing the *a priori* structural conditions of all the particular sciences that were themselves dependent upon contingent experience, Fichte deliberately adopts a different strategy.

He concerns himself not with the question as to how science, considered in regard to its objective validity, is related to the world, but rather with the question as to how science as an organised system of knowledge can be conceptualised as a *unity*. The systematic construction of science is reduced to a fundamental principle, and is thus theoretically analysed as a specific problem of grounding. And it is the next step that Fichte takes that is the really decisive one. For the theoretical analysis is now repeated at a meta-level, where he abstracts from all particular content and interrogates the source of the systematic form of knowledge as such. A science of science is necessary precisely in order to explain how the specific material sciences can acquire the required unity on the basis of an original fundamental principle. This 'science of science' is what is called the *Doctrine of Science*, a discipline that dissolves the traditional form of philosophy by explaining and elucidating the constitutive problem of a first principle of knowing.

At this point, we cannot possibly appeal to any purely given *fact*, but only to a certain *act* that originates in the spontaneity of spirit itself. This reveals an ego that is self-positing with regard to its own knowing and its existence precisely because it is no longer dependent upon anything else already posited. This theoretical meta-discourse concerning the formal grounding processes of knowledge is supposed to illuminate how the ultimate grounding function of this uniquely self-related principle can indeed perform the required task. From a historical perspective, we could say that Fichte has taken up the central theme of Spinoza's metaphysics in order to reformulate its characteristic definition of substance as *causa sui* in terms of a theory of subjectivity, in terms of the self-positing ego. But a historical observation of this kind by itself proves nothing with regard to the real issue here. It merely helps us to elucidate the conceptual effort involved in discovering an intrinsically self-grounding principle or acquiring an original and fundamental insight into the process of grounding as such.

With this discovery of the specific structure of the ego, Fichte certainly believed he could immediately tackle the problem of providing a theoretical grounding for scientific knowledge. For our own purposes here, it is thus permissible to distinguish between the *formal strategy* underlying the idea of a 'Doctrine of Science' and its actual realisation in practice, without doing serious injustice to the subtlety of Fichte's philosophical considerations. Such a distinction between form and content is certainly required if we are to understand the inner consistency of Schlegel's extension of Fichte, even though this also led him deliberately to dissolve into fragments a system that was still in the process of construction. In all good conscience, Schlegel could effectively abandon the systematic form of the *Doctrine of Science* without provoking the accusation that he had thereby simply destroyed the subtle textures of thought that Fichte himself had woven out of Kant's original proposals.

V

The core *content* of these speculations concerning the structure of the ego, which Schlegel retained in his romantic transformation of Fichte, had nothing effectively solid or substantialistic about it. It was rather the *ultimate intensification of form itself*, and indeed the form that irreducibly remains as long as we continue to hold fast to the originative power of self-activity. Fichte himself had appealed to this in order to establish the universally compelling necessity of a principle that was capable of grounding the process of grounding without itself falling victim to the problem of infinite regress. Thanks to the textual materials, the new historical-critical edition of Schlegel's works has recently made available to us, it is now much easier to grasp the significance and character of his engagement with Fichte's thought. Thus we read in a note that Schlegel made during the period of his intense study of Fichte: 'The *Doctrine of Science* is not the history of nature and the history of freedom – the doctrine of the formation of the pure ego; rather it presents us with the insights and observations of a free-floating and happily wayfaring mystic'.[10] Or again: 'One cannot understand *the Doctrine of Science* if one has no sense for chaos. The *Doctrine of Science* is Fichte's *Werther*'.[11] Schlegel is naturally well aware of the witty provocation involved in thus identifying the strictly systematic thinker with the extravagant novelist.

[10] KA XVIII, p. 35, No.175.   [11] Ibid., p. 38, No. 220.

But he is obviously also convinced that he has properly grasped the real import of Fichte's philosophical innovations, and is not merely striking out on a clever path of his own here.

In the fragment of 1799 entitled 'On Philosophy – For Dorothy', where his ideas are presented once again in epistolary form, Schlegel writes as follows: 'You will never find the results of the most profound reflection, and extended as it were into infinity, expressed in such an accessible fashion and with such clarity as you can in Fichte's latest exposition of the *Doctrine of Science*.[12] I find it interesting that a thinker whose one great goal is the *scientific* presentation of philosophy, and who perhaps commands the *technical facility* of thinking [*das* künstliche *Denken*] more surely than any of his predecessors, can also nonetheless be so enthusiastic for the cause of universal *communication* [Mitteilung]. I believe this accessible character [*Popularität*] reveals how philosophy itself is advancing towards *humanity* [Humanität] in the true and great sense of the word, one that reminds us that a human being must wish to live amongst other human beings and, to the extent that the human spirit fully extends its reach, will ultimately come home to itself once more'.[13]

The scientific status of philosophy in alliance with its popular and accessible character, the most elaborate accomplishments of reflection coupled with the promotion of humanity through general communication – this is the central governing idea behind Schlegel's interest in Fichte's *Doctrine of Science*: the concept of an emerging tendency. For such a 'tendency' naturally discloses the indispensable perspective of a future where domains and activities that have hitherto been segregated from one another will finally come to interact reciprocally. The standard interpretation of the relationship between Fichte and Schlegel claims that while the former is essentially concerned with the absolute ego, the latter is only interested in the empirical ego. And the conflation of these two perspectives is consequently deemed responsible for the alleged misunderstandings that ensue between the systematic thinker and the literary ironist. The underlying concept of a perpetually extended process of reflection is supposed to remain essentially unchanged, even though the relevant agent of reflection is surreptitiously reversed in each case. Even Walter Benjamin's 'Dissertation',

---

[12] Schlegel is clearly referring to Fichte's *Attempt towards a New Exposition of the Doctrine of Science* of 1797/98 (GA I, 4, p. 169 ff.).
[13] KA VIII, p. 57 f.

a pioneering work as far as Schlegel scholarship is concerned, and one that attempted to emphasise the element of modernity in the German romantics, seems largely to concur in this perspective.[14]

In my opinion, the situation is actually rather different. The Schlegel passage we have just cited presents the author of the *Doctrine of Science* itself as a 'happily wayfaring mystic' who possesses a system ruled by chaos, as one who effectively prepares the way for the aesthetician without remotely trying or expecting to do any such thing. As far as *the status of subjectivity* is concerned, it is not a question of two different modes of the ego – namely, the absolute and the empirical ego. It is rather that the strategy of the *Doctrine of Science* itself presents itself quite differently when viewed from the perspective of the art theorist. Fichte seeks his ultimate grounding principle in an act that no ego can repudiate without meaninglessly repudiating itself at the same time. But Schlegel regards this idea as the symptom of a much broader tendency of the age, one that will never finally be satisfied no matter how often Fichte rewrites the *Doctrine of Science* in his efforts to 'compel the public to understand'.

The man who inspired this new approach, and who generally felt himself exposed to misunderstanding, responded directly to the *different perspective* involved here in a remarkably perceptive letter. On 16 August 1800, Fichte wrote to Schlegel: 'I am glad you have decided also to give serious attention to the form of the *Doctrine of Science*, as you put it, and to lecture upon the work from this point of view. In your own ideas, which I have thought over once again in this connection, I believe that I can still detect traces of a conflation between the *philosophical mode of thinking*, which must indeed be realised in life itself, and *philosophy* in the objective sense, namely philosophy as a science. The idealistic standpoint as scientifically articulated can never pass over into the domain of life. This standpoint must be described as thoroughly unnatural'.

VI

The fundamental romantic intention is indeed to allow thought to *pass over into life*. This is precisely what the key concept of an emergent historical tendency is intended to express. In order to clarify this claim, I shall conclude by examining one of Schlegel's most famous fragments, and specifically in its briefer preliminary formulation. This version was

---

[14] W. Benjamin, *The Concept of Art Criticism in German Romanticism*, Bern 1920 (cf. *Gesammelte Schriften* I, 1, p. 28 ff.).

not published in the *Athenäum*, but it does clearly reveal the original impulse that Schlegel believed he had received from Fichte. The early formulation is this: 'The three greatest tendencies of our age are the *Doctrine of Science, Wilhelm Meister* and the French Revolution'.[15] In the well-known published version, this provocative triple reference is followed by the further observation: 'One who takes offence at this conjunction, one who holds no revolution important that is not loud and material in character, has yet to raise himself to the higher and farseeing standpoint of the history of humanity'.

It is obvious that this simultaneous allusion to a decisively formulated system of philosophy, a modern novel, and a profound political transformation, that includes reflection on the nature of art within the narrative itself can only be made from the elevated standpoint of a comprehensively conceived history of humanity. For the aphorist naturally foresees the banal objection that the three phenomena in question really belong to entirely different spheres. Schlegel desires to dissolve the boundaries that are implied in our usual understanding of politics, art and philosophy, and thus to anticipate a development that can only arise from implicit tendencies in the present that must first be intensified. The literary interventions of the critic are expressly conceived as an authentic contribution to encouraging and unifying the tendencies in question.

What is immediately striking about these three parallel manifestations of the age is their fundamental and shared feature of *incompletion*. The phenomenon of the Revolution encapsulates this paradoxical character insofar as this 'most terrible and grotesque product of the age, in the most bizzarely imaginable fashion, weaves the deepest prejudices and the most violent presentiments of the latter, thrown together in a terrifying chaos, into a monstrous tragi-comic spectacle of humanity'.[16] In his 1798 essay *On Goethe's Meister*, Schlegel hails Goethe's novel as intensely topical for much the same reason: 'Our usual expectations of overall unity and interconnection of parts are disappointed by this novel just as frequently as they are fulfilled. But one who harbours any genuine and systematic instinct or sense for the universe, any presentiment of the world as a whole, ... will everywhere feel the personality and living individuality of this work'.[17] And lastly we find the following judgement of Fichte's *Doctrine of Science* in one of Schlegel's

---

[15] KA XVIII, p. 85.   [16] KA II, p. 248.
[17] Ibid., p. 134.

jottings: 'If Fichte's system is genuine mysticism, then it must annihilate itself – for mysticism knows nothing of limitation, distinction, and so on. Everything flows onwards, unstoppable and unbounded, in an eternal cycle'.[18] In short, all three phenomena reveal how the process of history is driven on mysteriously and without end in an irresolvable concatenation of order and chaos. It is therefore not surprising that Schlegel also employs his three examples of the tendencies of the time as an occasion for discussing the role of misunderstanding and the infinite task of further understanding. He does so in a short essay that explicitly reflects upon the fate of an author's fragmentary utterances and the way in which they themselves require further supplementary understanding on the part of the reader. It may be noted in passing that this quite extraordinary essay, *On Unintelligibility*, which appeared in Schlegel's journal the *Athenäum*, clearly anticipates the entire theory of the deconstructive school from Derrida through to de Man.

Here Schlegel tells us that the word 'tendency' as used in the fragments has been misunderstood: 'This is already itself a cause for irony. For it might be understood in the sense that I simply regarded the *Doctrine of Science*, for example, merely as a tendency, as a preliminary attempt, like Kant's *Critique of Pure Reason*, and one that I myself hoped to realise more effectively or finally to complete ... I shall therefore leave this irony to itself and clearly declare here that in the dialect of these fragments, the word signifies that everything is still only a tendency, that the age is the age of tendencies. Now whether I believe that all these tendencies could be correctly pursued and brought to completion by myself, or perhaps by my brother, or by Tieck, or by anyone else belonging to our group, or only by one of our sons, by a grandchild perhaps or great grandchild, by some grandchild way down the line, or only at the Last Judgement, or indeed never – all this is vouchsafed to the wisdom of the reader that really represents the proper place for this question. . . . Here, too, the very best thing we can do perhaps is to magnify the difficulty; once this has reached its greatest pitch, it will collapse and vanish, thereby allowing the process of understanding to begin. We have still not gone far enough in being prepared to give offence: but what is not currently the case, can still become so'.[19]

---

[18] *Phil. Fagmente*, 'Zur Wissenschaftslehre', 1796 (KA XVIII, p. 10).
[19] KA II, p. 366 f.

Expressed without the irony, we may say that misunderstanding was obviously inevitable in the first place. Unintelligibility is thus the primary and permanent predicament of all hermeneutics. Unintelligibility must be intensified, *and the offence continually magnified*, until the *skandalon* reaches its peak. This alone can open up a perspective, through all the further instances and examples of understanding, through all succeeding generations down to the end of history, upon a task that is simultaneously a task for humanity itself. This task envisages the unification of art and life, the intensification of social existence through the exercise of reflection, and a corresponding expansion of the horizons of humanity through the interventions of the critic. The impulse of aesthetic modernism in the twentieth century has in turn attempted to appropriate this perspective that was first suggested by the prophetic thinkers of the final decade of the eighteenth century. In light of the text we have just cited, we all clearly form links in that infinite chain of those who find themselves driven to ponder the significance of the apparently unintelligible and thereby to reinforce the intrinsically problematic tendency of modernity itself – and this holds for you, my readers or listeners, for me even as I speak to you, and for all who will unforeseeably follow us in turn.

10

THE DIALECTICAL SIGNIFICANCE
OF ROMANTIC IRONY

Friedrich Schlegel wrote in the *Lyceum Fragments* that 'philosophy is the authentic home of irony'.[1] And he likewise regarded ironic philosophy as the appropriate expression of that anticipated unification of poetry and philosophy that constituted the early romantic credo itself.[2] It is therefore impossible to ascribe irony exclusively to one or the other of these domains. Irony hovers intangibly in an intermediate space between both. In the same context, Schlegel also defines irony as 'logical beauty', and continues: 'Wherever we philosophise in spoken or in written dialogue, rather than in an entirely systematic fashion, there irony should be pursued and encouraged'. And a little later he writes: 'It is poetry alone that can be raised from this perspective to the very heights of philosophy'.

The following remarks will attempt to clarify precisely this *dual thesis*: that irony should always be pursued and encouraged whenever we are not philosophising in an entirely systematic fashion, and that poetry is correspondingly capable of rising to the level of philosophical speculation through the medium of irony. As is well known, the principal difficulty here lies in doing full methodological justice to splinters and shards of thought that gleam with insights that are deliberately left ungrounded and uncompleted. What we are confronted with is neither a belletristic offering that could simply be enjoyed aesthetically without pausing to reflect upon some further intellectual content, nor an example of philosophical argumentation the steps of which could be carefully followed, reconstructed and possibly contested as such. Schlegel

---

[1] F. Schlegel, *Kritische Friedrich Schlegel Ausgabe*, ed. E. Behler et al. (Paderborn 1958–), vol. II, p. 152.
[2] E.g. ibid., p. 267.

expresses himself in 'fragments' precisely in accordance with his claim
for some intermediate space of discourse that lies between poetry and
philosophy: 'Like a little work of art, a fragment must be entirely detached from the surrounding world, completely enclosed within itself
like a hedgehog'.[3] Anyone attempting to interpret such a fragment is
inevitably confronted by its own immanent defensiveness, and may risk
injury from its protective spines. Since our theoretical inquiry necessarily proceeds un-ironically, it can all too easily appear more foolish
than its intended object. I must expose myself to this unavoidable risk
nonetheless.

Viewed from the perspective of the history of philosophy, Schlegel's
call for ironic presentation effectively invokes the Platonic figure of
Socrates in contrast to Fichte's attempt to ground transcendental philosophy systematically in a *Doctrine of Science*. The objective style of the
ancients and the most profound revolution accomplished by the new,
indeed newest, thought are suddenly brought into closest proximity
with one another. The appeal to irony is demanded by the present
moment, and arises from a view of history shaped by a contemporary
articulation of the 'Querelle des Anciens et des Modernes'. Insofar as
irony appears here as a historically necessary phenomenon, it is more
than simply an expression of the sophisticated verbal culture that was
once possessed in Athens and that one would dearly imitate now in
Jena or Berlin. Irony is more than an ornament that a literary mind
might naturally furnish for the latest dogmatic positings of philosophy simply because the proclamations of Fichte, most un-ironical of
all philosophers, come across as all too unadorned. Irony is rather a
necessity, a form of expression that must be adopted by anyone who
properly grasps what the spirit of the time demands.

'The method of philosophy must be Socratic', so Schlegel claims in
his lectures on transcendental philosophy of 1800/01, and this because
'the spirit of true philosophy will never be reawakened until the art of
pursuing a philosophical dialogue [*wissenschaftliches Gespräch*] has been
rediscovered and actively realised in the most effective possible form'.[4]
Or expressed even more succinctly: 'Irony is the duty of all philosophy
which is not yet history and is not system'.[5] The playful but considered
form of dialogue developed in the verbal culture of the ancients is itself

---

[3] *Athenäums-Fragmente*, KA II, p. 197.   [4] KA XII, p. 103.
[5] *Philosophical Fragments* (1797), Part II, No. 678, KA XVIII; cf. No. 823: 'A History of Irony
amongst the Ancients with Regard to a Critique of Philosophy'.

therefore a systematic vehicle for appropriately articulating a philosophy that as yet is still advancing, on Fichtean foundations, towards its future completed form.[6] Irony thus marks an intermediate state of philosophy where the latter is no longer confined within traditional parameters, but has not yet attained its ultimate goal.

With its demand for radically autonomous thought, Fichte's idealism had initiated an enthusiastically welcomed transformation of the outmoded scholastic form of traditional philosophy. With the recognition that we owe everything in theory to the absolutely spontaneous activity of the ego, the act of philosophising is no longer bound to the given limitations of the present or to those hitherto observed in the past. In Schlegel's eyes, this had opened the way to quite new possibilities. The spirit must now be encouraged to pursue infinite tasks and activities of its own, to accomplish unforeseeable achievements and discover ever more intense forms of expression for itself.

This broadly pedagogic perspective upon the imminent *future*[7] certainly emphasises what is novel, interesting and unparalleled about it, but it is a future that is projected in the light of the conviction that everything it may bring arises from the spirit's now finally awakened capacity for self-determination and self-realisation. The early romantic anticipation of the spiritual accomplishments of the future involves an essentially universal historical dimension insofar as the expected explosion of activity in all the arts and sciences simply represents the actualisation of a principle that, since Fichte, we have properly come to grasp. The *progressive universalism* of a philosophy intrinsically entwined with poetry fulfils through its own 'agility'[8] and 'invention'[9] what has long been recognised as the very essence of the human spirit: that activity that is essentially directed towards itself. This is the significance of Schlegel's eighth Habilitation Thesis: *Non critice sed historice est philosophandum.*

While philosophy has already been pursued critically, and will eventually be properly pursued historically, irony for the present remains the appropriate medium of philosophising. Schlegel's *Lectures on Transcendental Philosophy* attempt to explain this position in this way[10]: critical philosophy is mistaken in attempting to determine its limits and justify

---

[6] Cf. 'Concerning the Form of Philosophy', KA III, p. 97ff.
[7] Cf. *Philosophical Fragments*, Part II, loc. cit., Nos. 961 and 947.
[8] E.g., *Lectures on Transcendental Philosophy*, KA XII, p. 95.
[9] KA II, p. 263.   [10] KA XII, p. 96.

its method before it actually sets to work because one cannot examine the powers of thought without *employing* those powers. 'It is only
in the process of development that one learns to know the powers in
question'. And no limits can really be set to reason in the first place.
This is demonstrated precisely by the idealism that effectively begins by
moving beyond the alleged or antecedently given limits of reason. In
full agreement with his idealist contemporaries, Schlegel proposes the
following 'basic principle': 'A philosophy which does not begin with
the whole will hardly be able to elevate itself to it'. In the context of
such an elevation to the whole, criticism must now give way firstly to
polemic – the explicit definition and defence of idealism over against
opposing philosophies – and secondly to the insight that the philosophy that aims to think from the perspective of the whole never presents
that whole of which it remains, at most, itself a part. Although the text
of Schlegel's lectures does not explicitly say so, it seems clear to me
that it is self-criticism in this second sense that provides the basis for the
ironic attitude recommended – that is, the open recognition that we are
striving to envisage a fundamentally overarching whole against which
all our philosophical efforts must inevitably appear small and modest in
comparison. The deliberate reduction of the individual's own effective
contribution here, the capacity to withdraw or relativise that contribution, itself serves precisely to broaden our perspective upon the 'whole'
that is at issue.

   In attempting to develop a new philosophy that would finally transcend the limitations imposed by Kant's critical position and focus emphatically upon the future without carefully securing its own foundations first, Schlegel's ironic approach cannot easily be reconciled with
Fichte's philosophy at all. Of course, on the widely accepted view of
the matter, Schlegel was directly inspired by the Fichtean idea of an
absolutely free ego that annihilates reality qua given, and simply posits
its own being instead. Thus in a rather typical account of the 'Romantic
School', Haym writes as follows: 'The doctrine of irony is the application
to the aesthetic world of the idea of the ego as systematically developed
by Fichte'.[11] With this depiction of a subjectivity vainly dissolving all
substantial content, Haym is merely repeating a verdict that found an
often responsive echo in the nineteenth century[12] ever since it was first

---

[11] Berlin 1870, p. 260.
[12] E.g., F.Th. Vischer, *Über das Erhabene und Komische* (1837), ed. W. Oelmüller (Frankfurt
   am Main 1967), p. 180f.

formulated in Hegel's lectures on aesthetics.[13] There is certainly no doubt that Schlegel never failed to emphasise the radical transformation represented by Fichte's system of philosophy and thus to compare it with the French Revolution itself. Those who were offended by the paradoxical concatenation of the 'greatest tendencies of the age' had simply failed to 'raise themselves to the elevated and farseeing standpoint of the history of humanity'.[14] It is quite clear from many of his remarks in the correspondence with Novalis that Schlegel was also personally very impressed by the general effect of Fichte's thought.[15] And Schlegel explicitly confessed the essential encouragement he had received from that quarter. With a humorous allusion to Fichte's first important philosophical work, Schlegel explains that he is currently working out 'the foundations of a universal doctrine of wit'. Nor is the joke an inappropriate one since Schlegel is indeed effectively engaged in translating the *Doctrine of Science* onto the level of romantic irony.

And, in fact, Fichte was not someone who thought that philosophy was currently in a state of transition towards something greater that would only subsequently emerge. From the beginning, he was quite convinced that he would himself succeed in accomplishing the fundamental renewal and providing the final articulation of philosophy, of completing the work that Kant had initiated but not concluded. The unusual title '*Wissenschaftslehre*' explicitly expresses the definitive claim to have translated the traditional ambitions of philosophy into the absolutely valid form of 'Science'. The general title of Fichte's early programmatic essay of 1794, *On the Concept of the Doctrine of Science or of So-called Philosophy*, a work that proved to be so important for the beginnings of idealist thought, already underlines the same idea. From the summit attained by 'Criticism', philosophy is finally in a position to become 'Science'.

But this requires formulation of a *fundamental principle* that is capable of supporting the totality of genuine knowledge. And this could only properly be secured if the principle in question were immediately certain and essentially independent of anything else. For otherwise we should require yet another principle in order to grasp the supposedly initial principle, and so on and so forth in an inevitable and infinite

[13] Hegel, *Ästhetik* I (Werkausgabe, vol. 13), p. 92ff.; *Geschichte der Philosophie* I (Werkausgabe, vol. 18), p. 460.

[14] KA II, p. 198.

[15] E.g. the letters of 8 July 1796, 5 May 1797, 8 June 1797 (ed. M. Preitz, Darmstadt 1967, p. 59, 88, 94).

regress of argumentation. In order to avoid this, the relevant principle must be capable of internally generating its own content as well as its own form. What the principle claims, and the precise way in which it claims, should belong together in an indissoluble unity. This condition is satisfied if both these aspects arise as originally and simultaneously connected. For then the fundamental principle could be said to produce itself precisely as the one fundamental principle that would be entirely unconditioned by anything else. It is this systematic intention to provide an ultimate grounding for all knowledge that directs our attention to that fundamental act of self-positing that we encounter immediately in the ego. Everyone can discover within himself the prior accomplishment of an original act that has already transpired, an act through which the ego creates itself insofar as it bestows existence upon itself precisely by virtue of self-positing. Fichte's systematically constructive intentions lead him therefore not towards the thought of a free and ungoverned play of frivolous subjectivity[16], but rather to the inexorable and irreducible necessity of an original act. This structural unity of theory and practice, which can be read off from the fundamental experience of self-consciousness itself, thus provides a novel response to the problem of resolving the problem concerning the fundamental principle of philosophy in general.

Now it is indeed clear that Schlegel's own interests are focussed elsewhere and that he therefore has no good reason to pursue Fichte's attempt to *construct a system* on the basis of the concept of the ego. But I do not believe one can simply say, as it generally is said, that Schlegel has essentially applied Fichte's concept of the ego to *aesthetic* phenomena. For the lectures on transcendental philosophy already mentioned contain a third part where, under the title 'Philosophy of Philosophy', Schlegel draws a number of conclusions that are entirely incompatible with the general aim and structure of the *Doctrine of Science*.[17] In a spirit quite contrary to the essential pathos of Fichte's work, Schlegel himself

---

[16] I. Strohschneider-Kohrs has quite rightly freed Schlegel's concept of irony from these associated connotations (*Die romantische Ironie in Theorie und Gestaltung*, Tübingen 1960, e.g., p. 37). In this connection, she can appeal to Walter Benjamin's perceptive interpretation, which had already emphasised the objective significance of irony as anchored directly in the work of art itself (*Der Begriff der Kunstkritik in der deutschen Romantik*, Bern 1920, now in Walter Benjamin, *Gesammelte Schriften* I 1, pp. 81ff.; *The Concept of Criticism in German Romanticism*, in Walter Benjamin, *Selected Writings*, ed. M. Bullock and M.W. Jennings (Cambridge Mass. 1996), vol. 1, pp. 116–200).

[17] KA XII, p. 91ff.

starts from the claim: 'All philosophy is relative'. And he continues thus: 'Now the claim that all philosophy is relative – for over and beyond any combination of ideas it will still be possible to discover a higher one, and so on and so forth into infinity – also immediately implies the claim that all philosophy is infinite'. 'Truth arises when opposed errors neutralise one another. Absolute truth cannot be admitted; and this is the original testimony for freedom of thought and freedom of spirit. If absolute truth were to be found, the task of spirit would thereby be complete, spirit would inevitably cease to be since it can only exist insofar as it is essentially active. But if indeed all truth is merely relative, we can abandon ourselves to speculation in confidence and hope; every series of attempts that is founded upon something genuinely real leads to truth. We cannot say any more than this. If we but succeed in destroying error, then truth arises of itself'.

This *infinite progress of the active spirit* unfolding through the destruction of errors defines the essentially polemical method of philosophy already discussed. Schlegel also compares this approach with that of universal scepticism before his reflections eventually arrive at the concept of *dialectic*: 'In the more precise sense, philosophy is dialectical. Philosophy is supposed to be concerned exclusively with the development of the understanding, is supposed to refute errors ... Everything that relates to the art of developing our understanding in common and to the destruction of errors is dialectical. By virtue of developing our understanding in common, philosophy is dialectical and not logical. Philosophy in the broader sense is utterly unlimited. Philosophy is the whole and embraces everything that relates to the whole. All those who pursue the arts and the sciences must be philosophers – that is, philosophers according to the spirit; but not dialectical, which is rather for philosophers in the narrower sense.'[18] 'In the Socratic age, philosophy was dialectical ... The method of philosophy should be Socratic'.[19]

This is where the essential point of difference between Schlegel and Fichte is clearly revealed. Fichte's *Doctrine of Science* was a philosophical system, modelled after a Spinozistic example, and expressly designed to provide absolute grounding for all theoretical and practical knowledge on the basis of an ultimate self-generating principle. The dialectical model of philosophising, paradigmatically represented by the Platonic *Dialogues*, presents us rather with an infinite process of approximation to truth through the relative overcoming of existing errors. The process

[18] Ibid., p. 97. [19] Ibid., p. 103.

does not simply flow exclusively from a single fundamental principle, but is rather dependent upon an essentially shared and continuous effort to see through the one-sided partialities and finite limitations of our current perspectives. This presupposes a certain urbane and liberal approach to collaborative philosophical discussion, requires wit and polemical verve, and operates with an explicit historical awareness of unforeseen and unforeseeable intellectual developments. With this entirely unsystematic conception of philosophy, the method of irony thus comes to assume a clearly defined function for itself. Irony is anything but an arbitrarily employed and merely ornamental device; it is rather the appropriate form for the sustained and ongoing projection of that infinitely distant 'whole' that lies beyond all the finite standpoints it is possible for us to assume.

In the posthumously published *Philosophical Fragments* that date from 1797, around the same time as the critical fragments that make up the *Lyceum of the Fine Arts*, Schlegel therefore describes irony as the 'surrogate of an infinitely advancing process'[20], as the 'epideixis of infinity, of universality, of the sense for the world-all'[21], as something that is 'impossible unless one possesses a sense for the universe'.[22] 'The article of faith for the philosophy of the universe is precisely *that* world ... But wherefore this antithesis? That world is already here. For as long as we continue to speak of this and that world, we fail to possess any sense whatsoever for the world. – Is there indeed any other name for my irony, and is not this irony really the innermost mystery of the Critical Philosophy?'[23]. 'Critical Philosophy', 'Transcendental Philosophy' and 'Idealism' are all expressions that Schlegel borrows from the terminological resources of Fichte, while imperceptibly giving them a dialectical significance that is essentially directed against Fichte himself.

The real distance from Fichtean speculation is clearly revealed by the way in which Schlegel reinterprets Socratic irony. He presents the latter as the appropriate manifestation of the *infinite character* of the task that philosophy must face though never actually complete at any specific point of history. 'There must be infinitely many analogies for idealism, and that is why we can hardly speak of its truth without recourse to irony; idealism is infinitely true but the infinitude of this truth is never completed'. Ironic displacement does not revoke this truth, but rather first demonstrates its greatness. Wherever seriousness and playfulness pass

---

[20] KA XVIII, Part II, No. 995.   [21] Part III, No. 76.
[22] Part IV, No. 76.   [23] Part IV, No. 1067.

over inseparably into one another, we find ourselves walking the appropriate path of permanent self-overcoming in the light of something that is greater still. The 'self-parody' that 'mediocre harmonising minds' find so intolerable is a criterion for the superiority of the dialectical path, which alone can lead us to authentic insight. The outstanding Lyceum fragment that is expressly concerned with Socratic irony describes this path, where it is always impossible to say everything, as follows: 'Irony sustains and provokes a feeling of the irresolvable conflict between the conditioned and the unconditioned, between the necessity and the impossibility of a complete communication. Irony is the freest of all forms of licence since it allows one to go quite beyond oneself, but it is equally the most binding since it is unconditionally necessary'. This space of free play, created by the displacing distantiation from every definitive claim, assists the course of the issue, and is far from simply offering an open arena for an essentially arbitrary subject.

There is, however, one aspect of Fichte's doctrine that suggests a certain parallel to the dialectic. This concerns not the absolute ego, but rather the process of 'self-limitation' that is first made possible through the absolute ego. After unfolding the principle of the ego itself in §1 of the *Doctrine of Science*, Fichte introduces the formal opposition between the ego and the non-ego in §2. In §3 he then attempts to articulate the unity of the ego and the non-ego, the unity of the positing of all reality and the opposition to this positing, that is implied in the originally posited ego. In this connection, 'the identity of consciousness, the single absolute foundation of our knowledge'[24] cannot be abandoned – that is, no unexplained external interference that might limit the reality of the ego can be admitted. On the contrary, the ego as such must impose a limitation upon itself, without thereby entirely destroying itself once again after it had posited itself in the first place. And this is only possible insofar as the ego directs its own activity against itself. The concept of *restriction* [*Schranke*], governing the unity of both aspects and thereby also reciprocally relating them, is supposed to facilitate the compatibility of positing and opposing. Thus they are what they are insofar as they constitute an opposition, but they remain compatible with one another insofar as the opposition possesses, in the form of 'restriction', a shared term that is common to both.[25]

[24] Fichte, *Grundlage der gesamten Wissenschaftslehre* (1794), GA I, p. 269.
[25] Ibid., p. 270.

Setting up a restriction thus restricts something. Restriction here signifies the partial but not total negation of a certain reality. The execution of this activity is partial because, although it is directed against itself, it still leaves a persisting remainder behind. It therefore presupposes the concept of 'divisibility' or 'quantifiability', which can never be fixed as a specific quantity but rather implies the perpetual establishing of restrictions between any divisible parts. It is this *divisibility* of the original substance of the ego that therefore enables us to think positing and oppositing as immanently connected with one another. According to the demands of Fichte's formula: 'The ego opposes in the ego a divisible non-ego to a divisible ego'.[26] Fichte's solution to the problem of reconciling two mutually conflicting tendencies through recourse to the concept of *quantification* is a very remarkable one. For the specifically delimited ego is not identical with one that merely lacks a specific part of itself, and it is rather as if we were to cut pieces out of a cake without the cake thereby changing at all. Divisibility permits a limitation that has no effect upon the original whole and fails to transform its essential character in any way. This denial of qualitative transformation, which accompanies the relevant delimitation of the original ego, means that the delimitation can be repeated indefinitely. This implies the potentially infinite continuation of a process that effectively changes nothing with respect to the relations involved. That is why Fichte can say: 'It must be a system and One system; what is opposed must be connected, as long as there remains something opposed, until absolute unity can be produced; but this of course ... can only be produced through a completed approximation to the infinite, and that is intrinsically impossible'.[27] This is what Hegel vividly characterised as 'the bad infinite'.[28]

Does this impossible production of absolute systematic unity correspond, then, to Schlegel's literary project? In Schlegel's *Literary Annotations* from 1797/98, we can certainly read the following: 'A work is only properly possible as a system. Every other species of composition is incapable of closure, but can only come to an end or simply be broken off; must therefore always end in an annihilating or ironising manner'.[29] I would suggest, despite external appearances, that the au-

---

[26] Ibid., p. 272.   [27] Ibid., p. 276.

[28] Hegel, *Wissenschaft der Logik*, ed. Georg Lasson, I, p. 128 ff.; *Hegel's Science of Logic*, trans. A.V. Miller (London 1969), p. 139.

[29] *Literary Notebooks*, ed. H. Eichner (Frankfurt am Main 1980), Nr. 893.

thentic source of Schlegel's conception of dialectic does *not* in fact lie in the reciprocal relationship of activity and negation outlined by Fichte in Section 3 of the *1794 Doctrine of Science*. For the reciprocal determination of an infinitely perpetuated process here is grounded and sustained by the primordial certainty of the self-positing ego. Expressed in Fichtean terms: the absolute thesis necessarily precedes the relative connection between antithesis and synthesis – that is, of opposing and of the mediation of opposing. Without the self-positing ego, the reciprocal determination of positing and opposing would remain ungrounded.

But the process of irony, which Schlegel also describes as a 'constant alternation' of self-creation and self-destruction'[30], possesses no such basis. Rather, it actively rises into a state of *groundless floating*. The productive and freely creative ego posits a reality, and revokes that reality at the same time. It cannot appeal to any original supporting principle that would simultaneously guarantee reality or its repudiation, which would therefore transform both activities into a purely quantitative relation of reciprocal divisibility. The self-positing activity of the ironist is not something that is already partial or half-hearted in advance. Nor is the process of revocation deliberately restricted to the other aspect of the activity in order that the two contrary tendencies might ultimately concur by virtue of the 'restriction' common to both. The ironist posits everything and revokes everything since this is the only way in which he can fundamentally allude to the *all-encompassing whole* that always transcends him and all his achievements.

Fichte's *Doctrine of Science* begins with an absolute principle that the ironist must necessarily regard as something yet to be achieved. In the context of the romantic conception of literature, the dialectic of reciprocal determination is thus effectively presented from a reversed perspective. The absolute is always already there, and is first differentiated as an infinite progress only through the constantly renewable process of opposition within unity, an opposition constantly recuperated and mediated by that unity. Irony arises through consciousness of the absence of the unity that is intrinsically sought for and striven after. And the contradictions in which reflection so easily and perpetually entangles itself merely serve to renew and to intensify the yearning for the system, or definitively closed work, that we do not yet possess.

[30] KA II, p. 172.

One can also derive this contrasting perspective analytically by examining the concept of system involved here. The mediating Fichtean perspective of divisibility logically presupposes the *concept of totality*, which alone permits us to interpret the relevant delimitations precisely as divisions of a whole that is already given. Fichte's constructive insight was to dissolve the fundamental limits imposed by Kantian critique in a double manner: by internalising the problematic limiting notion of the 'thing in itself', which was supposed to indicate a world beyond that of the human understanding, and by reinterpreting it as a 'restriction' that the absolute ego opposes to itself as finite ego precisely in the form of the non-ego. The ego therefore makes a double appearance: in its absolute role as the inaugurator of being and in its relative role as the autonomous reduction of posited being through the positing of restrictions. The absolute itself, which effectively fulfils the grounding function of Spinoza's substantialistic conception even though it is here characterised by the fully spontaneous activity of subjectivity, thus provides the ultimate framework for this process of self-limitation. On this premise, all of reality appears as the gradually differentiated manifestation of the one all-encompassing substance.

In contrast to this approach to philosophical construction, dialectical philosophy works with a different perspective upon the concept of totality. For here, totality stands at the *end* rather than at the beginning. The self-differentiating processes are not regarded as so many successive limitations of a whole that is already given, but rather as the progressive annulment of limitations leading towards a whole that is yet to be attained. There is thus no need to introduce in the first place such restrictions and limitations grounded in an activity that is paradoxically directed against itself. Just how the latter can reverse its own original tendency towards self-activity, just where the 'opposited' dimension of its own directed activity can come from – all of this can hardly be explained by considerations deriving from the authentic significance of this activity. It can only be explained by reference to the need for a constructive system that itself generates such distinctions. Dialectical philosophy does not face these difficulties because it does not have to attempt to derive opposing from positing, or to derive nothing from being. Dialectical philosophy starts rather from the multiplicity of given limitations, and attempts to move beyond them precisely through developing its own insight into the reciprocally determining character of all such limitations.

But this repudiation of any absolutely prior fundamental principle implies the need for a *representative* figure to guide us along the appropriate path. And that is the ironist. If there is now no absolute ego to provide the secure basis for the never-ending process of limitation and division, then dialectical movement of thought, which constantly relativises all our supposedly definitive insights, must always retain an orientation towards the whole that is yet to be attained. For Schlegel, irony reminds us that the whole, as long as it remains unavailable to us, must still be envisaged as an ultimately binding task that transcends every particular act of reflection and every particular standpoint. Without this orientation along the path, one that permits no strict deductions on the basis of an absolute principle and merely challenges the relative truth of limited positions, reflection would indeed abandon itself to an ungoverned pleasure in mere negation. If an abstract nay is simply opposed to any and every yea, if all seriousness is simply dissolved in playful wit, then the process of reflection loses all its direction and finally ends up by merely *enjoying itself* as such.

This is of course precisely the charge that Plato made against the Sophists and Hegel directed against the protagonists of Romantic irony. For it is the latter who specifically pursue 'the self-conscious dissolution of all that is objective'[31], as Hegel claims in the review of Solger, where he critically analyses the typically modern over-emphasis on subjectivity in general. It is surprising to see how Hegel interprets romantic irony, which for Schlegel provided an essentially corrective perspective for a philosophy genuinely oriented towards the whole, as merely an expression of arbitrariness and wilful caprice. His misunderstanding here is total. Whereas the romantic ironist actually wanted to sustain through literary means our openness to a systematic philosophy yet to be achieved, the systematic protagonist of absolute spirit regards this simply as an evasion of serious thought that shuns genuine engagement with the basic issue and revels in 'the superiority of subjective consciousness with respect to all things'.

When he discussed antiquity and Socratic irony in his lectures on the history of philosophy[32], Hegel treated this 'manner of comporting oneself in society' simply as a subjective mode of behaviour between

---

[31] Hegel, 'Solgers nachgelassene Schriften und Briefwechsel', *Werkausgabe*, vol. 11, p. 233.
[32] Hegel, *Werkausgabe*, vol. 18, p. 458ff. *Hegel's Lectures on the History of Philosophy*, trans. E.S. Haldane and F.H. Simson (London 1892), vol. 1, pp. 397ff.

individuals that must eventually be turned through intellectual discipline into dialectical method as such. For irony itself lacks any substantive grounding, and its purely local character challenges what some
particular individual happens on occasion to believe. It simply assumes
that someone believes this or that claim or brings specific presuppositions to the discussion in question. But for Hegel, the decisive task
is to examine these presuppositions as such and thus to advance the
objective knowledge of the matter at issue precisely by clarifying the
presuppositions that are necessarily made in all situations of dialogue.
What we are compelled to think in the case of any specific concept is
for Hegel precisely what constitutes the specific concept in question,
and it is not therefore something that can be relegated to an apparently arbitrary way of understanding things now in one sense and now
in another.

Hegel goes on to confront the irony of Socrates with the more recent career of irony originally inspired by Schlegel. As in the lectures
on aesthetics, here too he castigates the hypertophried ego of Fichtean
philosophy that is allegedly responsible for the modern loss of genuine
substantial content amongst the romantics. He presents his own contrasting model of authentic dialectic that will finally fulfil the method
whose immature beginnings are exemplified by Socrates. 'The simple
element in Socratic irony is this: that he permitted the response which
he elicits, just as it is immediately assumed and entertained, to reveal its
own validity. (All dialectic permits what is allegedly valid to reveal itself
as if it were so, permits its inner destruction to develop immanently –
the universal irony of the world)'.

What is the significance of this remarkable translation of a subjective
comportment of interlocutors onto the level of *objective processes within
the world*? It signifies a different attitude, which the philosopher is encouraging us to adopt. For if we can successfully translate the ironic
attitude of purely free-floating reflection amongst individual subjects
into an objective process of refuting essentially limited presuppositions,
we shall thereby have submitted ourselves to the inexorable logic of the
dialectical method. Irony is then no longer a merely personal stylistic
device, but something that demands real insight into the matter at issue.
Hegel describes irony as the 'universal irony of the world', revealing as
it does that nothing is quite as it originally appears to be, because all of
our initial conceptions harbour inevitably limited perspectives, involve
necessary presuppositions that must, with equal necessity, be further
clarified and recuperated within the developing process of knowledge.

Now I wish to claim that precisely this 'irony of the world', which is pre-eminently supposed to advance the great task of knowing in the Hegelian sense as opposed to the careless play of the ever triumphant arbitrary subject, actually comes very close to Schlegel's own intentions in the matter.[33] Romantic irony is therefore a literary manifestation of dialectic, which has far less in common with Fichte's attempts at ultimate grounding and philosophical deduction than it does with Hegel's speculative method. Hegel simply failed, or did not really wish, to perceive this *parallel* because he was so concerned with challenging the vanity of modern subjectivism in its resistance to substantial content, with demonstrating that the reflective process of dialectic itself can properly lay claim to the required content.

Thus it is that Hegel's image of Socrates comes to assume such an ambivalent character. On the one hand, irony anticipates the dialectic by facilitating the move from a subjective form of reflection towards the elaboration of an objective method: Socrates is a forerunner of Hegel. On the other hand, Socrates is a Sophist and thus a forerunner of that modernity that celebrates the cult of individuality: Schlegel is an intensified example of an ancient theme. Following in Hegel's tracks, Kierkegaard would later dispel this ambivalent judgement insofar as he identified the infinite negativity of the subject with the figure Socrates and thereby turned him into the very prototype of the modern romantic that Hegel held he never really was.

---

[33] For the whole relationship, cf. the substantial article by Ernst Behler, 'Friedrich Schlegel und Hegel', *Hegel-Studien* 2, 1963.

11

IS THERE A HEGELIAN THEORY OF
AESTHETIC EXPERIENCE?

I

The question expressed in my title addresses a question located in the intermediate space between Hegel's philosophy of art and Kant's *Critique of Judgement*. And it thereby assumes an inevitably paradoxical appearance. For at first sight, it should be obvious that an aesthetic theory like Hegel's, oriented as it is to the structure of the *work* of art, will naturally neglect the analysis of the *effect* produced upon the subject by aesthetic phenomena and concentrate rather upon identifying the essential character of art itself. On this conception of aesthetic theory, there seems little place for the concept of aesthetic experience. On the other hand, one cannot straightforwardly claim that Kant's transcendental derivation of the judgement of taste from the reflective activities of the faculty of judgement itself provides a theory of aesthetic experience either. In order to address this question adequately, we must attempt, at least initially, to separate Kant's own approach from its predominantly epistemological context, and develop it somewhat further in the direction of a substantive definition of art. But then we shall also have to revise Hegel's decisive identification of the essence of art as the 'sensuous appearing of the Idea' if we are to discover traces of something like aesthetic experience within his own systematically expounded concept of art.

In the following remarks, I shall attempt just such a mutually illuminating analysis of the two theories. Insofar as we must also recognise the specificity of the conceptual approach each theory takes to the problem of art, we cannot rest content with any purely external comparison between them. We must rather attempt to see if a systematic comparison of both theories can help to shed clearer light upon the specific

quality of aesthetic experience itself. In my view, this demands a careful
examination of the so-called 'symbolic form of art'. The discussion originally
conducted within the Hegelian school as well as that of more recent interpreters has generally focussed much more closely upon Hegel's conception of the 'classical' and 'romantic' forms of art. This itself expresses
a justified sense that the symbolic form that Hegel himself characterised
as 'pre-art' cannot easily be reconciled with the governing perspective
of a systematic interpretation of art in terms of the category of spirit.
And the question concerning the 'symbolic' seems to be particularly
remote from the modern preoccupation with the controversial thesis
of 'the end of art' – something allegedly produced when independent
reflective content comes to invade and destroy the traditionally unified 'work'. The symbolic form of art, which comes first with respect
both to historical development and to the conceptual explication of
art, is certainly difficult to accommodate within Hegel's fundamental
conception of dialectical mediation. But that is what makes it a suitable
candidate for discussion in the light of our original question.

Before briefly sketching the further course of the argument, I should
like to emphasise what I am *not* attempting to do here. In the *first* place,
it is not my intention to provide a kind of doxographic contrast between
Kant and Hegel. That has often carefully been done before. In the
second place, I am not offering a philological contribution to the question concerning the lecture materials that Hotho edited so cleverly
to produce a unified and readable version of the constantly modified
courses on aesthetics given by Hegel on several occasions.[1] For the
present, at least, we shall have to make do with Hotho's text, just as
we have always similarly had to rely upon the *Corpus Aristotelicum*. Fully
aware that we have no completely authentic or properly authorised
text at hand, we can still undertake successful philosophical enquiry
on the basis of the materials that have come down to us. Any other
alternative, even if feasible, would probably yield far less fruitful results.
The philological analysis of the traditional Aristotelian corpus as pursued by Werner Jaeger and his school should surely serve as a terrible

---

[1] A. Gethmann-Siefert regards Hotho's interventions in the text, which go far beyond the
usual editorial procedures, as so significant that she claims: 'The 'aesthetician' Hotho still
continues, under the mask of his teacher Hegel, to exert an influence upon contemporary
philosophical discussions in the field of aesthetics' ('H.G. Hotho', *Hegel-Studien*, Beiheft
22, 1983, p. 237). Yet Hotho's own originality, as far as we can see, is so slight in comparison
with his teacher's that the student's reproduction of Hegel does not appear decisively to
distort the teacher's views anyway.

warning in such matters. In the *third* place, I shall not attempt the kind of reconstruction of intellectual development that has become so common today. For however instructive it may be to observe a thinker's ideas in the process of emergence, it must also be possible to grasp the relevant content of an idea independently of its genesis. Intellectual reconstruction cannot replace the task of conceptual understanding, for it is always only on the basis of some prior understanding that one is able to identify what is relevant from the abundance of scattered, sometimes fragmentary and often insignificant documentary material available to us.[2]

Here I shall undertake instead a structural analysis of Hegel's thought as expressed in the lectures on aesthetics. The analysis will not content itself with simply following the suggestive path of the dialectical movement, but will attempt, guided by the contrasting Kantian analysis of the issues, to reveal a persisting trace of aesthetic experience, which Hegel never systematically develops and that perhaps cannot ultimately be fully accounted for within the context of a Hegelian philosophy of spirit. In the *first* place, we must clarify with reference to the Kantian position precisely what we are to understand by 'aesthetic experience'. In the *second* place, we need to explicate the basic substantive premises that clearly distinguish Hegel's undertaking from Kant's analysis of the specific logic of the judgement of taste. In the *third* place, we must examine the character of the symbolic form of art where there is a sense in which we cannot yet speak of 'works' because the intrinsic inadequacy of form here still involves a quest for the appropriate content. In the *fourth* place, finally, we shall have to answer the natural question as to why the romantic form of art, which in dissolving the unity of form and content typically exhibited in classical art corresponds in a sense to the symbolic form of art that also seems to anticipate it, cannot itself be regarded as the authentic candidate for exemplifying 'aesthetic experience'.

II

We can interpret the concept of 'aesthetic experience' in terms of what Kant describes, employing the terminology of our cognitive faculties,

---

[2] The reader is referred to the studies by Klaus Düsing ('Idealität und Geschichtlichkeit der Kunst in Hegels Ästhetik', in *Zeitschrift für philosophische Forschung* 35, 1981), Otto Pöggeler ('Die Enstehung von Hegels Ästhetik in Jena', in *Hegel-Studien*, Beiheft 20, 1980), and A. Gethmann-Siefert (*Die Funktion der Kunst in der Geschichte, Hegel-Studien*, Beiheft 25, 1984).

as 'reflective judgement'. Since I have presented my interpretation of this question in some detail elsewhere[3], I shall confine myself to a brief summary here. In his transcendental analysis of consciousness, Kant locates the faculty of judgement, which mediates the particular with the universal, between the faculties of reason and the understanding, and proceeds to reinterpret the principal function of 'determining judgement' in the light of purely 'reflective judgement'.

In the case of determining judgements, we subsume a given particular under a given universal or relate a given sensuous content to its appropriate conceptual form in the interests of cognition. In the case of reflective judgements, on the other hand, we seek a universal that is not given in order to apply it to some particular that is, or attempt to move intelligibly from an appropriate sensuously given content to something like universality in general, even though in this case we possess no determinate universal that would make objective cognition possible. Since the movement of reflection here is not governed by any concept, it can only acquire orientation from the mediating function of the faculty of judgement itself. The faculty of judgement, in responding to a given content, thereby becomes aware of its own intrinsic function. For in performing its work it already presupposes a certain potential for the very order that it itself brings about through the act of judging. That is why things appear to accommodate themselves spontaneously to our cognitive intentions and why we can consider nature heuristically as an intelligibly articulated structure. This produces an immediate sense of unburdening that can be aesthetically enjoyed in its own right.

But there must be some *stimulating factor* for this sense to arise. What precisely transpires when we find ourselves in those states that we describe as 'aesthetic' and that can effectively be interpreted by the subtle means of Kant's conceptual approach? Something must have happened so that the transcendental processes of consciousness typically involved in the exercise of the faculties of cognition suddenly find themselves effectively suspended in relation to the objects of experience. These faculties thus enter into a kind of suspended state, where they become aware of their own functional relationships with one another. It is quite

---

[3] Firstly in my article 'Über einige Bedingungen gegenwärtiger Ästhetik' in R. Bubner, *Ästhetische Erfahrung*, Frankfurt am Main 1989. In this connection, the reader is also referred to the writings of H.R. Jauss, who pursues a similar argument from the perspective of literary history and criticism. For a representative selection of relevant articles, cf. his collection *Ästhetische Erfahrung und literarische Hermeneutik* (Frankfurt am Main 1982). Most recently: H.E. Allison, *Kant's Theory of Taste* (Cambridge 2001).

true that no specific knowledge – either of the object or the subject – is produced in this state, but it does facilitate a fundamental insight into the essential character of cognition in general. This insight is not theoretically grounded in any way, but rather arises from a situation in which everything appears as if already predisposed to cohere with human knowledge. Unless we are prepared to deceive ourselves, this is clearly something that we cannot bring about consciously. We can only find ourselves in this situation through some extraordinary experience that permits the transcendental assumption that such an encounter with objects corresponds to our own cognitive potential.

Since it would be entirely illegitimate to make this claim simply on the basis of extravagant metaphysical speculation, we must attempt to find a concrete basis for it instead. But what is at issue here is not merely some particular case of knowledge, but rather the entire inter-connected structure of our knowledge considered from the perspective of the overall 'technology of nature'. The stimulating factor that first allows the faculty of judgement to become aware of itself as such must possess the peculiar capacity of presenting the whole through the in-dividual case. On the one hand, the experience in question must be a real experience rather than a dreaming delusion. On the other hand, it must also sufficiently transcend normal experience as to permit a suc-cessful encounter with the world as such without need of any further conceptual elaboration of the empirically given.

It is quite clear that all aesthetic gain falls exclusively to the *sub-ject* that is cognitively oriented to the world. The world immediately presents itself to the subject as if it were fashioned entirely with a view to the purposes of the latter. But in order to render this remarkable state of affairs intelligible, the capacity for such a reflective perspec-tive cannot simply be ascribed to the faculty of judgement alone. For the *object*, in relation to which we find ourselves in an aesthetic state, must be structured in such a way that the universal can manifest itself in the particular, that the individual can shed light upon the whole, or that reality can reveal itself as the medium of our purposes. These are all different and partially inadequate ways of describing something for which we lack the adequate categories. For the aesthetic state of the subject cannot in principle offer an explicit object of cognition precisely because it essentially reflects the very process of cognition itself.

But given the general structure of his own theory, Kant was not re-ally in a position to address this issue properly. And that is not simply because the modestly limited perspective of the critical theory of knowledge prevented him from attempting a corresponding determination of the object. For he also had absolutely no way of effectively explicating the intrinsic character of what it is that mediates between universality and particularity. That is why he takes refuge in allusions to a 'supersensible substrate' of nature. Although we are said to know nothing about this substrate in itself, it is nonetheless supposed to provide the ultimate ground for such mediation. In this connection, we must also remember that for Kant himself, aesthetics represents one branch of *the more general question of teleology* that still remained to be clarified in terms of the critical theory of knowledge. From the historical point of view, modern aesthetics effectively emerges out of the traditional concerns of a cosmology that had come to find itself radically displaced in the new scientific age.

The openness of Kant's theory with respect to identifying the relevant objects of aesthetic experience is connected inextricably with the entire transcendental approach itself. But this perspective effectively disappears if we now turn to the massive *underlying assumption* that supports Hegel's aesthetics. For Hegel replaces aesthetic experience with the idea of the sensuous incarnation of spirit, procuring an adequate intuition of itself in and through a product created specifically for that purpose. The original parallel between aesthetics and teleology is thereby dissolved, and with it that priority of natural beauty over artistic beauty that Kant was forced to uphold given the cognitive model underlying his analysis of the judgement of taste. In view of the superiority that is now ascribed to the spiritual ideal of beauty, Hegel can only regard the beauty of nature as an imperfect reflection of something greater.

III

Hegel elevates art to the systematic level of *spirit* precisely in order to make it an appropriate object of *philosophical science*. Along with religion and philosophy, art belongs to the absolute because it is not concerned with the essentially deficient realm of finitude. Art is one of the actually existing forms in which spirit finds itself entirely at home because it can here, and without remainder, essentially mediate itself with its own truth. And that is why the intuitive dimension that intrinsically belongs to art as the sensuous manifestation of the Idea cannot simply be defined in terms of the perceptual activity of the subject. This dimension must rather be defined directly in terms of the undiminished spiritual content of art itself. The external form that is brought forth by spirit as a means of intuiting its own character is the *work of art*. And given the systematic construction of Hegel's theory, it is the work of art that now assumes an exemplary burden of proof for the entire argument. If there were not actual 'works', Hegel's idealist conception of art would remain ungrounded.

Hegel thereby relinquishes two lines of thought that had traditionally served to define the concept of the 'work' – one deriving from classical philosophy and one from a particular development of Christian theology. In the classical context, the concept of the work was understood pre-eminently in a *technical* sense, and the task was essentially to provide appropriate guidelines for the actual production of the object. What must the maker be able to do in order to produce something that stands forth in its own right and yet resembles something other than itself? Existing reality provides the original standard to which the *ergon* stands in an essentially mimetic relation. The Christian concept of creation, on the other hand, eliminates this presupposition since it is now the omnipotent God who first creates the world out of nothing. The notion of artistic *genius* developed since the Renaissance is a descendant of this view insofar as the artist, although a created being himself, is specifically made in the image of God, and thereby also possesses an independent capacity for original creation in his own right. Like an 'alter deus', the artist produces new realities of his own through the authentic works of art that he creates.

Now Hegel shows little interest either in the mimetic technique of art or in the genius as a creator of alternative worlds. He employs the concept of 'work' solely in terms of the appropriate medium for the objective expression of the principle of spirit from the perspective of which his entire system is articulated.[4] This medium must be capable of presenting itself in terms of sensuous intuition without effectively obscuring the essential spiritual content. The sensuous character of the work of art is a showing [*Schein*] that cannot impede the process of spirit precisely because it is posited by spirit itself. And it is this that also facilitates the transition from the actual expression of spirit in art to the more reflective forms of religion and philosophy. For the original spiritual character that constitutes all works of art can ultimately be

---

[4] E.g. Hegel, *Ästhetik* I (*Werkausgabe*, vol. 13), p. 27f., 48f., 114f; *Hegel's Aesthetic*, trans. T.M. Knox, vol. 1 (Oxford 1975), p. 12f-, 29f-, 82f-.

trusted to overcome the medium of sensuous appearance itself: the essence liberates itself into its own form.

This concept of the work allows us to present all manifestations of art according to the schema of ascent, culmination and decline. And this yields the 'symbolic', the 'classical' and the 'romantic' as the three relevant *forms of art*. The unity of form and content in the work, a concept presupposed throughout the entire analysis, is sought for in symbolic art, is perfected in classical art, and is finally dissolved in romantic art. This differentiated concept of the work offers us an overall perspective upon the different epochs of art and thus introduces an essentially *historical* dimension to the ancient idea of an eternally valid standard of beauty. And this is of course why Hegel has earned the title of 'the father of art history'.[5] But this concept of work also allows a systematic interpretation of the individual arts as distinctive ways of embodying the aesthetic ideal itself. And this suggestion concerning the internal relationship between the various arts is one that is susceptible of further elaboration and finds a certain confirmation in twentieth century attempts to relate the arts to one another more actively.[6]

Now the *symbolic form of art* assumes a rather peculiar place within this triadic scheme in a number of respects.[7] Ever since the celebrated *querelle* concerning the respective merits of the ancients and the moderns, the paradigm of classical antiquity had generally been pitted over against the typically modern appeal to innovation. And Schiller had then interpreted his own relation to Goethe by formulating the contemporary version of this debate in terms of the 'naive' and the 'sentimental'. A generation later, Hegel develops the idea of the Romantic movement that already began with Schlegel, and thereby comes to distinguish the 'classical' and the 'Romantic' forms of art as he does.[8]

But Hegel also introduces the symbolic form of art, a concept that had played no role in these earlier discussions, as an antecedent stage

---

[5] Cf. Ernst Gombrich, 'Hegel und die Kunstgeschichte', *Neue Rundschau* 88, 1977.

[6] Cf. Adorno's thesis concerning the 'internal fraying' of the arts in modernity ('Die Kunst und die Künste', in Th.-W. Adorno, *Ohne Leitbild*, Frankfurt am Main 1967).

[7] This seems to have been overlooked by Paul de Man when he hastily interprets Hegel's aesthetics as 'theory of symbolic form', which, despite this symbolic approach it shares with Romanticism, has very little to contribute to 'understanding our own modernity' (P. de Man, 'Sign and Symbol in Hegel's Aesthetics', *Critical Enquiry* 8, 1981/2, p. 764).

[8] For more on this entire issue, cf. the chapter on 'Hegel and Goethe' included in this book.

in relation to the other two generally acknowledged forms of art. In this connection, he was probably influenced by the work of one of his Heidelberg colleagues – namely, by Friedrich Creuzer's *Symbolism and Mythology of the Ancient Peoples, and especially of the Greeks*.[9] But Hegel also makes use of considerable material from the Orientalist scholarship of his time, whereas Creuzer had mainly concerned himself with Greek culture. But what is especially striking in Hegel's account is the structural peculiarity of the symbolic form of art insofar as, strictly speaking, this does not yet properly involve the concept of the 'work' at all. The very *distance of symbolic art* with respect to the governing concept of the work makes it a prime candidate for elucidating our question concerning the traces of aesthetic experience in Hegel's philosophy of art.

IV

Under the name of the 'symbolic', Hegel includes a broad range of phenomena, from spontaneous and religiously motivated symbolism, through forms of the sublime, to the playful and instructive uses of fable, metaphor and didactic poem, and so on. We can already discover some relevant suggestions in this direction in one particularly interesting chapter of Creuzer's work that presents certain 'ideas for a physics of the symbol and of myth'.[10] But Hegel succeeds in bringing such observations, covering as they do a surprisingly broad range of phenomena, into an illuminating systematic connection with one another.

With reference to the marginal forms conceptualised within a general theory of genres, Hegel interprets the historical legacy of Persian, Indian and Egyptian art as a kind of naive product in direct contrast with the more reflective creations of spirit. This opposition between

---

9 Cf. Hegel's letter to Creuzer of 30 October 1819 and the remarks by Karl Rosenkranz concerning Hegel's excerpts from Creuzer's work (*Hegels Leben*, 1844, p. 15). This insufficiently explored relationship has been discussed by J. Hoffmeister in his article 'Hegel und Creuzer', *Deutsche Vierteljahrsschrift* 1930. Cf. also H.-G. Gadamer, 'Hegel und die Heidelberger Romantik', in his collection *Hegels Dialektik* (Tübingen 1971). For the latter essay, see H.-G. Gadamer, *Hegel's Dialectic: Five Hermeneutical Studies*, translated by P.C. Smith (New Haven: Yale University Press 1976). It should be noted that Creuzer's pioneering approach by no means went uncontested at the time: cf. J.H. Voss, *Antisymbolik* I (Stuttgart 1824).

10 As already evident in the first edition (Leipzig/Darmstadt 1810), which was subsequently expanded and often reprinted. Surprisingly, Hoffmeister does not discuss the earlier edition. Hegel himself referred to the second edition of 1812, which contains the relevant chapter in volume I (§26 ff., pp. 52–102).

naive and reflected forms of art in turn enables Hegel to respond to Kant's theory of the sublime, which had been systematically displaced by the exclusive Hegelian emphasis upon the domain of fine art. Here I shall ignore the questions raised by this unexpected combination of such heterogenous approaches, as well as that concerning the adequacy of Hegel's actual interpretation, although the general plausibility of this new concept of symbolic art depends entirely upon such considerations.[11] For we might well ask why anyone should ever have dreamed of combining oriental cultic practices, the products of didactic poetry and the hallowed doctrine of the sublime in some dialectical triad in the first place.

I shall concentrate instead simply on the basic motivation behind the entire analysis, which essentially interprets all the phenomena of the symbolic as a progressive *search* for the appropriate form in which to express a significant content. In the first place, this implies that symbolic art possesses a dynamic character, one that is quite different from that belonging to the internally differentiated forms of classical art and the self-dissolving tendency of romantic art. For the classical and the Romantic form of art both presuppose the stability of the enduring work. In symbolic art, on the other hand, there is no proper 'work' in which the spirit might find its adequate expression. The symbolic form of art gestures towards something that never fully coincides with itself. It is quite true that some sensuously perceptible object is always interpreted from the perspective of spirit in symbolic art and is never simply taken up unaltered and thereby left in its original natural condition. But what is directly and sensuously presented to us in symbolic art is precisely something that spirit has *not yet* been able fully to appropriate for itself. The inner and the outer still stand in some unresolved tension with one another, and it is 'imagination', as Hegel explicitly says, that must bridge the persisting disparity between them. Adoration of the divine in terms of some natural object, the Egyptian pyramid as the ultimate paradigm of the symbolic, the massive temple architecture, the Sphinx as the incarnation of all that is intrinsically enigmatic, elaborate manifestations of allegorical allusion – these are all perfect examples of the still uncompleted struggle between outer form and inner content. Symbolic art, as Hegel says, represents the 'spiritual task that falls to

---

[11] Peter Szondi rightly describes Hegel's sections on didactic poetry and the like as the 'least inspired' passages of the entire work (*Poetik und Geschichtsphilosophie* I, Frankfurt am Main 1974, p. 390).

self-deciphering spirit even though it actually fails to accomplish here its own deciphering'.[12] What is the precise meaning of this Hegelian claim?

If symbolic art presents us with no completed work, we must interpret the sensuous object in question *as if it were* a work. The spiritual significance that is not properly realised in visible reality must nonetheless be bestowed upon the latter. But this presupposes a subject that perceives things as if they were more than mere things. The spiritual task of 'deciphering' derives therefore from an original projection that itself lends to the intrinsically meaningless object the very meaning subsequently to be read off from it. This problem does not arise in the same way in the case of a work of art, where external manifestation is entirely fused with intrinsic meaning and the actual existence of the object is the very work of spirit itself. Here the sensuous presence of the object already harbours, without detour, what calls to be deciphered. The subjectivity of the producer and that of the recipient alike can properly withdraw into the background because the aesthetically interpreted reality and the appropriate understanding of the latter essentially coincide within the work of art: spirit finds fulfilment precisely in intuiting itself.

The symbol, on the other hand, inevitably brings *subjectivity* into play because the lack of any unified 'work', understood as a kind of full spiritual self-presence, must be compensated through the express achievements of human imagination. The imagination of the artist bridges the distance between the sensuously given object and the substantial spiritual content, which, not being immediately given as such, must now be imaginatively constructed in response to the object. Whatever the artist may have thought in bestowing ever-changing forms on god and animal or in fashioning his devotional *stelae*, in producing the sublime poetry of the psalm or the ingenious allusions of the parable – without the labour of the recipient who is appropriately touched and affected by such forms, all symbolic art would remain entirely powerless. And there is more we can say here too. For the artist of pre-Greek mythology disappears entirely into the anonymity of an unquestioned religious context, whereas in the subsidiary forms of didactic poetry, he later succeeds in expressing a conscious and deliberate awareness of what he is doing.

But it is the imaginative capacities of the *recipient* that are the ultimate key for unlocking the significance of the symbolic form of art. For it

---

[12] Hegel, *Ästhetik* I, p. 456f; *Hegel's Aesthetics*, vol. 1, p. 354.

is only by imaginatively developing a meaning not already present that the recipient is capable of transcending the given as a mere thing. The latter is neither a natural object simply in its immediate state, nor a result of the regular technical manipulation that is directed solely towards the transformation of nature. To take the visible as something that points pre-eminently towards the invisible involves the spontaneous contribution of the percipient who first activates the symbolic function. The kind of explanations offered by systematic commentators or the interpretations subsequently provided by philosophers intent on filling out their preconceived schemata have absolutely no role to play in this connection. For we cannot speak of 'symbolism' unless the subject in question actually has an aesthetic experience occasioned by the relevant phenomena.

The self-deciphering activity of the spirit transpires precisely there in the face of art that is perceived symbolically in search of a content that is not manifested in the given form without remainder. And we should always privilege this approach over against the purely conceptual *ex post* thematisation of art. We learn more about symbolic art from our never-ending efforts to decipher it than we do from a philosophical interpretation that undertakes to explain, on systematic grounds, why the symbolic approach remains a search that can only come to rest with the classical work of art. It therefore seems that we can find a place, at the heart of Hegel's conception of art, for 'aesthetic experience', as a specific relation to the aesthetic on the part of the subject, without appealing to any external, say Kantian, ideas.

It is worth noting that Hegel actually praises Kant, who is otherwise generally rebuked, *en passant* in his introductory remarks on the 'symbolism of the sublime'. The reduction of all determinations to the subjective domain, Hegel observes, must 'be regarded as correct according to its universal principle in *this* regard, namely that sublimity is not itself contained in any object of nature but only in our own feeling to the extent that we are conscious of our superiority over the nature within us and thereby also over the nature outside us.'[13] In contrast to the beautiful, the sublime possesses a kind of relation to the Ideas of reason that is intrinsically unsuited to external representation. This is because nothing in the world of appearance can properly do justice to that which is superior in principle to anything belonging to nature. The content therefore necessarily negates the realm of appearance,

[13] Hegel, *Ästhetik* I, p. 467f; *Hegel's Aesthetics*, vol. 1, p. 363.

particularises the latter and ultimately brings it to vanishing point. If Hegel is thereby not so much describing the sublation of art in spirit as such, but rather projecting an intrinsic possibility of art itself, then his approach here stands in obvious contrast to his principal thesis concerning art as the sensuous manifestation of the Idea.

Now Hegel, of course, does not share the strict separation between 'reason' and the 'understanding' that underlies Kant's own distinction between the 'sublime' and the 'beautiful'. If the sublime represents the relationship of phenomena to our moral vocation as rational beings, then the beautiful presents the universal structures involved in our actual cognition of the world. Both forms can only be realised in terms of the effect they exercise upon our own feeling. Whereas the beautiful presents that harmony between the world and cognition that produces delight, the sublime arises from the experience of an incongruity that can never be overcome. This latter can only be brought into the strange equilibrium of 'negative pleasure' by reference to the world-transcending capacity of the moral subject. But lines of thought like these are entirely and essentially foreign to Hegel's whole approach. And his astonishing admission of the correctness of Kant's theory can only signify that art that still falls short of complete articulation as a work claims its existence here by virtue of the aesthetic experience of the conscious subject. But this merely consolidates Hegel's evaluation of the symbolic as a form of pre-art, and further underlines the focus of his own aesthetic theory upon an ontology of the 'work'.

V

Lastly we must respond briefly to the objection that these aspects of aesthetic experience that we have uncovered in Hegel cannot be restricted to his theory of the symbolic, but may equally well be extended to apply to his analysis of *romantic* art. This raises a further issue that we have not yet addressed but that certainly helps to explain the recently renewed interest in the concept of aesthetic experience as such. For have we not all been effectively influenced by the new kinds of art that have emerged after Hegel, and were therefore in principle quite inaccessible to his thought? From the revolutionary artistic upheavals at the close of the nineteenth century through to the expressly transgressive experiments of the present, art in general has clearly followed a very different course from that anticipated by Hegel. The comprehensive orienting capacity of art, far from being overtaken by that of philosophy, has itself come to assume a leading role in articulating our view of the world as a whole.

The confidence once invested in the systematic possibilities of philosophical synthesis has vanished, and the successor disciplines that followed afterwards – the special sciences in their entirety, characterised as they are by the ever-increasing specialisation and the further division of intellectual labour – have proved incapable of providing any unified image of reality as a whole. In modernity, therefore, it is the *arts* that have come to fulfil this function of more easily facilitating a real understanding of our world and of ourselves. The *arts* are capable of specifically serving these spiritual and intellectual needs at the requisite level of universality precisely because, unlike the highly specialised modern disciplines, they are accessible in principle to all human beings even though they also self-consciously interpret and develop our experience in accordance with the requisite demands of the epoch. Does this itself not strongly suggest that we could learn something significant from Hegel's perceptive engagement with the self-conscious art of the romantic age?

The answer to the original objection is simply this: romantic art cannot properly be grasped in Hegelian terms without presupposing his own governing concept of the *work*. For everything Hegel says about the progressive dissolution of unified form as independent and self-conscious 'reflection' gradually comes to penetrate art itself is still oriented essentially to the central ideal of an ultimate reconciliation between form and content. Hegel's analysis of the Romantic 'dissolution' of art has been rightly praised as an extraordinarily subtle one. But this does nothing to alter the fact that Hegel, like Goethe, still regards romantic art simply as a richly developed deviation from classical art, and this is essentially because Hegel's theoretical gaze is entirely governed by the concept of the 'work'. Furthermore, it is quite inadequate, it seems to me, to restrict the range of specifically aesthetic experience solely to that which precisely *fails* to fulfil the meaning of a work in its entirety. The role of subjectivity must rather be regarded as constitutive for aesthetic experience as such. It should not simply be acknowledged as an inevitable but ultimately undesirable factor that threatens to lead us away from the proper path of proper ontological insight.

I should like to say a final word about the fascination that is exercised in this connection by modern art. It is certainly true that we can describe the path it has taken as a reflective and deliberate dismantling of the concept of the 'work'. The play of transient impressions, the use of multiple perspectives, the introduction of concrete objects as a substitute for creative intervention, the incorporation of trivial products of popular culture, the celebration of the obvious and the common-place, and so on – all of these procedures can be interpreted in terms of such deliberate dismantling, and this has of course been done many times before. But it may be worth asking if this concentration upon the now vanished ideal of the 'work' does not falsify the original character of artistic expression. For while the latter certainly follows the general movement in the direction of 'autonomy', it simultaneously resists interpretation in terms of obsolescent assumptions from the past. The principle of aesthetic autonomy answers to the idea that art alone can decide what art is. In the contemporary situation, emancipated from the claims of ontology, the interest for the symbolic, as a kind of pre-art that inevitably eludes the concept of the work, offers us a conceptual approach that is free of 'substantialist' commitments and one that is therefore capable of responding positively to the unpredictable and changing character of all manifestations of art. For in the meantime, we have certainly learnt one thing at least: the essence of art cannot be explained through the presumed logic of its own history.

12

HEGEL AND GOETHE

I loathe this notorious 'and': for the Germans love to say
'Goethe and Schiller'. . . . Yet there are even worse cases of
'and', for with my own ears I have heard speak, though only
amongst academics, of 'Schopenhauer and Hartmann'.

Nietzsche, *Twilight of the Idols*

I. Introductory Remarks

A certain feeling of embarrassment naturally descends on anyone who
dares to tread on hallowed ground. And the rather arbitrary coupling of
intellectual heroes, connected often enough by little more than 'and'
in the title of some public lecture, rightly invites our scepticism. 'Hegel
and Goethe' – could there be a more hackneyed sounding theme than
this? It is certainly no easy matter to dispel such reservations. Yet this
particular conjunction of names also exercises an obscure fascination
of its own if we regard them as naming more than the actual historical characters they serve to designate. If we look beyond the classical
pantheon, if we look beyond the prince of poets in Weimar and the
absolute professor of philosophy in Berlin, we can see that Goethe and
Hegel effectively serve to embody two fundamentally different conceptions of art. For this contrast ultimately represents the impossibility of
reconciling the poetical and the philosophical approach to art itself.

The fascinating issue lies therefore beneath the obvious surface.
And we can only uncover it if we ignore the largely contingent connections between the life and thought of two eminent individuals and
refrain from the usual edifying attempt to establish some harmonious
relationship between their respective ideas. And dutiful attention to
the existing material on this question merely serves to strengthen this

conviction. In the traditional annals of intellectual and cultural history, both writers have been compared and considered as the natural culmination of the classical period of art and philosophy in Germany.[1] Critical studies of the modern age from Karl Löwith[2] to Hans Mayer[3] have effectively treated the pair as *dioscuri* fully capable of representing the fate of the nineteenth century itself. And Marxist interpreters such as Georg Lukács[4] and Ernst Bloch[5] have regarded both as exemplary forerunners with respect to a properly 'realist' conception of the world.

The contrasting and incommensurable dimension of the relationship between Goethe and Hegel has been entirely ignored in this connection.[6] Yet examining this aspect of the problem would, it seems to me, prove to be an illuminating task. In opposition, therefore, to the general tenor of previous discussions of this question, I should like to pursue an analysis that might more appropriately be entitled 'Hegel contra Goethe, Goethe contra Hegel'. The argument will proceed in four steps. Firstly, I provide a necessary brief account of the relevant historical connections between the poet and the philosopher.[7] Secondly, I attempt to clarify the fundamental respective positions of both in relation to art in general. Thirdly, I undertake to elucidate the central role played by the universal categories of the 'classical' and the 'romantic' in both Goethe and Hegel. Fourthly, and finally, I try and articulate the principal difference between them by reference to *Faust*, specifically paying attention to both parts of Goethe's great poem.

II. The External Association of Hegel and Goethe

It is very easy to provide a brief account of the factors connecting Hegel and Goethe as specific individuals. As a minister in the Weimar

---

[1] For example, J. Hoffmeister, *Goethe und der deutsche Idealismus* (Leipzig 1932).

[2] K. Löwith, *Von Hegel zu Nietzsche. Der revolutionäre Bruch im Denren des 19. Jahrhunderts* (first published 1941; Stuttgart 1958). ET: *From Hegel to Nietzsche, trans.* by D.E. Green (London 1965).

[3] Cf. 'Goethe, Hegel und das neunzehnte Jahrhundert', in H. Mayer, *Goethe* (Frankfurt am Main 1973). Cf. also Mayer's early inaugural address in Leipzig, strongly influenced as it is by Lukács and Bloch, 'Goethe und Hegel' (1947).

[4] Georg Lukács, *Goethe und seine Zeit* (Bern 1947), 'Faust-Studien'; ET: *Goethe and His Age*, trans. R. Anchor (London 1968), ch. 8: '*Faust* Studies', pp. 157–253; and Lukács, *Probleme des Realismus* (Neuwied 1965).

[5] Ernst Bloch, *Subjekt-Objekt. Erläuterungen zu Hegel* (Berlin 1952).

[6] But cf. B. Sandkaulen's entry 'Hegel' in the *Goethe-Handbuch* (1995).

[7] In this respect, cf. the detailed account provided by R. Honegger, 'Goethe und Hegel', *Jahrbuch der Goethe-Gesellschaft* 11, 1925.

government, Goethe had direct educational responsibility for the official cultural and intellectual life of the Dukedom. This included the affairs of the University of Jena, where Hegel had sought refuge in 1801 in order to escape the depressing conditions of employment as a private tutor in Frankfurt and to establish some influence for himself as an academic teacher of philosophy. The relations between the still largely unknown lecturer and the relevant authorities were initially restricted exclusively to issues connected with his professional academic employment. It is embarrassing today to read the begging letters this 'most humble servant' Dr. Hegel was obliged to address, 'with sentiments of the highest regard', to His Excellency the Minister of Culture. The letters are sometimes concerned with the possibilities of academic promotion, sometimes simply with securing a regular annual salary. After Jena, and without Goethe's assistance, Hegel proceeded first to Bamberg to take up a post as newspaper editor, then to Nuremberg to become a School Director, and finally, more than ten years later, to Heidelberg, where he was appointed as a Professor of Philosophy.

This period in Heidelberg marked the beginning of a new phase of co-operative intellectual interest between the two men. In the *Encyclopaedia of the Philosophical Sciences* of 1817, Hegel expressly endorsed the cause of Goethe's *Theory of Colour*. Goethe was gratified by this welcome show of support for a controversial theory that employed poetic means to champion the immediate qualitative perception of sensible phenomena over against the explanatory procedures of natural science typically adopted by Newton. As Goethe himself had put it: 'We believe that we may deserve some gratitude on the part of the philosopher insofar as we have sought to trace the phenomena back to their original sources, to there where they simply manifest themselves as they are, there where there is nothing more to be explained from them'.[8] Hegel himself reports this expression of thanks, that had certainly not been proffered immediately, and openly praises, in marked contrast to the 'barbarism' of Newton's theory of optics, the 'clear and fundamental and indeed learned manner in which Goethe has illuminated' the ultimate nature of light.[9] And it is quite true that Goethe's general approach certainly answered to one of the first ambitions of idealist

---

[8] J.W. von Goethe, *Entwurf einer Farbenlehre, Einleitung* (*Naturwissenschaftliche Schriften*, Hamburger Ausgabe XIII, p. 327).

[9] G.W.F. Hegel, *Enzyklopädie der philosophischen Wissenschaften* (1817), 1830³, §320; *Hegel's Philosophy of Nature*, tr. A.V. Miller (Oxford 1970), §320, pp. 195 passim. Also cf. Hegel's letter to Schelling of 23 February 1807.

philosophy, already formulated in its early days – namely, 'to bestow wings once more upon the physics that advances so slowly and laboriously by means of experiment'.[10] Goethe in turn now gladly acknowledged the support offered to his theory by a now recognised philosopher of the day, and a brief scholarly exchange of views ensued as a result.

The third phase of the association between Hegel and Goethe belongs to the last decade of both their lives during the 1820s. Hegel had been called to Berlin, where he largely dominated the recently founded University, and soon became a important focus of intellectual interest even beyond the borders of Prussia. By this time, Goethe, still resident in Weimar, had become an Olympian celebrity who was regularly sought out by hosts of foreign visitors. The association in question has now become one between two extremely well-known figures: addresses are ceremoniously exchanged and the respective fame and mutual respect of both are further communicated to the world through third parties who are far less celebrated than either. In 1821, Goethe honours Hegel by presenting him with a goblet and the accompanying dedication: 'Fairest greetings to the Absolute from the Primal Phenomenon in earnest of a friendly welcome'. On his return trip from Paris in 1827, Hegel visits Goethe at home and is honoured to find himself seated alongside the now somewhat deaf Grand Duke Karl August himself.[11] Hegel dies in 1831, a year before Goethe. Goethe's poem on Faust, on the second part of which he was still working right up to the final weeks of his life, would soon provide the Hegelian School with an opportunity for elaborating the appropriate relationship between poetry and philosophy. Hegel himself never lived to see the completion of Goethe's greatest work.

III. Philosophy and Art

Biographies like these must first be interpreted if they are to claim our interest in anything more than a neutral account of contingent

[10] The so-called 'Earliest System Programme of German Idealism' of 1796–97. It is still widely disputed whether the authorship should be ascribed to Hegel or Schelling (for the current state of research on this question, cf. *Das Älteste Systemprogramm. Studien zur Frühgeschichte des deutschen Idealismus, Hegel-Studien*, Beiheft 9, ed. R. Bubner (Bonn 1973); Chr. Jamme/H. Schneider, eds., *Mythologie der Vernunft* (Frankfurt 1984); F.P. Hansen, *'Das Älteste Systemprogramm des deutschen Idealismus'. Rezeptionsgeschichte und Interpretation* (Berlin 1989). Cf. the essay on 'Schelling's Discovery and Schleiermacher's Appropriation of Plato' included at the beginning of this book.

[11] Cf. Hegel's letter to his wife of 17 October 1827.

details concerning some particular life. Goethe is a rare case of the creative writer who carefully and deliberately transforms his own life into part of the artistic *ouevre* itself. His autobiography, as its title suggests, represents an essentially inextricable entwinement of 'poetry' and 'truth'. Looking back from the perspective of a fairly late stage in his life, Goethe here sets out his original artistic intentions, his aesthetic judgements, his maxims for the conduct of life, his developed theoretical views – all embedded within the narrative of his own childhood and youth.

In this work, Goethe also takes the report of a conversation with a friend of his youth as a retrospective opportunity for presenting his own mature attitude to philosophy in general. I quote the relevant passage at length because it is particularly helpful in approaching our second question concerning the proper basis for any meaningful comparison between Hegel and Goethe. In Book VI of *Poetry and Truth*, Goethe writes: 'My friend began to introduce me to the mysteries of philosophy [. . .] But, alas, these matters simply refused to make the same sort of sense in my own mind. I asked questions and made demands that he promised to answer later and satisfy in future. However, our main difference of opinion concerned my assertion that there was no need for a separate philosophy since it was already completely contained in religion and poetry. By no means could he agree to this, trying on the contrary to prove to me that both of the latter essentially required a philosophical basis, something that I obstinately denied, and in the course of our discussion I found arguments to defend my own view at every step. Since poetry is predicated upon a certain belief in the impossible, and religion upon a similar belief in the unfathomable, I felt that the philosophers were in a very poor position when they attempted to prove and explain poetry and religion in philosophical terms. And one could very quickly demonstrate from the history of the subject how each philosopher had rejected the fundamental principles of the others, and how the sceptics had ended up declaring everything to be without ground or foundation'.

Goethe's brief sketch of the 'The Relationship of Philosophy with Regard to Religion and Poetry' expresses a perspective that is more or less the exact reverse of the systematically grounded arrangement of the three forms of 'absolute spirit' in Hegel.[12] The objections raised by the protesting philosopher in Goethe's account can effectively be

---

[12] Cf. the similar remarks in Goethe's conversation with Eckermann of 4.2.1829 where he explicitly refers to Hegel.

formulated in Hegelian terms. If we develop this counter-argument to
Goethe's own position somewhat further, we could express it in the
following way. The existence of poetry and religion, or of art in the
broadest sense, does not render philosophy superfluous. On the contrary, it is the specific historical emergence of art and religion that
confronts philosophy with its greatest challenge. Once the absolute has
initially presented itself as clothed in the beautiful form of aesthetic
appearance, once its presence has already been sensed in the religious
faith of the community, we still require the philosophical labour of the
concept in order to liberate the absolute from its own inadequate forms
of expression in art and religion and thereby bring it into a total and
transparent consciousness of itself as spirit.

Goethe suggests that the ultimate task of poetry and religion is somehow to hint at the impossible and to evoke the unfathomable. Hegel
himself interprets this ultimate horizon in terms of his operational concept of the 'absolute'. Now the real meaning of this concept cannot
fully be defined by reference to traditional substantialist metaphysics.
Rather it represents an abstract term at the philosopher's disposal for
everything that lies beyond the finite limitations that characterise the
world of the abstract 'understanding'. On this interpretation, the ultimate purpose of poetry and art is to accomplish what is impossible
from the perspective of the understanding, to present what transcends
the limits of reality so conceived. In assuming this transcendent function, art cannot rely upon the solid reality of the objectively given but
must essentially trust to its own resources. And religion relates in a
similar way to the unfathomable and sublime, which lies above and beyond all grounds and reasons. Since all our merely finite attempts to
grasp this dimension necessarily fail, we must here rely entirely upon
'faith'.

Hegel's philosophical speculations arose specifically from close consideration of this kind of *irrational* relationship to the absolute. If the
absolute, precisely in order to be and to remain truly absolute, forces
every approach to it onto an essentially irrational level, if it simply demands a blind belief on our part because of the limited and inadequate
nature of the human understanding, then the entire relationship remains fundamentally ambiguous and incomplete. The finitude that was
expressly to be overcome in the light of the absolute is not really overcome at all. This finitude reappears in the medium of faith since the
original recourse to faith with regard to the absolute was itself an expression of the inadequacy of our own conceptual powers. We seek refuge

in faith because we can find no better or more appropriate means of approaching the absolute. This 'faith' cannot represent an adequate attitude to the absolute, but merely expresses the fundamental disparity that results from the dualistic relationship between consciousness and its object.

To take the problem of the absolute seriously, for Hegel, means developing a proper mode of approach that is superior to that of 'faith'. The true absolute intrinsically requires us, as it were, to adopt a better and more adequate relationship towards it than the typical posture of mere faith. The truly appropriate way of comprehending the absolute can be described as the way in which the absolute would essentially comprehend itself. Hegel defines this definitive manner of comprehending the absolute in terms of 'spirit'. And the task of elaborating this approach falls precisely to a philosophy whose rational resources extend beyond the reach of the finite categories of the understanding. The inappropriate relationship to the absolute expressed by faith must be overcome in principle. That is why art and religion, properly considered, both require their own ultimate overcoming and sublation in and through philosophy. It is not merely that philosophy succeeds in accomplishing what they could not – namely, in comprehending rather than irrationally believing in the absolute. But philosophy also enables us to analyse these other inappropriate alternatives and to deduce art and religion as imperfect prefigurations of philosophy itself. Hegel's position is thus the very opposite of Goethe's. In Hegel's view, there is a specific need for philosophy in its own right precisely because neither poetry nor religion is capable of perfectly expressing what philosophy itself has to say.

The contrast between the two approaches can readily be developed on the basis of the short passage we have quoted, even if Goethe himself does not expressly underscore its significance. Hegel's own approach, as sketched here, was systematically developed at the end of the *Phenomenology of Spirit*, and his later system of philosophical aesthetics was also constructed in terms of this carefully explicated hierarchical relationship between art and philosophy. Art and philosophy belong so intimately together because philosophy clearly expresses what art can only intimate through the sensuous image. But the philosophical concept acquires a natural superiority in this connection insofar as philosophy perfects a preliminary truth that art itself presents in an immediate and unreflective fashion. With the appearance of philosophy, art can now be clarified conceptually, articulated systematically in terms of its different methods and media, and defined with respect to its essential function and character. And this is precisely the task of philosophical aesthetics, and one that cannot be fulfilled by art itself.[13]

Art is accomplished with a certain immediate naivety and in ignorance of what art really is. The philosophical knowledge of what art genuinely represents is inevitably articulated and justified from a higher standpoint. The world of art itself is abandoned once theoretical aesthetics begins. Nor is this inner hierarchical relationship between art and aesthetics simply systematic and functional in character. For it serves to express a specifically *historical* process as well. The undiminished claims of philosophy can only be articulated in the modern epoch, and indeed in the age of idealist thought that began with Kant and is consummated, for Hegel, in his own speculative dialectic. The age of the sensuous manifestation of truth through the imagery of art, the way in which earlier epochs had effectively interpreted reality as a whole, is thereby regarded as something that is now in principle overcome. We no longer need art in order to interpret the world now that we possess the appropriate conceptual means of grasping its essence. The tentative interpretive achievements of art, falling short of definitive knowledge as they do, therefore belong to a stage of human history that has now been superseded.

Hegel's famous thesis concerning art as *essentially a thing of the past*, an aspect of his aesthetic theory that has had considerable impact on the contemporary discussion, does not imply the actual cessation of artistic production. Hegel was well aware of the vigorous artistic activity characteristic of his own age, and indeed participated critically in these developments himself. But in Hegel's eyes, art has now lost the world-historical role it formerly used to play. 'The specific character of artistic production and its works no longer fully satisfies our highest need; we have advanced beyond the point where we can venerate works of art as something divine, or fall in prayer before them; the impression they make upon us now is a more reflective one, and what they stir within us now demands a higher touchstone and a more comprehensive form of preservation. Thought and reflection have passed over beyond the realm of fine art as such.'[14]

---

[13] Ernst Gombrich has rightly identified Hegel as the real 'father of art history' ('Hegel und die Kunstgeschichte', *Neue Rundschau* 88/2, 1977).

[14] Cf. Hegel, *Ästhetik* I, Werkausgabe (Suhrkamp), vol. 13, p, 24; *Hegel's Aesthetics*, tr. T.M. Knox (Oxford 1975), vol. 1, p. 10.

Hegel thus regards the *West-Eastern Divan*, a subtly reflective and autarchic late work of Goethe's, as a typical example of the art of his own time.[15] The complex interplay between East and West, the conjunction of immediate experience and remote historical precedent, the free handling of given forms, the recessive tone of subjective interiority – all of this provides an excellent example of how art may still be produced after its original historical role has vanished. If it is true, as Hegel says, that 'art can no longer be regarded as the highest form in which the truth procures existence for itself'[16], then it is thereby effectively relieved of its former task. Self-consciously aware of its own historical character and no longer restricted to any authoritatively binding content, art can now concern itself with its own possibilities. We shall see how *Faust II*, the final work of Goethe's and one that only appeared after Hegel's death, was interpreted by the Hegelian School as a good example of artistic production after the end of art. Once the serious tragic themes of *Faust I* have been left behind, art emphatically comes into play precisely through the sovereign exercise of all the aesthetic means at its disposal.

IV. Art and Nature

We may pause now that the systematic structure of Hegel's aesthetic theory has been outlined with regard to its basic features. The contrast between Hegel's conception of art and that of Goethe could hardly be greater, and indeed the poet himself once effectively confessed: 'I have never possessed any receptivity for philosophy in the proper sense'.[17] And in a letter to Schiller, he wrote as follows: 'I find that philosophy destroys poetry, and that because it confronts me with an object. I can never relate to anything in a purely speculative sense, but must always seek out some corresponding intuition for every claim, and that is why I flee immediately to Nature'.[18] In contrast to the kind of philosophical consummation of art and its ultimate purpose that is implied in Hegel's schema, Goethe here presents a fundamental conflict between art and philosophy. The concept destroys poetry precisely because it attempts to determine and define the 'object' and repudiates the original intuition in which *art and nature are immediately presented together*.

---

[15] See, Section VII f.
[16] Hegel, *Ästhetik* I, p. 141; *Hegel's Aesthetics*, vol. 1, pp. 102–103.
[17] Goethe, 'Einwirkung der neueren Philosophie', Hamburger Ausgabe XIII, p. 25.
[18] Goethe's letter of 19 February 1802.

The 'intuition' that Goethe constantly seeks and demands, this direct contact with the undiminished phenomena themselves, overcomes the conceptual abstraction through which the object stands over against ourselves as something alien.[19] It is only the direct immersion in intuition that opens up the possibility of a genuine approach to nature and art alike. And both spheres mutually illuminate one another. The artist must keep to the actual phenomena that nature presents to us, while the scientist properly engaged with nature can be inspired aesthetically as well.[20]

It is impossible to overemphasise the importance of this relationship to nature in Goethe's conception of art, for it surely marks the most obvious difference between Hegel's position and his own. For Hegel, nature appears as the 'other' of spirit, and must be thematised within the 'Realphilosophie' precisely in terms of this opposition. Art, on the other hand, belongs to the domain of spirit and represents the first, though not yet self-conscious, form in which absolute spirit itself is manifest. In aesthetic theory, spirit recognises itself in art and thereby releases the latter from its bondage to the domain of sensuous appearance. For Goethe, on the other hand, nature represents an essential corrective over against the claims of entirely autonomous thought. It binds spirit back to the realm of intuition, returns it to something that always eludes the total control of spirit itself.

And yet nature does not simply appear here as the radically 'other'. This kind of rupture only arises through the act of self-conscious reflection that separates the one from the other. But the fundamental and original relationship between intuiting and intuited, our own sensuous contact with the phenomena themselves, avoids such separation in the first place. That is why the nature disclosed to intuitive perception has not yet been reified into a mere object of scientific knowledge. Nature sustains the consciousness that is open to the concrete and particular content of experience in an unbroken relationship to the universal context of its own life. It is this mediating character that effectively brings art and nature together on a single level in Goethe's eyes.

To clarify the relevant comparison a little further, I should like to cite a couple of quite marginal texts that are particularly instructive here

---

[19] Cf. *Zur Farbenlehre*, §716 ff. (*Naturwissenschaftliche Schriften*, p. 482 f.).

[20] For example, *Italienische Reise* (28.1.1987): 'My instinct tells me that they [the Greeks] followed the same laws as Nature, and I believe I am on the track of these'. ET: *Italian Journey*, trans. W.H. Auden and E. Mayer (New York 1970), p. 168.

precisely because of their occasional character. Karl Rosenkranz, Hegel's first biographer, came across some interesting remarks in Hegel's unpublished notes and papers. He cites an early passage from the Jena period concerning the poetic intuition of nature in contrast to the perspective of philosophical knowledge, and one that explicitly alludes to Goethe's poem on *Faust*.[21] It concerns the dialogue with the Earth Spirit in the scene 'Wood and Cave' where Faust expressly greets nature like a friend. Hegel remarks on this as follows: 'Nature is a whole as far as our living, or if you like, *poetic* intuition is concerned. The manifold phenomena of nature here pass before our eyes as a procession of living beings and we can recognise our brothers in the bush, the air, the water. For this poetic intuition, nature is an absolute whole, a living whole. But this living character presents itself in its actual configuration as a specific individuality. The living beings here are inwardly identical, but their being is one of absolute externality in relation to one another. Each one exists independently, and their movement in relation to one another is absolutely contingent. In this, their individualised life each opposes the other with the exactly same right, and insofar as the infinitude of their singular existence proves to be their own *destruction*, this existence itself is not intrinsically justified as such. And our intuition involves a *certain sense of pain* '.

Philosophy analyses this poetic intuition of nature conceptually and identifies a contradiction between the vitality of life in general and its individual manifestations. Intuition is confronted with a plurality of living shapes that all equally present themselves as part of a totality, even though each one, as intuitively perceived, possesses a specific existence all of its own. Since the supposedly absolute character of life is dissolved in the sheer multiplicity of individuals, it is impossible to remain within the poetic intuition presented to us here. To transcend the apparent self-destruction involved requires a mediation beyond the capacities of immediate intuition. The absolute connected structure of life can only be clarified through the sublation of its own individual forms. But intuition itself is insufficient to accomplish or reveal this necessary 'sublation'. On Hegel's interpretation, therefore, the intuitive orientation to living things themselves already drives us on beyond the domain of intuition proper. Thus, with respect to what it was intended to accomplish,

---

[21] Karl Rosenkranz, *Hegels Leben* (1844; reprinted Darmstadt 1963), p. 187. Otto Pöggeler has examined the emergence of Hegel's conception of art during the Jena period in his article 'Die Enstehung von Hegels Ästhetik in Jena' (*Hegel-Studien*, Beiheft 20, 1980).

the poetic perspective itself cannot ultimately be retained except at the cost of 'a certain sense of pain'.

In direct contrast, we might cite a passage from one of Goethe's letters that reveals a total lack of understanding for Hegel's dialectic and the associated approach to nature that it logically demands. The conceptual analysis of natural phenomena appears simply barbarous in Goethe's eyes. As he writes to Th.J. Seebeck on 28 November 1812: 'I happen to have come across a passage from the 'Preface' to Hegel's Logic. This is what he says. 'The bud disappears in the bursting-forth of the blossom, and one might say that the former is refuted by the latter; similarly, when the fruit appears, the blossom is shown up as a false manifestation of the plant, and the fruit now emerges as the truth of it instead. These forms are not just distinguished from one another, they also supplant one another as mutually incompatible. Yet at the same time their fluid nature makes them into moments of an organic unity in which not only do they not conflict, but each is as necessary as the other; and this mutual necessity alone constitutes the life of the whole'. It is surely impossible to say anything more monstrous: the attempt to deny the eternal reality of nature with a wretched sophistical jest seems to me quite unworthy of a rational individual.

'If the earthly outlook of the empiricist makes him blind to Ideas, we must simply pity him and leave him to pursue in his own way, although we ourselves can still certainly profit from his researches. But when an excellent thinker who clearly grasps an Idea and really understands its true worth, and the higher value it embodies, actually expresses a monstrous approach to nature, jestingly produces a sophistical caricature of nature itself, destroying and denying it by recourse to artificial and self-refuting words and phrases, then one simply does not know what to say ... And yet I should be very sorry to lose Hegel. But what can one hope from a Logic that supposes, if the arid words of its 'Preface' are to be trusted, that the right and true conclusion can only arise from false premises like these'.[22] Goethe's instinctive faith in intuitively accessible reality is as incapable of responding to the logic of the absolute concept and the violence it inflicts upon the world of nature as Hegel's thought in turn is unable to rest content with a purely poetic attitude to nature.

---

[22] Goethe makes a mistake about the title here. The quotation is actually from Hegel's *Phenomenology of Spirit*, and specifically from the beginning of the 'Preface', which was, however, intended to introduce not merely this work, but the system in its entirety.

The immediacy that belongs to the content of all intuitive percep-tion explains why Goethe himself constantly emphasises the *equivalent status of art and nature*.[23] Nature itself invites us to contemplate pure phenomena that point beyond particular experience and embody the paradigmatic ideal of reality. And artistic activity, in analogy with this, proceeds in an essentially symbolising fashion. 'It makes a very great difference whether the poet seeks the particular in the universal or beholds the universal in the particular. The former yields allegory, where the particular is regarded simply as an illustration, as an ex-ample of the universal. But the latter reveals the proper nature of poetry, which expresses something particular without thinking upon or referring us to the universal. If this particular is grasped in a re-ally living manner, the universal is simultaneously given too, without our becoming explicitly aware of it as such, or only subsequently so. That is true symbolism, where the particular represents the universal, not as its dream or shadow, but precisely as a living moment of the revelation of the unfathomable'.[24] The living revelation of the unfath-omable in the *symbol* holds intuitive perception to the domain of the particular. It is the particular that simultaneously discloses the univer-sal and thus obviates any speculative attempt to transcend this domain and determine the universal rationally in terms of purely philosophical knowledge.[25]

The philosopher whom Goethe chiefly likes to cite in support of his own perspective is of course Kant rather than Hegel.[26] And Goethe is

---

[23] Cf. 'Einleitung in die Propyläen'; 'Über Lakaoon'; 'Über Wahrheit und Wahrschein-lichkeit der Kunstwerke' (Hamburger Ausgabe XII, pp. 42 ff., 56, 72).

[24] 'Maximen und Reflexionen', No. 751 (HA XII).

[25] Hegel certainly recognised that this was indeed the case, as a passage from one of his own less well-known reviews indicates: '... For Goethe perceptively demands that a work of art, a product of nature, a specific character, and so on, should be grasped in its own right and in its concrete individuality, likewise that the underlying concept and enjoyment of the same should not be disturbed or ruined through external com-parison, through theory, or through the one-sided procedures of that kind of abstract reflection that had early and persistently plagued his mind'. But Hegel goes on to say that we should 'not simply content ourselves with this in the case of totalities quite dif-ferent from the work of art, of fundamental principles, laws, thoughts, of any content that is universal in nature rather than concretely sensuous in character, and attempt to apply these sensible demands inappropriately and without proper conscious thought to such different kinds of objects' (*Berliner Schriften*, ed. J. Hoffmeister, Hamburg 1956, p. 387 f.)

[26] For example, 'Einwirkung der neueren Philosophie', loc. cit., pp. 27–34; Goethe's con-versation with Eckermann of 11 April 1827.

entirely justified in appealing here to the *Critique of Judgement*, which indeed emphasises the intimate connection between the work of art and the realm of natural form. For both discharge the same function in relation to our human capacity for understanding. Kant speaks of the activity of reflective judgement, which is provoked alike by works of art and by the organic products of nature. For the sensuously given particular here facilitates an immediate representation of the universal that cannot be divorced from the particular itself. This parallel between art and nature, arising from our conscious response to experience, naturally implies no metaphysical assumptions concerning the essence of nature considered in itself and independently of its effects upon human beings. But from the perspective of the faculty of judgement itself, activated equally through the perception of works of art and the purposive phenomena of nature, art resembles nature and nature resembles art.

This original parity between art and nature does not arise by accident. Nature presents itself as purposive to us when it seems to correspond to our own intentions even though we cannot say why this is so. Our inability to provide any theoretical explanation actually harbours an aesthetically felt experience of surplus. On the other hand, art is also supposed to resemble nature. This relationship explains the priority that Kantian aesthetics ascribes to natural beauty as against the beauty of art. Works of art are not openly and obviously supposed to bear any mark of artificial production upon them. They must be oriented rather towards the paradigm of nature, which spontaneously reveals itself to us as beautiful. The beauty of nature thus provides the exemplary model for the production of the work of art. But it requires 'genius' to build the bridge between art and nature – that is, to create works of art entirely in accordance with the inner laws and rules so wisely embodied, in a way we cannot hope to understand, in living nature itself.

Genius is Kant's name for the extraordinary and philosophically inexplicable talent that elicits the formative principles of nature or allows itself to be governed spontaneously by those principles. The indispensable role of genius thus indicates the rationally incomprehensible character of this bridge between art and nature. Although he did not explicitly pursue, with the same clarity of Kant, the fundamental problem of an aesthetic theory essentially oriented to the perception of nature, Goethe certainly shares Kant's basic assumption about genius as far as the appropriate task of the artist is concerned: 'Nature operates according to laws, prescribed by herself in harmony with the creator, art according to rules which concur with those of genius'.[27]

The Kantian element in Goethe's theory of art permits us to articulate a further contrast with Hegel's aesthetics. For Hegel's interpretation of art inevitably repudiates the most essential features of Kantian aesthetics: the parity of art and nature in relation to the faculty of judgement, the priority of natural beauty over artistic beauty, the central role of genius. As we have already pointed out, nature for Hegel belongs to a lower sphere than art in the general construction of the system. The autonomy of art, grounded as it is in the power of absolute spirit, makes every manifestation of natural beauty essentially derivative from the ideal of beauty only properly actualised in the free realm of art itself. The hierarchy suggested by Kant is thus reversed in favour of artistic beauty.[28] And once the priority of nature has been abandoned, the central role formerly played by genius in relating art and nature to one another also disappears. A fully self-conscious philosophy now takes over from all such claims.[29] For it is in philosophy that spirit fully recognises itself and thereby also allows us to grasp the spiritual character of art in an appropriate conceptual manner.

It is hardly surprising that the weakest point in Hegel's entire philosophy of art lies in its undervaluation of that *perceptible-intuitive dimension* upon which Goethe had laid such emphasis. Strictly speaking, the domain of intuitive perception loses any function for an aesthetics of absolute spirit. The dimension of vivid sensuous presence is clearly what is most remote from the perfected self-consciousness of spirit. Spirit can only be what it is through a process of total reflective mediation, and even in its inception has long since abandoned the level of immediate sensible intuition. This approach is already quite clear from the structure of the *Phenomenology of Spirit*, which begins with the elementary immediacy of sense-certainty (where the ego is a 'pure intuiting')[30] and concludes with the total mediation of knower and known in and

---

[27] 'Maximen und Reflexionen', No. 723.
[28] With reference to Goethe, cf. Hegel, *Ästhetik* I, p. 173f; *Hegel's Aesthetics*, vol 1, pp. 128–129.
[29] Ibid., p. 44f; *Hegel's Aesthetics*, vol. 1, pp. 25–26.
[30] *Phänomenologie des Geistes*, ed. J. Hoffmeister (Hamburg 1952), p. 84; *Phenomenology of Spirit*, tr. A.V. Miller, pp. 61–62.

as 'spirit'. But even within Hegel's aesthetic theory, the category of intuition plays no effective role either.[31]

Hegel famously defined the beautiful as the *sensuous manifestation* of the Idea. The concept of manifestation or 'appearance' [*Schein*] here is based upon logical considerations[32] and is designed to explicate the phenomena of art on a properly conceptual level. In Hegel's *Science of Logic*, 'appearance' is that form of reflection where the spiritual essence is not yet entirely present to itself as such, but is already determinative even in its absence. 'Appearance' is related to the essence, which at first merely 'seems' to show itself here. This renders the category of appearance fully transparent and allows us to pass on to a further stage of the analysis. Hegel employs this complex structure of thought in interpreting the relationship between art and philosophy. For it is precisely the Idea that shows itself in the form of art. But once this 'showing' has been seen for what it is, the content of the Idea demands to be grasped conceptually in its own right. The sensuous moment that complements the concept of appearance is a rhetorical concession that is never seriously redeemed. The Hegelian theory of aesthetics is systematically incapable of doing adequate justice to the sensuous and intuitive moment that is ineliminably involved in every experience of art.[33] The theoretical sublimation that Hegel offers has always already transcended our actual encounter with the concrete givens of aesthetic experience.

V. The Opposition between the Classical and the Romantic

The tendency to emphasise the pure autonomy of sprit is further articulated in an important way through the fundamental distinction between the *classical* and the *romantic*. It is true that the classical and romantic types of art are preceded in Hegel's analysis by the *symbolic* form of art, introduced essentially to facilitate the typical triadic exposition demanded by the dialectic. But he also made it abundantly clear that the symbolic is merely a kind of 'pre-art',[34] where form and content still fall apart and thereby point towards a perfect aesthetic mediation beyond its own

---

[31] The thorough index produced by H. Bartsch, *Register zu Hegels Vorlesungen über die Ästhetik* (Mainz 1844), has no entry for the term 'intuition'. But cf. Hegel, *Ästhetik* I, p. 55 and frequent references elsewhere.

[32] But cf. Hegel, *Ästhetik* I., p. 21; *Hegel's Aesthetics*, vol.1, p. 8.

[33] Ibid., p. 49f.; *Hegel's Aesthetics*, vol. 1, pp. 28ff. In this connection, compare with 'Is There a Hegelian Theory of Aesthetic Experience', Chapter 11 in this book.

[34] Ibid., p. 393; *Hegel's Aesthetics* vol. 1, p. 303.

resources. Hegel's *symbolic* form of art roughly corresponds, in Kantian terminology, to the sublime, and refers historically to the development of Eastern art before the emergence of classical Greek art. In this limited sense, the concept of the symbolic[35] has nothing in common with the symbolising artistic approach of Goethe, which itself is ultimately focussed upon classical art. If we therefore ignore the peculiar role of the symbolic form of art in the structure of Hegel's aesthetics, we can see that Hegel and Goethe characteristically concurred in their evaluation of the classical and the romantic forms of art and continued to regard them as appropriate categories for understanding all previous and contemporary art. The dichotomy between the classical and the romantic can also shed further light upon our question concerning the relationship between the poet and the philosopher.

The older Goethe summarised his position, not without a certain feeling of pride, in one of his discussions with Eckermann: 'The concept of classical and romantic poetry that has now spread over the whole world and occasions so many quarrels and divisions, came originally from Schiller and myself. I laid down the maxim of objective treatment in poetry, and would allow no other; but Schiller, who worked very much in the subjective way, deemed his own approach to be the right one, and composed his essay upon *Naive and Sentimental Poetry* in order to defend himself against me. He proved to me that I, against my will, was romantic, and that my *Iphigenia*, through the predominance of sentiment in it, was by no means as classical or as conceived in the spirit of antiquity as many people supposed. The Schlegels took up this idea and carried it further, so that it has now been disseminated throughout the world, and now everyone talks about classicism and romanticism, something to which no one gave any thought fifty years ago.'[36]

This programmatic distinction between two aesthetic categories, which initially arose as a poetological dispute and was then eagerly popularised by third parties[37], appears in retrospect as a statement of

---

[35] Gadamer traces this concept of symbol back to the influence of Hegel's friend and colleague Friedrich Creuzer. Cf. H.-G. Gadamer, 'Hegel und die Heidelberger Romantik', in his volume of essays, *Hegels Dialektik* (Tübingen 1971), p. 75ff.; English version in Gadamer, *Hegel's Dialectic*, translated by P.C. Smith (New Haven: Yale University Press 1976). On Creuzer, cf. Hegel, *Ästhetik* I, p. 402ff.; *Hegel's Aesthetics*, vol. 1, pp. 310ff.

[36] Goethe's conversation with Eckermann of 21.3.1830.

[37] Goethe is alluding here to Fr. Schlegel, *Über das Studium der griechischen Poesie* (1795) and to A. W. Schlegel, *Vorlesungen zur Geschichte der klassischen und romantischen Literatur* (1802–3).

fundamental principle. Goethe is alluding to his earlier debate with
Schiller, clearly documented in their correspondence of 1794, in which
Schiller so perceptively diagnosed his own artistic character and that
of his antagonist Goethe. The essay *On Naive and Sentimental Poetry* of
1795 was the effective fruit of that debate.[38]

But one must also recognise that these discussions concerning the
'classical' and the 'romantic' effectively resume an entire tradition of
poetological-aesthetic debate pursued throughout the early modern
period: the 'Querelle des Anciens et des Modernes'.[39] Ever since the
Renaissance and the Humanist cultivation of antiquity, the question
concerning the unrivalled status of the ancients in relation to the independent rights of the moderns had been a burning issue. Schiller
raised this traditional controversy onto a much more self-conscious
level. The terms 'naive' and the 'sentimental' historically reflect the
opposition between antiquity and modernity, reflect both the remoteness of the classical paradigm and the yearning for its re-establishment
in the present.

In this context, the 'naive' signifies an immediate sense for the
natural: for everything we no longer expect from a world of deliberate calculation and artifice, for an inspired capacity for simplicity
as opposed to the distorting interference of reflective thought. The
'sentimental', on the other hand, expresses an overt sense of lack,
that yearning to recover the lost unity with nature that so preoccu-
pies the modern artist. Whereas Schiller regarded himself as a 'sentimental' poet, he saw Goethe as personifying the principle of the
'naive'.[40] But both types of artist can only be defined against the background of a Greek antiquity that was once capable of harmoniously
uniting nature and art but is now irretrievably lost to us.[41] Naive

---

[38] This kind of personal stylisation of two mutually incompatible principles of art has been
continued by other writers right down to Thomas Mann's early novella, *Schwere Stunde*
of 1905.

[39] Cf. H.R. Jauss, 'Schlegels und Schillers Replik auf die "Querelle des Anciens et des
Modernes"', in his book, *Literaturgeschichte als Provokation* (Frankfurt am Main 1970).

[40] Cf. Schiller's famous letters to Goethe of 23 and 31 August 1794. Their contemporaries
clearly saw things rather differently. Ludwig Tieck, for example, wrote to A.W. Schlegel
in November 1798 about Schiller: 'His verses as verses acquire an infelicitous tone, he
wants to sound like Goethe and he hardly manages any better than Hans Sachs, he just
sounds uncommonly obvious and trite instead ... He should, it seems to me, entirely
avoid making people think of Goethe where his own work is concerned'. (*L. Tieck und
die Brüder Schlegel. Briefe*, ed. E. Lohner, Munich 1972, p. 34).

[41] In the letter of 23 August 1794, Schiller writes to Goethe as follows: 'Had you been born a
Greek or even an Italian, surrounded from infancy by an elevated nature and an idealised

and sentimental art simply represent different reactions to the same loss.[42]

Hegel himself later interprets the issue in these terms: 'One feels that at one period of his work, Schiller busied himself with thought more even than was advantageous for the naive beauty of his own works. Deliberate concentration upon abstract reflections and even an interest in the philosophical concept is noticeable in many of his poems. For this he has been reproached, and especially blamed and deprecated in comparison with Goethe's invariable directness and objectivity, steadily undisturbed by the concept. But in this respect Schiller, as a poet, only paid the debt of his time, and his complicity here turned out only to the honour of this sublime soul and profound mind and only to the advantage of Science and knowledge.'[43]

For his part, Goethe basically understood Schiller's distinction in terms of the difference between two kinds of native poetic talent, and fully accepted Schiller's interpretation of their respective artistic roles.[44] In later life, Goethe reported that it was only his relationship to Schiller that properly enabled him to clarify his own profound and instinctive sympathy for Kant's philosophy of nature and art as expounded in the *Critique of Judgement*. He summarised the significance of the discussions with Schiller as follows: 'Our conversations proved thoroughly productive or theoretical, and usually both: he preached the Gospel of freedom, I wished to see the rights of nature upheld undiminished. [. . .] But I was not content simply to emphasise, in my obstinate and self-willed fashion, the advantages of the Greek approach to poetic art in

art, your own path would have been made infinitely shorter, perhaps even unnecessary altogether. With your very first perception of objects there would simultaneously have arisen an understanding of the necessary form. And the great style would then have developed in you on the basis of this initial experience. But here and now, born a German, with your Greek spirit transplanted into this northern world, you were faced with the choice of becoming a Nordic artist or of recreating in your imagination through intellectual power the art that reality withholds from it and thereby giving birth to Greece once more, as it were, from within and in a rational way' (Cf. *Correspondence between Goethe and Schiller 1794–1805*, trans. by L. Dieckann, Peter Lang 1994, p. 5).

[42] *Über naive und sentimentalische Dichtung*, in F. Schiller, *Schriften zur Philosophie und Kunst* (München 1959), p. 163 ff.; *On Naive and Sentimental Poetry*, in *German Aesthetic and Literary Criticism*, ed. H. B. Nisbet (Cambridge 1985), pp. 180–232. Cf. P. Szondi, 'Poetik und Geschichtsphilosophie. Zu Schillers Abhandlung "Über naive und sentimentalische Dichtung"', in R. Koselleck/W-D. Stempel, eds., *Geschichte–Ereignis und Erzählung*, Poetik und Hermeneutik V (München 1973).

[43] Hegel, *Ästhetik* I, p. 89f., and II, p. 114 ff.; *Hegel's Aesthetics*, vol. 1, pp. 507–508.

[44] In Goethe's reply to Schiller of 27 August 1794, he already refers to ' . . . your letter in which with a friendly hand you grasp the sense of my existence . . . '

general, and of the poetry that derived from and continued to base itself upon the latter, and I exclusively regarded that approach as the only proper and desirable one to take. This in turn provoked him to further penetrating thought on the subject, and it is to this argument that we effectively owe the existence of his essay on *Naive and Sentimental Poems* [sic!]. Both approaches to poetry should peacefully acknowledge one another, and their contrasting character, and thereby grant each other an equal status. In this way, he laid the first foundations for an entirely new aesthetics: for the expressions *hellenic* and *romantic*, and whatever other synonyms that were soon contrived, can all be traced back to this discussion concerning the relative preponderance of a real or ideal treatment in art'.[45]

This conviction concerning the *paradigmatic status of antiquity* underlies the concept of the classical that Goethe never subsequently abandoned. That original living unity of art and nature remains paradigmatic for an epoch that is no longer capable of the natural immediacy of Greek art. The face that art presents should be almost natural in character, following classical example, never attempting to mediate form and content in an obviously calculating way or provoking a distracting distance between the viewer and the work. The priority of 'realistic treatment' in this sense is opposed to the purely 'ideal treatment'. The two approaches correspond to the contrasting distinction between 'symbol' and 'allegory' as presented in the passage from the *Maxims and Reflections* we have already quoted. The first represents the immediate intuition of the universal in the particular, while the second begins with the abstract universal and subsequently seeks the particular that can exemplify it. Goethe makes it transparently clear that he aspires to emulate the symbolising approach he associates with antiquity, and names Schiller as a typical representative of the alternative approach. We can find abundant examples illustrating Goethe's commitment to the 'classical' and his polemical disparagement of the 'romantic' as a decadent artistic development. The lack of understanding that Goethe revealed in relation to the younger generation of poets amongst his romantic contemporaries derives from the interpretive schema that rather crudely declares that 'the classical is the healthy, the romantic is the sick'.[46]

---

[45] 'Einwirkung der neueren Philosophie', loc. cit., p. 28f.; cf. also 'Shakespeare und kein Ende', HA XII, p. 291f.

[46] 'Maximen und Reflexionen', No. 863; similarly 865 and 867.

Although we have found more than sufficient evidence to contest the traditionally assumed parallel between Hegel and Goethe and to emphasise the fundamental difference between them, we can nonetheless see that they share a similarly canonic conception of genuine art. The reciprocal assurance of solidarity they both proclaimed, always so fondly cited by past interpreters, rests exclusively upon this categorial ranking of classical and romantic art, which is shared by poet and philosopher alike. It is beyond question for Hegel, just as for Goethe, that the fundamental aesthetic concept of the beautiful essentially coincides with the 'classical'[47], and that the classical ideal itself has been bequeathed by the Greeks. The perfect unity of form and content in classical art signifies neither more nor less than what is here expressly brought to appearance, and nothing appears that fails to signify its own meaning. The structure of total self-mediation so characteristic of Hegelian spirit explicitly manifests itself here in external form. Classical art embodies the spiritual entirely intact, and in the only way genuinely appropriate to the essence of spirit itself.

The symbolic 'pre-art' that is represented by oriental and pre-classical art necessarily falls short because of the characteristic disparity between form and content here. The unfathomable content exceeds the possibilities of the given form, which is thereby degraded to the status of a mere sign for something else. The romantic form of art, the form of the dissolution of art itself, on the other hand, disrupts the harmonious equilibrium of the classical ideal by introducing the kind of self-conscious and abstract reflection that cannot adequately be captured in sensible or plastic form at all. Between these two extremes, the unsurpassable and perfect incarnation of the spiritual element finds exemplary expression in the duly delimited and proportioned form of classical art. The *images of the Greek gods*, successfully individuating the universally spiritual in plastic form as they do, represent the culminating point of Greek art for Hegel. In this connection, we should note a striking, almost hymnic, reference to Goethe on Hegel's part that clearly underlines their shared aesthetic perspective here: 'In their beauty, these gods appear therefore raised above their own corporeality, and thus there arises a divergence between their blessed loftiness, which is a spiritual kind of inwardness, and their beauty, which is external and corporeal. The spirit appears utterly immersed in its

---

47 Hegel, *Ästhetik* II, p. 13; *Hegel's Aesthetics*, vol. 1, p. 427.

external form and yet simultaneously turned back entirely within and upon itself. It is like the wandering of an immortal god amidst mortal men'.

'In this connection, the Greek gods produce an impression, despite all difference, similar to that made upon me by Rauch's bust of Goethe when I first beheld it. You too have seen it, this lofty brow, this powerful commanding nose, the free eye, the round chin, the affable and well-formed lips, the intelligent placing of the head with a glance sideways and a little upwards; and at the same time the whole fullness of sensitive friendly humanity, and in addition these finished muscles of the fore-head and the face, expressive of the feelings and the passions, and, in all the vitality of the bust, the peace, stillness and majesty of an elderly man; and now along with this the leanness of the lips, which retreat into a toothless mouth, the looseness of the neck and cheeks whereby the bridge of the nose appears still greater and the sides of the fore-head still higher [. . . .] It is a firm, powerful, and timeless spirit, which, in the mask of encircling mortality, appears about to let this veil fall away.'[48]

A startling and striking image: Goethe himself as a Greek god! Here Hegel sees what he is looking for: the return of the classical in the present. In strongly marked contrast, one can then consider his per-ceptive analysis of *romanticism*, which advances far beyond the tradi-tional conceptual opposition between the ancient and modern, the naive and the sentimental, and begins to probe the essence of more modern forms of art. Hegel's diagnosis of romanticism brings into play a certain historical and conceptual perspective, which has proved fruit-ful and illuminating right up to the present.

The parts of Hegel's aesthetics devoted to the discussion of romantic art have subsequently been taken up and developed in relation to post-classical and post-romantic artistic developments in the period after his own death and that of Goethe. A particularly good example of this is the young Georg Lukács, whose *Theory of the Novel* of 1916 successfully applies Hegel's conceptual analysis to the narrative character of late nineteenth century literature. Another good example would be the modern discussion concerning Hegel's thesis of the 'end of art'. If the end in question actually coincides with the dissolution of the romantic form of art, then Hegel's thesis might paradoxically shed further light

---

[48] Ibid., p. 84; *Hegel's Aesthetics*, vol. 2, pp. 483-4.

upon contemporary aesthetic developments in what we would have to describe as art after the end of art.[49]

Hegel's *historical* perspective upon the romantic form of art implies an inevitable serial relationship between the classical and the Romantic: the latter can only be understood as the dissolution of the former. The older distinctions, between ancient and modern, naive and sentimental, simply assumed the reality of two different kinds of artistic production, and interpreted the relationship between them in terms of legacy or transmission. There were once the ancients and there are now the moderns, just as sons historically succeed their fathers according to the processes of nature. The argument was concerned solely with the dependent or independent legitimation of the modern form of artistic production in relation to the tradition.

Hegel, on the other hand, defines the romantic as a stage that follows on from the classical in a historically necessary fashion. This perspective upon the classical, which locates artistic perfection in an irretrievably distant past, is precisely what elevates it to the paradigmatic status that the designation 'classical' now expressly bestows. Classical art only counts as classical once it has passed away. And we know that it has passed away when a new shape of art has effectively usurped its place. This new shape of art follows on intelligibly from the classical insofar as its immanent tendency is to negate and dissolve the unity characteristic of classical art.

At this point, Hegel's historical perspective is supplemented with a *conceptual* one. It is impossible to provide a precise account of the historically necessary sequence of these forms of art without invoking a purely conceptual and non-historical principle capable of determining the exact relationship between them. That is why the concept of spirit must be introduced here. It is part and parcel of the concept of the spiritual content of art that it should ultimately come to full consciousness of itself. Spirit is properly spirit only when it knows itself as such. The process of elevating this spiritual element into its own pure form opens up a certain distance with regard to its external artistic manifestation. The more the spirit comes to consciousness of itself, the more it relinquishes the beautiful 'covering' originally vouchsafed by the classical

---

[49] For example, D. Henrich, 'Kunst und Kunstphilosophie der Gegenwart', in W. Iser, ed., *Immanente Ästhetik. Ästhetische Reflexion*, Poetik und Hermeneutik II (München 1966). Cf. also my essay 'Über einige Bedingungen gegenwärtiger Ästhetik', in the collection *Ästhetische Erfahrung* (Frankfurt am Main 1989). Arthur Danto has often discussed this theme (cf. his *The Philosophical Disenfranchisement of Art*, 1986).

form of art. Thought now becomes autonomous and destroys the self-contained harmony of the work as self-conscious reflection invades and ultimately transcends the sensible immediacy of the art object itself. The 'romantic' essentially designates this process in which the spiritual content of art effectively abandons its sensuous form of manifestation as the beautiful and passes over into a purely intellectual form of existence as the 'concept'. Romantic art is still art, though it no longer enjoys the aesthetic autarchy that belongs to classical art. At the same time, romantic art is not yet pure thought, though its artistic form is indeed already permeated by reflection.

This is how the historical and conceptual moments are connected in the relationship between the classical and the romantic forms of art. The romantic historically succeeds and displaces the classical insofar as it marks the transition from the beautiful realm of art proper to the philosophical realm of thought.[50] Once this transition has been definitively accomplished – and according to Hegel this transpires in his own time and by means of his own system – art has effectively ceased to play its former world-historical role as the immediate manifestation of absolute spirit. Artistic activity may well continue, of course, but philosophy now fulfils the task once discharged by art. The sensuous manifestation of the Idea has been overcome through the self-certain and transparent grasp of the Idea. Philosophical aesthetics breaks the hold of art by facilitating the fully conceptual expression of what merely appeared in immediate form as art. The establishment of a truly philosophical aesthetics simultaneously crowns and definitively concludes the age of art.

VI. Some Philosophical Responses to *Faust*

In the period of elevated philosophical claims that sprang directly from the perfected Hegelian system, the question was already asked whether it was possible to conceive of a form of art that might unite the aesthetic

---

[50] A.W. Schlegel's attempt to develop a comprehensive historical perspective upon romantic poetry as a whole was still essentially motivated by the need to justify specifically modern literature over against classicist preconceptions. The independent rights of the modern were to be defended by identifying 'the inner principle [*das Gesetzmässige*] behind its advance and its levels of development ... that pervasive inner affinity through which its works can already be seen in their unity to form a recognisable whole, albeit one that is still developing rather than yet concluded' (*Geschichte der romantischen Literatur*, 1802–3, in A.W. Schlegel, *Kritische Schriften und Briefe*, vol. 4, ed. E. Lohner, Stuttgart 1965, p. 15f., p.19f.)

principle and the autonomous character of thought.[51] Such an expressly philosophical form of art would effectively give the lie to Hegel's pronouncement concerning the end of art. And the beautiful domain of aesthetic semblance that had been officially relinquished would then rise again, enhanced by the very resources of further Hegelian speculation. In this context, it is hardly surprising that Goethe's *Faust* became a privileged object of discussion for such lines of thought. For Hegel himself had apparently spoken with great respect of Goethe's poem as a case of 'absolute philosophical tragedy'.[52]

H.F.W. Hinrichs, one of the later Hegel's students, soon claimed to be able to identify fundamental concepts of Hegelian philosophy in the Faust poem.[53] And his *Aesthetic Lectures on Goethe's Faust as a Contribution towards a Systematic Consideration of Art* saw their proper task as that of 'developing the true content of the tragedy in the medium of thought'. Hinrichs undertook his analysis on the basis of the following conviction: 'The proper judgement of art in general cannot content itself with an approach conducted purely in terms of representation [*Vorstellung*], but must rather present and comprehend the content of the work of art, that first presents itself in and through the realm of representation, as ultimately arising from the essential character of the realm of thought'.[54] This crude and intellectualising attempt at conceptual appropriation, which neglected the aesthetic quality of the work itself, was soon followed by other more or less barbarous adaptations or violent

---

[51] As in the work of Ch. H. Weisse for example. Following on from the classical and romantic ideals of art, he explicitly envisages a 'modern ideal' of art that is self-consciously aware of itself as such, an art that has now acquired absolute status in its aesthetic purity and universality. This art discloses new creative possibilities both 'for understanding the historically existing and given world and for expressing intimations of and demands for further forms and manifestations of beauty in the future' (*System der Ästhetik als Wissenschaft von der Idee der Schönheit*, 1830, reprinted Hildesheim 1966). The Hegelian claim concerning the end of art was obviously widely reported even before the actual posthumous publication of the relevant lectures on aesthetics by Hegel's student H.G. Hotho in 1835, and in this connection Weisse comments as follows: 'In particular it is now the students of Hegel who declare the standpoint of their master, as the necessary outcome of the historical development of philosophy, to be the absolute one, and defend it against every direct and indirect assault not so much by skilfully and bravely engaging with the enemy as by simply closing their eyes tightly and holding their arms out at the ready. They have taken on the futile task of demonstrating, before this freely and splendidly dawning day of further ideal and artistic development, spreading its pure and illuminating rays in every direction as it is, that this sunlight is nothing but nocturnal darkness' (p. 304).

[52] Hegel, *Ästhetik* III (Werkausgabe 15), p. 557; *Hegel's Aesthetics*, vol. 2, p. 1224.

[53] Halle 1825.   [54] Ibid., p. v f.

readings of the poem.[55] The explicitly 'philosophical' interpretation
of Faust became a favourite pastime for essayists of mediocre talent
until F.Th. Vischer, the only independently minded aesthetic theorist
in the Hegelian tradition, finally put paid to these 'deeper-meaning-
diggers'.[56] Vischer simply objected to Hinrichs and others: 'What is
the task here? Not to provide a philosophical commentary – the poem
should be intelligible on its own without this kind of assistance – but
to raise our first impression – namely, the aesthetic impression – which
must already be transparently clear, onto the level of philosophical consciousness and to explicate the reasons for this impression'.[57]

   This tendency of philosophers to try and appropriate Goethe's *Faust*
actually goes right back to the beginning of the nineteenth century.
The historian Heinrich Luden relates how he had come across Vischer's
review of the Faust literature of the Hegelian School, which was 'still
playing the same old song' and 'speaking merely to the initiated'.[58]
And in this connection, Luden explicitly remembered a conversation
he had had with Goethe in 1806. 'Faust' was the subject under discussion
and Luden was telling the poet all about the 'Jena Wisdom' of his academic colleagues. For under the influence of Schelling, Hegel and the
Schlegel brothers, they were all describing Goethe's 'Faust Fragment',
the only version of the poem available to the public at the time, as a
'great, sublime, indeed divine tragedy', as a 'divina tragoedia'.[59] 'The
spirit of the entire history of the world will find itself represented here in
this tragedy, should it ever be completed; the latter will prove a true image of the life of humanity itself, effectively embracing the past, the
present and the future. Mankind has been idealised in the figure of
Faust; he is the very representative of humanity'.[60]

---

[55] Cf. the highly informative dissertation on this subject by H. Titze, *Die philosophische Periode
     der Faustforschung* (Greifswald 1916; reprinted Leipzig 1973).

[56] 'Die Literatur über Goethes Faust' (1839), in F. Th. Vischer, *Kritische Gänge* II, ed.
     R. Vischer (München 1920).

[57] Ibid., p. 202.

[58] H. Luden, *Rückblicke in mein Leben* (Jena 1847), p. 24ff.

[59] The parallel with Dante's *Divina Commedia* also appears in Schelling's essay 'Über Dante
     in philosophischer Beziehung' which was published in the *Critical Journal of Philosophy*
     that was co-edited by Hegel and Schelling (No. 2, 1803). 'On Dante in Relation to
     Philosophy', in *German Aesthetic and Literary Criticism*, ed. D. Simpson (Cambridge 1984),
     pp. 140–148. From the perspective of the philologist, on the other hand, Erich Auerbach
     has insisted that the two works 'are mutually quite incomparable and have nothing
     whatsoever in common with one another' (E. Auerbach, 'Entdeckung Dantes in der
     Romantik', *Deutsche Vierteljahrsschrift* 3, 1925).

[60] Cf. Schelling's remarks in his lectures on the *Philosophy of Art* of 1802 4: 'So far as
     one can judge Goethe's 'Faust' on the basis of the published fragment that is available

'My friends conceded that the actual poet of Faust may not have entertained this idea at all, and indeed perhaps entertained a quite different one, but they claimed that this idea nonetheless formed the real basis of the poem, irrespective of his conscious will or intention, and that it essentially permeated the work throughout'. Goethe's own response, in Luden's account, to the straightforward expectation that the author himself was surely the one best fitted to reveal the fundamental concept behind the work, gives pause for thought: 'The whole splendour of the poet's task would be destroyed by revealing any such thing. For the poet should not attempt to explain himself or provide some careful analysis of his own compositions in terms of everyday prose. He would cease to be a poet if he did so. The poet brings his creations into the world; it is the task of the reader, the aesthetic theorist, the critic, to investigate what he intended with these creations'.[61]

Once the compulsory pursuit of specific philosophical ideas in such epoch-making poetry had become the fashion in the Hegelian School, there was simply no stopping this general approach. And as we shall see, nothing has really changed in this respect since. Heinrich Heine rightly ridiculed this national passion: 'I would hardly be a German if, in mentioning 'Faust', I were not ready to offer further explanatory observations of my own on the subject. From the greatest thinker down to the smallest tradesman, from the established philosopher down to the graduate struggling for his doctorate, everyone likes to exercise his own cleverness in relation to this book'.[62]

If we too follow the custom, and exercise whatever philosophical insight we possess in relation to Goethe's drama, we should certainly begin by clearly distinguishing between the two parts of the tragedy. Hegel himself, as we pointed out, was only familiar with *Part One* of *Faust*, while *Part Two* appeared shortly after his death. Hegel's only detailed mention of the Faust figure is found in one chapter of the *Phenomenology of Spirit*, a work that was itself completed around the same time as *Faust Part One*. The chapter in question is entitled 'Pleasure and

---

to us, this poem is nothing other than the purest and innermost essence of our age: form and material alike fashioned from what the time as a whole has harboured within itself and even from what it bore and perhaps still bears unborn within it' (Schelling, *Sämtliche Werke* V, p. 446). Cf. also Schelling's quotation from *Faust* in his *Vorlesungen über die Methode des akademischen Studiums* (Lecture 10) and Hegel's reference to one of the scenes from *Faust* during his Jena period as discussed earlier (K. Rosenkranz, *Hegels Leben*, p. 187).

[61] H. Luden, op. cit., p. 28f., 32, 37.

[62] *Die romantische Schule* (1835/6), in H. Heine, *Prosa* (München 1961), p. 424.

Necessity' and refers to the scene in Faust's study where Mephistopheles prophesies as follows: 'Have but contempt for reason and for science, / Man's noblest force spurn with defiance, [...] / The spirit which he has received from fate / Sweeps ever onward with unbridled might, / Its hasty striving is so great / It overleaps all earth's delights. / Through life's wild course I'll drag him, / Through shallow triviality / [...] And were he not abandoned to the devil, / He must needs perish' (*Faust Part One*, 1851–1867). Hegel cites the passage rather freely and comments thus: 'Consciousness thereby plunges into life and realises the pure individuality in which it first appears. It does not so much make its own happiness as take it directly and enjoy it. The grey shades of science, laws and principles, which alone stand between it and its own reality, vanish like a lifeless mist that cannot contend against the living certainty of its reality. It takes its life much as a ripe fruit is plucked in coming to meet the hand that takes it'.[63] But the consciousness immersed in pleasure thereby consigns itself in truth to a blind necessity. The individual's attempt simply to realise itself alone in this way is inevitably fated to dissolve into something quite universal after all. The pleasure that is enjoyed only confirms its entrance into a circle of necessity that ultimately destroys its supposedly emphatic individuality.

It is obvious that the figure of Faust vividly represents merely one quite specific stage of consciousness as it traverses the appearing shapes of spirit on the path that finally leads to absolute spiritual self-certainty. Ignoring the other themes of Goethe's poem, Hegel has simply focussed on the way in which the immediate pursuit of pure individuality suddenly finds itself subjected to a higher law than it initially acknowledged. But this allusion was naturally not enough to satisfy the desire for a fully-fledged philosophical reading of *Faust*. The tendency of certain philosophers to interpret their thought in terms of Faust, already ridiculed by Heine, has continued to flourish. In Marxist aesthetics, Goethe's *Faust* has been regarded as a work that effectively combined an intellectual grasp of reality with a vivid poetic expression of early modern history. A rather crude and undifferentiated conception of 'realism' set the stage for bringing Hegel and Goethe together as progressive representatives of bourgeois ideology. The Marxist theory of history thus passes the appropriate judgements here concerning the assessment and evaluation of artistic questions.

---

[63] Hegel, *Phänomenologie des Geistes*, p. 262f.; *Phenomenology of Spirit*, p. 218.

VII. Phenomenological Faustiads

Whereas the older, typically Hegelianising, literature on Faust was primarily concerned with moral, theological and aesthetic questions and categories, the more recent theorists inspired by Marx have concentrated upon the problem of articulating an authentic understanding of reality in general. The earlier attempt to locate the Faust figure within the realm of objective or absolute spirit in immanent terms of the Hegelian system is now abandoned in favour of identifying a historical parallel between the Faustian aspiration for knowledge and the Hegelian reconstruction of all knowledge through philosophy. The parallel is easily and readily established once the all-embracing Marxist concept of ideology is employed to explain every phenomenon of the intellectual, artistic, scientific and philosophical superstructure. Now it is possible to interpret Goethe's *Faust* and Hegel's philosophy as equally important manifestations of a specific stage in the development of bourgeois consciousness. Viewed from the unified perspective of the ideological superstructure, all the fundamental contrasting differences between philosophical thought and poetic production we have already identified simply disappear from sight.

In this context, the comparison between Hegel and Goethe has generally been based upon considerations concerning the *Phenomenology of Spirit*. Hegel had intended this work to introduce his system by reviewing and examining in turn the claims to truth represented by all previous historical and existing forms of consciousness. This critical refutation of other positions was supposed to lead us to the standpoint of absolute knowledge that itself is no longer historically conditioned precisely because it has exhaustively clarified the historicity of knowledge itself.[64] In a famous passage in his Paris manuscripts, Marx, on the other hand, expressly repudiated the foundational ambitions of absolute knowledge as a case of exaggerated intellectualism, and identified the true significance of Hegelian dialectics as its conceptual and phenomenological sensitivity to the essentially historical realm. For Marx, the *Phenomenology* effectively depicts the real self-generating process of the human species, and should therefore be regarded as 'the true birthplace and secret of the Hegelian philosophy'.[65] This basic thesis, which clearly contradicts Hegel's own intentions and reverses the original systematic and

---

[64] Cf. my chapter 'Hegel's Concept of Phenomenology' included in this book.
[65] K. Marx, *Werke*, vol. 1, ed. H.-J. Lieber/P. Furth (Darmstadt 1962), p. 641 ff.

constitutive relationship between the *Logic* and the *Phenomenology* for the purposes dictated of a critique of ideology, has been unquestioningly accepted throughout Marxist thought, and has also inspired the kind of interpretive approach to Goethe's *Faust* that we have just mentioned. Georg Lukács, for example, claims to recognise 'the path of a poetic "phenomenology" of the human species in Faust's individual consciousness and fate'.[66] The tragedy is supposedly a microcosmic representation of the macrocosmic process of social progress and development. In a similar fashion, Ernst Bloch has attempted to uncover the 'Faust motif' in the very construction of Hegel's *Phenomenology* as a whole.[67] He speaks of the ascending dynamic that Faust shares with the phenomenological movement of consciousness insofar as both effectively traverse the entire world in ultimate pursuit of genuine self-knowledge. The interplay between consciousness and its own constant negation, personified in Faust and his Mephistophelian alter ego, is alleged to be the moving force behind the whole development.

As soon as we attempt to go beyond such vaguely plausible but sweeping analogies, however, the profound incoherence underlying this approach is quickly revealed. In the first place, it blithely ignores the undeniable fact that Hegel's phenomenological path through the shapes of consciousness only touches once, and very briefly, on the figure of Faust, and lends him a strictly limited role that soon vanishes in the following play of shapes. For the disappearance of self-consciousness into the universal precisely through the radical pursuit of its own self-realisation is a theme that is only treated in this one section entitled 'The actualisation of rational self-consciousness through its own activity'. This is the only phase of the phenomenological development of spirit that can be presented poetically by reference to Faust as an individual who repudiates all theory and seeks fulfilment in the fullness of life instead.

But quite apart from such philological observations, there are also substantive grounds for refusing to extend the Faust motif beyond its proper bounds. For we cannot really talk of an 'ascending dynamic' on the part of Faust, whereas the *Phenomenology of Spirit* would lose all meaning if each succeeding shape of consciousness did not emerge specifically from the self-reflexive overcoming of the immediately preceding

---

[66] Georg Lukács, 'Faust-Studien' (1941), in *Faust und Faustus* (Hamburg 1967), p. 147ff.

[67] Most recently in his essay, 'Das Faustmotiv der Phänomenologie des Geistes', *Hegel-Studien* 1, 1961.

position. Faust and his diabolical counterpart, on the other hand, remain essentially the same for all their passage through the world. They change their own particular location at will and confront the same reality, however manifold its forms, without thereby being changed themselves. In all their wanderings, the characters as such are not transformed, nor is the world itself drawn into a constant process of change and becoming. The restless haste with which one momentary experience is abandoned for another without any sense of progress, the exhausting and constant alternation of sensations without further end or purpose, is precisely what reveals the essentially tragic import of *Faust Part One*. And the transition to *Faust Part Two* changes nothing in this respect when the two protagonists return, in depersonalised form, and seem to act as allegorical representatives of humanity in general rather than as specific characters in their own right. There is nothing here that really corresponds to the crucial strategy of the *Phenomenology*.

The way in which Faust, in his ceaseless curiosity and hunger for new experience, variously comes into contact with the realm of magic, the narrowness of bourgeois life, with science and faith, with the domain of politics and the world of the court, with classical culture or the mythological cosmos – all of this follows a similar schema, and the vividly presented character of these themes derives entirely from the poet's own imaginative power. And if Faust has indeed grown in understanding towards the end of the poem, insofar as the restless individual pursuit of experience has ultimately given way to a more fulfilled life in the service of the public good, he must thereby endure the 'blinding' that now inflicts upon him the ceaseless 'care' of everyday existence.[68] And that is all the more reason why Faust must still be redeemed by divine grace in the elaborately choreographed mystery play of the poem's final scene.

Considered as a whole, the life of Faust on stage effectively moves between the two extremes of his initial pact with the devil and his eventual transfiguration in the pure spiritual realm of essence. There is an ever-present transcendent dimension, however playfully presented, which always lies behind and beyond the story of his earthly wanderings. The tragedy begins in heaven, where God the Father and Mephistopheles struggle for the possession of Faust's soul, and it also concludes in heaven, where the principle of the Eternal Feminine finally promises

---

[68] Cf. the still extremely informative study by K. Burdach, 'Faust und die Sorge', *Deutsche Vierteljahrsschrift* 1, 1923.

to elevate the protagonist. It may well be true that the dramaturgical structure of Goethe's work was influenced by Greek tragedy and its depiction of contending gods, by Baroque drama and its theatre of the world, and by the *Divine Comedy* of Dante. But there is no doubt whatsoever that Goethe denied his Faust any gradual liberation from earthly entanglements or any ascent to the absolute through the exercise of his own powers. And this effectively removes any real basis for a serious comparison between Faust's path through life and the movement that animates Hegel's *Phenomenology of Spirit*.

In this context, we should also mention a remarkable document that has caused a certain amount of confusion here. Karl Rosenkranz, Hegel's faithful student and biographer, cites a certain text[69] that he attributed to the Jena period when Hegel developed the systematic conception of the *Phenomenology of Spirit*, and gradually worked his way towards it with extensive preparatory studies and materials of one kind or another. The 'aphorism' in question refers explicitly to the figure of Faust, and interprets his lust for knowledge by reference to a whole range of moral and theological issues. Rosenkranz believed he had here discovered a 'Promethean confession' on Hegel's part, and was already quite prepared to speak of a 'philosophical Faustiad' in this connection.[70] But all attempts to construe any parallel between Goethe's *Faust* and Hegel's *Phenomenology* on the basis of this little text have had to be abandoned since philological research has definitively shown that we are not dealing with original Hegelian insights here at all. For the passage under discussion is actually a compressed series of excerpts from an anonymous review of the novels of F.M. Klinger, a review that had appeared in 1805 in a literary journal based in Halle.[71]

Rosenkranz himself had already pointed out that the text in question was difficult to relate specifically to Goethe's *Faust*. And he interpreted it as essentially representing the 'general German type of the individual in desperate struggle with current necessity'. Careful research into the relevant textual sources has revealed that the review, further abbreviated in Hegel's excerpt, brought together and discussed various themes from several of Klinger's novels, only one of which is concerned with the figure of Faust – namely, *The Life, Deeds and Infernal Journey of Faust*.[72] But

---

[69] K. Rosenkranz, *Hegels Leben*, p. 548ff.   [70] Ibid., p. 200.

[71] M. Baun/K. Meist, "Hegels 'Prometheische Confession'. Quellen für vier Jenaer Aphorismen Hegels", Hegel-Studien 8, 1973.

[72] Petersburg 1791.

we must still ask why Hegel should have transcribed parts of this review in the first place. Rosenkranz correctly realised that it was the intimate relationship between the principle of individuality and inexorable necessity that had attracted Hegel's interest, a relationship that is certainly addressed in Hegel's excerpt and is specifically elaborated later in the section of the *Phenomenology* that alludes to Faust. There is also some reason for thinking that the Jena text already presents in embryonic form certain of the basic ideas behind the immediately succeeding sections entitled 'The law of the heart and the frenzy of self-conceit', 'Virtue and the way of the world' and 'The spiritual animal kingdom'. Perhaps the review that Hegel had come across provoked a series of reflections, which then pointed towards the explicit analysis of the contradiction within the moral world that already hovered vaguely before his mind. Hypotheses of this kind can of course never be properly verified, and historical research into sources soon comes up against its limits in such cases. But this Jena document, difficult though it is to locate its precise significance for Hegel's thought, certainly offers no support for the idea of some internal and mutually illuminating relationship between the figure of Faust and the intention behind the *Phenomenology of Spirit*.

VIII. The Aesthetics of *Faust Part Two*

The *second part* of Goethe's *Faust* has always placed quite extraordinary demands on its interpreters. The dramaturgical relationship between the two parts cannot properly be determined without some ambiguity, and the complicated poetic structure of the last part itself has still never been fully clarified in immanent terms. And the kind of philosophical interpretations that simply search the stage for vivid embodiments of their own conceptual ideas break down completely in relation to the second part of Goethe's poem. It is not surprising therefore that the eloquent Hegelians, so adept at identifying categories of the dialectical system throughout Part One, simply fall silent when it comes to the interpretation of Part Two. Thus F.Th. Vischer delivered a devastating *ex cathedra* judgement upon this late and allegedly misconceived product of the poet's failing creative powers.[73] Even if Vischer was perhaps

---

[73] 'The whole of Part Two is a mechanical product, not something that has developed but something fashioned, fabricated, cobbled up' (F.Th. Vischer, 'Die Literatur über Goethes Faust', p. 207). Cf. Vischer's further remarks in 'Zum zweiten Teil von Goethes Faust' (1861) in *Kritische Gänge* II.

influenced by the Hegelian verdict that beauty belongs intrinsically
to classical forms, and that the self-consciously reflective works of the
modern age mark an inevitable decline in comparison, his total failure
to appreciate the aesthetic value of the later part of *Faust* is a very poor
testimony to the critic's effective grasp of art. Rosenkranz was milder
in his judgement, and attempted to come to terms with the *skandalon*
of Part Two in a different way. He interpreted the latter as a basically
misguided attempt to press the 'final result of an eclectic universalism'
into poetic form. 'Since the poet Goethe, unlike Herder or Hegel, was
unable to write a philosophy of history, he produced a poetical version
of one instead'.[74]

Such attempts to discover specific concepts behind the poetic images are clearly incapable of doing justice to the peculiar form and the
aesthetic principles of the second part of Goethe's tragedy. But the real
enigmas of this work in particular are thereby simply avoided. Even in
Germanistic studies, it has taken a long time for this awkward problem
to be directly and explicitly addressed. But it is now true that *Faust Part
Two* has come to receive closer attention than before. K. May, for example, expressly refrains from philosophical speculation about the work,
and exercises all the pedantic care the philologist can muster in interpreting the text exclusively 'on the basis of its own linguistic form'.[75]
W. Emrich, on the other hand, applies the concept of symbol to the developmental history of the text in order to unlock the work as a whole.[76]
M. Kommerell invokes the precedent of Baroque drama and its conception of the world as theatre, something that was certainly familiar
to Goethe in the work of Calderón.[77] H. Schlaffer, finally, rejects the
traditional approach to symbolism in favour of a concept of allegory
derived from Benjamin, and interprets the work in terms of modernity,
noting parallels between themes in *Faust Part Two* and the economic
processes of abstraction analysed by Marx.[78]

---

[74] K. Rosenkranz, *Goethe und seine Werke* (1847), Königsberg 1856[2], p. 444.

[75] K. May, *Faust II aus der Sprachform gedeutet* (1936), Frankfurt am Main 1972[3].

[76] W. Emrich, *Die Symbolik von Faust II* (1943), Bonn 1957[2].

[77] M. Kommerell, 'Faust zweiter Teil. Zum Verständnis der Form' (1937), in M.K., *Dame
Dichterin*, Munich 1967. Cf. also the study specifically influenced by Kommerell: D.
Lohmeyer, *Faust und die Welt* (1940), republished in revised form Munich 1975.

[78] H. Schlaffer's highly intelligent book (*Faust Zweiter Teil. Die Allegorie des 19 Jahrhunderts*,
Stuttgart 1981) nonetheless attempts to prove too much insofar as it also undertakes
to identify a potential diagnosis of modernity in terms of allegory even in Hegel's
aesthetic theory. Whereas Hegel condescendingly locates 'allegory' at the margins of
the 'symbolic form of art', Schlaffer thinks it possible precisely for allegory to evade

Now there is a whole series of remarks made by Goethe himself during the composition of the second part of *Faust* that expressly clarifies
features of its aesthetic structure and organisation. The prior publication of the 'Helen Act', before Part Two appeared in its entirety, bore
the subtitle 'A Classical-Romantic Phantasmagoria'.[79] The author remarked upon this as follows: 'I never doubted that the readers for whom
I effectively wrote would grasp the principal significance of the scene
straight away. It is time that the impassioned dispute between classicists
and romantics should finally be reconciled [*sich endlich versöhne*]. The
principal thing is that we should properly cultivate ourselves; the source
from which we do so would not matter, if we did not have to fear the
possibility of miscultivation by appealing to false models. For it is certainly a broader and purer insight into and around Greek and Roman
literature to which we owe our liberation from the monkish barbarism
of the period between the fifteenth and sixteenth centuries. Is it not
from this elevated school of thought that we have learnt to appreciate
everything in its true physical and aesthetic value, both what is oldest
and what is newest?'[80]

The attempted *reconciliation of the classical and the romantic* clearly
also characterises the aesthetic form that Goethe specifically adopts in
the difficult final part of the Faust poem. The actual material components of the poem are of secondary significance in this respect. The

the ominous 'end of art' in the context of the dissolution of romanticism – that
is, in the midst of the nineteenth century. Hegel, on the other hand, simply observed
soberly that allegory as allegory has 'nothing properly romantic about it' (Hegel, *Ästhetik*
I, p. 514).

[79] Cf. Goethe's letter to S. Boisserée of 22 October 1826: '... nothing but the fullness of
time could round off this work that now covers a good three thousand years from the
Sack of Troy to the destruction of Missolonghi: and one can also regard this as respecting
the "unity of time" in a kind of higher sense'.

[80] Goethe's letter to K.J.L. Iken of 27 September 1827. Eckermann records a rather similar
conversation of 25 January 1827: '"There is a whole world of antiquity in it", I said.
"Yes", said Goethe, "the philologists will have their work cut out". "I have no fear", I
said, "about the part dealing with antiquity; for there we find the most careful detail,
the most thorough development of the individual figure, where each says just what each
is supposed to say. But the modern romantic part is very difficult, for half the history
of the world lies behind it. And such extensive material can only be lightly suggested
and places considerable demands upon the reader". "Yet", said Goethe, "it all appeals to
the senses, and on the stage would certainly satisfy the eye; and more I did not intend –
as long as the crowd of spectators take delight in the spectacle, and at the same time
its higher significance will not escape the initiated, just as also happens with the Magic
Flute and other things". "It will produce a most unusual effect on stage", I said, "being
a piece that begins as tragedy and ends as opera"'.

scene of the spectacle is both modern Germany and ancient Greece. Various characters from Homeric epic, from the world of the Middle Ages, from the historical present suddenly find themselves anachronistically confronting one another. But the original chapbook, the *Historia von D. Johann Faustus* of 1587, already anticipated in part this kind of richly variegated stage presentation. Here at the intersection between Humanism and the Middle Ages, when monkish barbarism and the liberating insight into classical culture, to use the words of Goethe's letter, explicitly came into contact with one another, we already clearly witness the emergence of themes that Goethe takes up directly in the second part of his poem, like the role of Faust at the Imperial Court, Faust's marriage with Helen, or the invocation of the Greek heroes. But what the anonymous author of the chapbook had naturally suspected as the 'apish tricks and juggling arts' of an un-Christian sorcerer[81], here receives an entirely fresh poetic significance.

The 'principal significance' of the scene only reveals itself through the conscious confrontation of classical and romantic elements. The higher significance that transcends the explicit dramatic material itself lies in the total aesthetic impression arising from the successful unification of the classical and the romantic approach. The explicitly presented contrast between material components that are historically remote from one another and apparently quite disparate from the perspective of artistic content effectively relativises the initial appearance of mutually incompatible categories. The classical culture here cited as 'classical' and the Romantic setting here offered as 'romantic' mediate one another reciprocally and thereby dissolve the sharply defined limits between the two distinct approaches as traditionally understood.

With the second part of Faust, Goethe has aesthetically revoked precisely the theoretical distinction for whose subsequent influence he had regarded Schiller and himself as largely responsible. The separation between the naive and the sentimental, about which the two friends had earlier agreed during the years of their closest intellectual collaboration, has now been abandoned. *Faust Part Two* is neither a self-contained classical composition nor a romantic work suffused with the spirit of self-conscious reflection. On the contrary, it represents the aesthetic

---

[81] *Historia von D. Johann Fausten, dem weitbeschreyten Zauberer und Schwarzkünstler,* reprinted Stuttgart 1968, p. 97. The German text was translated into English in 1592 as *The Historie of the damnable life, and deserved death of Doctor John Faustus, Newly Imprinted, ... according to the true Copie printed at Franckfort.*

overcoming of this very categorial perspective, and thereby bids farewell to the so-called German 'epoch of art', which was essentially characterised by the clear significance of this distinction.[82] If, according to the previously established schema, the 'classical' perspective historically articulates the persisting validity of the paradigmatic art of antiquity and the 'romantic' perspective of the art of the modern age up to and including the present, then *Faust Part Two* essentially belongs to the *post-romantic* epoch. Perhaps one can say that this late masterpiece of Goethe first inaugurates such an epoch insofar as it creates quite new possibilities that can no longer be properly accommodated in terms of the traditional distinctions.

In the earlier discussion, we identified the only appropriate basis for comparison between Goethe's and Hegel's conceptions of art as their common perspective upon the dichotomy of classical and romantic. But if with his last great artistic creation, Goethe actually relinquishes this formerly shared ground, does this imply that he has also definitively escaped the systematic grasp of the Hegelian dialectic? Hegel, for his part, had certainly envisaged the emergence of post-Romantic forms of art. Indeed he could not avoid doing so after having interpreted

---

[82] The correspondence between Goethe and Schiller already provides a surprisingly accurate intimation of the kind of aesthetic problems that would eventually emerge in Goethe's attempt to continue and complete the story of Faust. With regard to his conception of 'Helen', Goethe writes on 12 September 1800: 'But the beautiful aspect of my heroine's situation attracts me so much that it disturbs me to think of now turning it all into a caricature. I really feel not the slightest desire to try and base a serious tragedy on what I have written so far ...' Schiller immediately tries to calm Goethe's concerns: 'You shouldn't be disturbed by the thought that it seems such a pity to barbarise to the beautiful forms and situations that come to you. This is something that could well arise repeatedly in the second part of Faust, and it may be a good thing to silence your poetic conscience in this respect right now. The barbaric character of the treatment, which the spirit of the whole piece demands of you, cannot itself destroy the higher content or extinguish what is beautiful, but merely serves to specify it in different ways and prepare it for a different psychological approach. It is precisely the more elevated and refined aspect of the themes that will lend the work a distinctive charm of its own.... There is a very significant advantage in proceeding deliberately from the pure to the more impure, instead of trying to ascend to the pure from the original basis of the impure, as is the case with the rest of us barbarians. You must therefore make a good fist [*Faust*] of *Faust* and emphatically assert your own rights throughout.' (Schiller to Goethe, 13 September 1800). Goethe responds in an affirmative tone: 'The consoling suggestion that you proffer in your letter, that it would not necessarily result in a wholly contemptible poetic monster if I were to combine the beautiful and the adventurous, has already been confirmed in my own experience insofar as this amalgamation has indeed yielded certain remarkable and visible effects which I take some pleasure in myself'.(Goethe to Schiller, 16 September 1800).

the reflective dissolution of the unified classical work of art in the extreme expressions of romantic art as heralding the end of the formerly
essential manifestation of spiritual substance in the domain of sensuous appearance. In terms of the actual production of art, Hegel's contemporaries themselves seemed to be aiding and abetting a process
that philosophical aesthetics had already diagnosed as a transition into
the pure sphere of the speculative concept. Since significant further
achievements can no longer be expected for historical and systematic
reasons, and since the perfected philosophy of absolute spirit now exists
in Hegel's own system, more flexible means of interpretation are obviously required in order to come to terms with the nonetheless persisting
activity of artists.

In this connection, Hegel speaks explicitly of a *tabula rasa*, which
permits the further reflective elaboration of all possible forms and
themes[83]. This implies that the subjectivity of the artist stands in an entirely free relationship to the essential variety of historically transmitted
but now substantively indifferent material. This marks the beginning of
the variable and playful citation that mirrors our total exposure to anything and everything through all-encompassing universal mediation.
The subjective facility for handling alternative forms passes over into a
kind of objective self-recognition in the comprehensive exploration of
all possible content. Hegel recognised this type of post-romantic play
with artistic possibilities in the *museé imaginaire* of the history of art, and
described it in terms of 'objective humour'. But he also left no doubt
that 'such final flowerings of art' must be regarded as powerless and reduced forms that stand at the end of a mighty history. In addition to the
work of Rückert, Hegel explicitly cites the *West-Eastern Divan* of the later
Goethe as an example of this openness to substantive indeterminacy.[84]

Thus Hegel writes: 'The solidarity with such a specific limitation of
subject-matter was cancelled by humour that could make every determinacy waver and dissolve and therefore made it possible for art to
transcend itself. Yet in this self-transcendence art is nevertheless a withdrawal of man into himself, a descent into his own breast, whereby art
strips away from itself all fixed restriction to a specific range of content

---

[83] Cf. the chapter on the end of the romantic form of art: *Ästhetik* II, p. 231 ff., and particularly p. 234 ff. and 239ff; *Hegel's Aesthetics*, vol. 1, pp. 602 ff., 604 ff., and 608 ff.

[84] Ibid., p. 242; cf. also *Ästhetik* I, p. 356, where in a very similar way Hegel praises Goethe's
West-Eastern Divan for the accomplished way in which it bridges the historical distance
between one age and another and incorporates what appears alien and remote into the
intimately personal domain. Cf. *Hegel's Aesthetics*, vol. 1, pp. 610–611 and 275 respectively.

and treatment, and makes Humanus into its new holy of holies – that is, the depths and heights of the human heart as such, mankind in its joys and sorrows, its strivings, deeds and fates. Herewith the artist acquires his subject-matter within himself and is the human spirit actually determining itself and considering, meditating, and expressing the infinity of its feelings and situations, a spirit to which nothing that lives within the human breast is alien any longer. This is a subject-matter that does not remain determined artistically in itself and on its own account; on the contrary, the specific character of the topic and its outward formation is left to capricious invention, yet no interest is excluded – for art does not need any longer to represent only what is absolutely at home at one of its specific stages, but everything in which man as such is capable of being at home'.[85]

One must bear in mind that Hegel himself was no longer able to witness the completion of Goethe's poem on Faust. Yet his own characterisation of art at the end of its period of historical influence could itself also be interpreted as a highly perceptive description of the poetic shape of *Faust Part Two*. On the conceptual perspective of the last great example of an aesthetics fundamentally based upon a philosophical system, this late work of Goethe's could not therefore be recognised as properly belonging to the relevant sphere of artistic production at all. The immediate followers of Hegel, as we have noted, actually came to this verdict. Their close historical proximity to the work in question may be partly responsible in this case for the fact that an essentially limited perspective completely failed to provide any appropriate response to Goethe's most powerful creation. It is very easy for later observers to know better after the event. Nonetheless it touches on fundamental questions concerning the validity of the categorial approach adopted by philosophical aesthetics, if such a significant manifestation of postromantic art as *Faust Part Two* can simply be classed amongst essentially playful experiments without a future and located at the outer edge of a vanished epoch.

It is all the more remarkable then to see how a later generation could appeal precisely to the later Goethe in attempting to formulate the ideal of a truly comprehensive work of art for the future. With his 'all-embracing work of art', conceived 'in an entirely modern sense', Richard Wagner hoped to put an end to the trivialities of contemporary opera and thereby bring traditional drama closer to its authentic and

---

[85] Hegel, *Ästhetik* II, p. 237f.; *Hegel's Aesthetics*, vol. 2, pp. 606–607.

highest fulfilment. In 1871, almost forty years after the appearance of Goethe's great final work, Wagner delivered his programmatic speech 'On the Purpose of Opera' before the Royal Academy of Arts in Berlin. Wagner here interprets his own activities as the direct consequence and continuation of the ultimate intentions of the poet. And it is not simply the rhetorical expression of a grand ceremonial moment when he explicitly recalls Goethe's sense that 'the exceptional prospects for a musically conceived drama initially disclosed to him by *Don Giovanni* now seemed dashed once he received news of Mozart's death'.[86] Wagner here suggests, transparently enough, that he is the person to fulfil these temporarily abandoned prospects once and for all. We are not called upon to adjudicate that question here. But Wagner's historical reference to Goethe is profoundly justified in substance. As Goethe himself had explicitly remarked with regard to Faust Part Two: 'The character of the music would have to resemble that of *Don Giovanni*, for Mozart should really have composed the music for my Faust'.[87] Above all, however, Wagner's genealogical self-justification displays in passing a greater sense for the aesthetic qualities of Goethe's drama than the whole Hegelian School in its obsessive intellectualism and poetic blindness could ever muster.

---

[86] Richard Wagner, *Ausgewählte Schriften* (Frankfurt a. M. 1974), p. 188ff.; for the example of *Faust*, cf. p. 184.

[87] Goethe's conversation with Eckermann of 12 February 1829, and similarly that of 29 January 1827. Cf. the commentary on *Faust* by A. Schöne (Frankfurt am Main 1994), p. 19f.

INDEX